# The Power of Restricted Stock

## The Definitive Guide to a Resurging Long-Term Incentive

Brent M. Longnecker, CCP, CBP
with Christopher S. Crawford

WorldatWork.

**About WorldatWork®**

WorldatWork is the world's leading not-for-profit professional association dedicated to knowledge leadership in compensation, benefits and total rewards. Founded in 1955, WorldatWork focuses on human resources disciplines associated with attracting, retaining and motivating employees. Besides serving as the membership association of the professions, the WorldatWork family of organizations provides education, certification (Certified Compensation Professional — CCP®, Certified Benefits Professional — CBP™ and Global Remuneration Professional — GRP®), publications, knowledge resources, surveys, conferences, research and networking. WorldatWork Society of Certified Professionals and Alliance for Work-Life Progress (AWLP) are part of the WorldatWork family.


ISBN 1-57963-1347



**WorldatWork.**

***The Professional Association for Compensation, Benefits and Total Rewards***

WorldatWork
14040 N. Northsight Blvd., Scottsdale, AZ 85260
480/951-9191 Fax 480/483-8352
www.worldatwork.org

# Acknowledgments

It's always great to be asked to write about one of your passions. Therefore, we'd like to thank WorldatWork for again asking us to address this issue, and also thank our wives, Teri Longnecker and Sarah Crawford, who have graciously allowed us the time to develop this book. Finally, we want to thank Mel Todd and the Todd Organization, of which Longnecker & Associates is now part, for encouraging us to write and backing these efforts 100 percent.

WorldatWork and the authors also would like to acknowledge the following individuals and/or companies for contributing to the completion of this book:

*Content Advisors*

Brice Simpson, Nathan White, Nicole Shanklin, April Canik and Tammy Hemphill, Longnecker & Associates, Inc.

Julie Long, Vice President of Human Resources — KCS Energy

Suzanne Smith, Vice President of Human Resources — Concurrent Computer Corporation

The Todd Organization

Wm. Jay Harrelson — Attorney at Law, Waller, Lansden, Dortch & Davis

*Technical Reviewers*

Cimi B. Silverberg, Frederic W. Cook & Co.

Gary Starzmann, CCP, CBP, SPHR, Mellon Human Resources & Investor Solutions

Guy Van Tiggelen, CPA, CCP, CBP, LifeBridge Health

*WorldatWork Staff Contributors*

Dan Cafaro

Rebecca Williams Ficker

Betty Laurie

Mark Anthony Muñoz

Barbara Parus

Rodney Platt

*Content Illustrators/Typists*

Addie Ballentine, Longnecker & Associates, Inc.

# Table of Contents

# Introduction

## Restricted Stock Awards — The Return of the Old Sheriff

They say that the Clantons ruled Tombstone, Arizona, until Wyatt Earp and his brothers restored law and order with the world's most famous gunfight at the OK Corral. Like the Clantons, options have "ruled the town." However, a gunfight of sorts has been taking place over the last several years, and the result is the return of an old sheriff named restricted stock awards (RSA).

This book is a sequel to the bestselling WorldatWork book, *Stock Option Alternatives: A Strategic and Technical Guide To Long-Term Incentives*. This book, however, is more specific because it deals with only one stock option alternative: restricted stock in its various forms. This is considered a key sequel since (1) restricted stock is the fastest growing long-term incentive in the United States today, (2) Microsoft has received significant press with the introduction of a variation known as the restricted stock unit (RSU), and (3) this long-term incentive (LTI) is multi-faceted and can be used in a variety of formats that can help any company more effectively attract, retain and motivate key talent critical to survival in today's marketplace.

In addition, much has happened (i.e., the gunfight for control) in the executive compensation field since the last book:

- The Financial Accounting Standards Board (FASB) has definitively decided to expense options. (Editor's note: As of this writing, there are schools of thought that would dispute when, how, and to what degree, expensing of options will be mandated; however, the writing clearly is on the wall.)
- The Internal Revenue Service (IRS) is launching a study to determine the extent of non-compliance in executive compensation, including the use of restricted stock.
- The Securities and Exchange Commission (SEC) has increased its involvement where new proxy rules have come out.
- The New York Stock Exchange (NYSE) came under heavy fire for a terribly excessive package belonging to its former CEO.

And one can bet there is more to come — especially with politicians starting to use executive pay as a key talking point.

Therefore, stock options have increasingly been replaced and/or supplemented with restricted stock. As a result, this book has been written for boards of directors, corporate officers, stock analysts, private business owners and other consultants who are dealing with executive pay and specifically want a better understanding of RSAs and RSUs. This book provides specific discussions about this award and details the tax, accounting and legal issues involved. Our intent is to provide an easy-to-understand guide of practical, yet technical, insight into any consideration given this specific compensation vehicle.

Finally, the Appendix includes an abundance of information and sample documents for review, including FAQs, a glossary of terms, a glossary of executive compensation abbreviations, sample documents and other resources for executive compensation practitioners. Whether you are the chair of the compensation committee, the CEO, a CFO, a vice president of human resources, an executive officer, a board member, a company owner, an analyst or a fund manager, and you need a better understanding of long-term incentives, this book is for you.

* * * *

One caveat — RSAs and RSUs are not the "be all and end all" in any package. This is no different than what we have been saying for years regarding options: Diversification and the maximization and understanding of the total package is critical. We strongly recommend readers investigate other insights into equity and equity alternative programs. Bruce Overton's *Executive Compensation Answer Book* is one of the best resources in this field, along with Bruce Ellig's *Complete Guide to Executive Compensation*.

In addition, WorldatWork offers four courses and two books that augment *The Power of Restricted Stock*, titled *Equity at Work: Constructing a Broad-based Stock Option Plan* and *Stock Option Alternatives*. Related courses offered by WorldatWork include:

- T11: Fundamentals of Equity-Based Rewards
- C6: Elements of Executive Compensation
- C6A: Advanced Concepts in Executive Compensation
- C12: Variable Pay — Incentives, Recognition and Bonuses.

# 1

# Restricted Stock Awards (RSAs)

## What Are Restricted Stock Awards?

A restricted stock award (RSA) is a stock grant by an employer to an employee whereby the employee's rights to the stock are subject to some type of restriction and risk of forfeiture. Restrictions often include an employment or length-of-service restriction, also known as time-lapse restricted stock (i.e., vesting over a three- to five-year period). Typically, the employee may not pledge, sell or transfer the shares of stock until the restrictions lapse; however, the employee receives dividends and voting rights during the restriction period. Upon vesting (or lapsing of the restrictions), the stock is released automatically to the employee. Until then, the stock is nontransferable and is subject to forfeiture; i.e., the employee terminates employment before vesting. As a result, the stock is usually held in an escrow or custodial type account and not released to the employee until vested. If the employer decides to award certificates, there will be a legend stating that it is restricted. Once the stated restrictions lapse, the employee obtains full ownership of the unrestricted shares that may be pledged, sold or transferred. In the event the employee does not meet the stated restrictions, the shares are forfeited.

**Example:** Executive 2 of Heidi Corp. received an award of 1,000 restricted shares of Heidi Corp. at no cost on May 1, 2003. The restrictions lapse in five years or on April 30, 2008, as long as Executive 2 remains an employee with the company. At the time of the award, the shares are worth $5 each, and over the five-year vesting period, the company has provided a $1 dividend. Once the restrictions lapse, the stock is worth $10. Assuming the executive has not taken an 83(b) election, the executive will recognize $11,000 of income on April 30, 2008, and Heidi will get a corresponding tax deduction of $10,000.

**FIGURE 1: How Restricted Stock works**

| *Timing* | *Years* | | | |
|---|---|---|---|---|
| | *1* | | *5* | |
| **Restricted Stock** | **Grant** | | **Restrictions Lapse** | |
| Fair Market Value: | $5 | → | $10 | |
| Dividends: | $0 | → | $1.00 | |
| Executive Investment: | $0 | → | $0 | |
| Executive Gain: | $0 | → | $11.00 | (Ordinary Income) |
| Executive Tax[1]: | $0 | → ($11 X .35) | $3.85 | Tax Due |
| Executive Net Gain: (After Tax) | $0 | → | $7.15 | Net Gain |

(1) Assumes the executive is subject to an ordinary income tax rate of 35%. If an 83(b) election was made within 30 days of the award, the executive would be taxed on the fair value of the stock at grant as ordinary income, with subsequent appreciation treated as a capital gain. 83(b) elections are not typically made because the executive cannot recover taxes paid at grant if he or she forfeits the shares or if the shares decrease in value.

## Why Offer Restricted Stock Awards?

Companies may choose to offer restricted stock to selected employees because it:

### *Attracts and Retains*

Restricted stock is a powerful retention tool if the stock award is of meaningful value, regardless of the number of shares. An employee who holds restricted stock immediately feels the value of the award given. In the event an employee terminates and forfeits his shares, these shares will become available as an attraction tool for the new employee.

### *Provides Dividend Payments to Employee Stockholders*

As opposed to other prevalent equity awards such as stock options, RSAs allow the recipient to receive dividend payments on the shares awarded. Because of this provision, many companies that return shareholder value via dividends, such as utilities or real estate investment trusts (REITS), have used RSAs to reward employees along with the shareholders.

### *Increases Stock Ownership*

Empirical studies indicate that the most effective way to link shareholder interests with that of executives is through direct equity ownership on behalf of the executive. RSAs provide this alignment through ownership accumulation often defined by ownership targets.

### *Supports Performance Goals*

The ultimate goal of all companies is to maximize shareholder value, defined by stock price plus dividends. While RSAs motivate employees to maximize shareholder value through increasing stock price and dividends, additional performance accelerators may be utilized to achieve critical short-term and/or long-term performance goals. These performance goals, such as customer service, business unit profitability and decreasing expenses, may or may not be immediately recognized by the stock market. For example, vesting periods may be accelerated in the event certain performance goals are achieved, which will provide increased motivation and reinforcement of the organization's overall goals.

### *Diversifies Long-term Incentive Awards*

RSAs often are utilized in tandem with other LTI vehicles to diversify against a volatile market. In the event a company's stock price declines for external reasons other than the company's performance, restricted stock allows for employees to retain value, while appreciation-only vehicles, such as stock options, lose their retentive capabilities.

### *Supplements Other Pay Practices*

Because RSAs have an element of retention and the charge to earnings is spread over a period of time, RSAs also are utilized to supplement other pay practices; for example, cash sign-on bonuses, supplemental executive retirement plans and/or annual incentives.

### *Discretionary Compensation*

RSAs also are a form of discretionary compensation; therefore, the company can choose who is eligible by using a process that does not have to be granted on any basis of equality. This allows the company to customize its grant process to its culture.

### *Easy to Understand*

Stock options have been deemed complicated. Most recipients had trouble understanding that they had to affect certain activity to realize any gain. As a result, many in-the-money options went unexercised. However, a full-value award that vests on a certain date and is transferred to the recipient at that time is much easier to understand, and therefore, more valuable to grant.

*Possibly Less Dilutive Than Options*

Since an RSA is a full-value award, it requires less to be granted than its stock option counterpart that is solely an appreciation vehicle. Typical grant ratios range from one RSA for 2.5 options to 1:6, depending on the type of model used and the stocks' volatility. However, options do result in cash inflow (the purchase) that can be used to offset dilution through a repurchase program. RSAs do not typically generate any cash inflow, since they are an outright grant.

## Prevalence of Plans

At the outset of 2004, RSAs are the fastest growing long-term incentive in the United States. It is estimated that nearly 90 percent of all publicly traded companies either have them or are considering adding them to their compensation package. Companies like Microsoft, Amazon, Altria Group, Dell Computer, Cendant and Daimler Chrysler AG are leading the way. (See Chapter 3: Drafting Behind the Peloton of Other Companies.)

With all the advantages RSAs have over traditional options, it's a wonder it's taken this long to get here.

## Purpose, Eligibility and Vesting

According to a survey conducted by PricewaterhouseCoopers on the subject of restricted stock, the following was found:

*Purpose*

The primary purpose of awarding restricted stock is to retain employees. (See Figure 2.)

*Eligibility*

The top eligibility criterium for RSAs is job level. Discretion runs a close second. (See Figure 3.)

*Restriction Period/Vesting*

As expected, the average restriction period is between three and four years with cliff vesting being preferred over graded vesting. In addition, the survey noted that the conditions for vesting are 93 percent for service and 7 percent for attaining specific goals.

**FIGURE 2: Purpose of Awarding Restricted Stock**

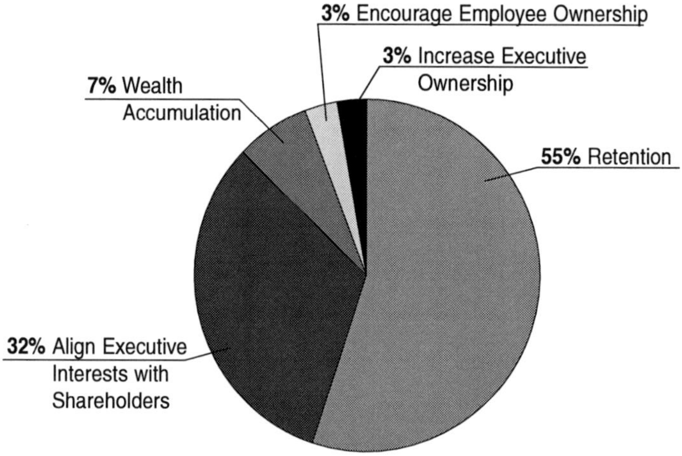


Source: PricewaterhouseCoopers

**FIGURE 3: Eligibility Criteria for Restricted Stock Awards**

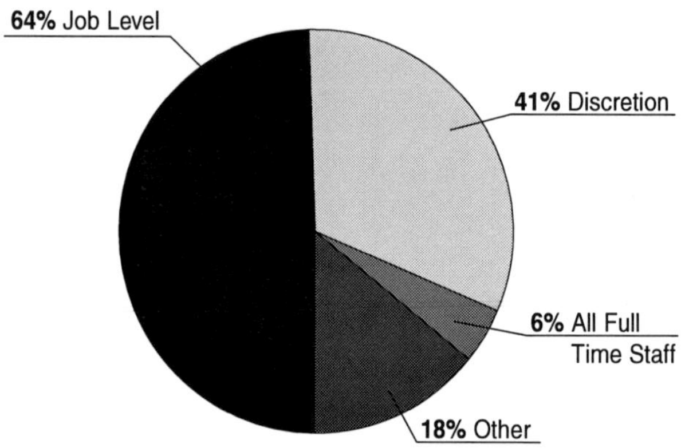


Note: Areas have overlap, so total is more than 100 percent.

Source: PricewaterhouseCoopers

## Advantages vs. Disadvantages

Any company considering implementing a restricted stock plan shou carefully at the advantages associated with this compensation vehicle. companies will have all the right situations in place, thus making RSAs the right vehicle to use. However, there are disadvantages that need to be considered to ensure the right decision for each organization. Specifically:

The following are some **advantages** of restricted stock:

- It promotes immediate stock ownership.
- The charge to earnings is fixed at the time of grant and can be budgeted and more easily planned for.
- Dilution is set at the grant date and does not vary as restrictions lapse.
- Fewer shares are required to deliver greater value (than options).
- If the stock price appreciates from the grant date, the company's tax deduction may exceed the fixed charge to earnings.
- It immediately aligns employees' interests with those of shareholders.
- It allows employees to receive dividends and voting rights.
- It is immediately recognizable to employees.
- If an employee terminates and forfeits shares, the shares are available to be used as an attraction vehicle for someone else.
- It offers employees potential long-term appreciation as the company grows.
- The award retains value even if the stock price drops.

The **disadvantages** of restricted stock include:

- There is a charge to earnings.
- There is immediate dilution of earnings per share.
- The employee incurs tax liability as shares vest, not at the exercise or sell date.
- If the stock price depreciates, the company's fixed-earnings charge exceeds the actual value delivered to the employee and the subsequent tax deduction.
- Unless performance accelerators are utilized for vesting, there are no performance-related criteria, except vesting to receive the award.
- Possible 162(m) issues could apply.

## Figure 4: Summary of RSAs

### Key Provisions

- Outright grant of shares to executives with restrictions as to sale, transfer and pledging
- Restrictions lapse over a period of time (e.g., three to five years)
- As restrictions lapse, executive has unrestricted shares which he or she may sell, transfer or pledge
- If executive terminates employment, all unvested shares are forfeited
- During restriction period, executive receives dividends and can vote the shares

### Earnings Impact

- Fair market value at grant charged to earnings over restriction period
- Subsequent appreciation not charged to earnings
- Immediate dilution of EPS for total shares granted

### Tax Impact on Executive (1)

- At grant — no tax
- As restrictions lapse — the current market value of vested shares taxed as ordinary income
- Dividends received during restriction period taxed as ordinary income

### Tax Impact on Company (1)

- At grant — no tax deduction
- As restrictions lapse — company receives tax deduction equal to executive's ordinary income
- At sale — no tax deduction
- Dividends paid during restriction period are deductible by company when paid

### Advantages

- No executive investment required
- Promotes immediate stock ownership
- Charge to earnings is fixed at time of grant
- If stock appreciates, company's tax deduction exceeds fixed charge to earnings
- Aligns executive's interests with shareholders
- Recognizable to most executives
- Offers executive potentially long-term appreciation as company grows

### Disadvantages

- Charge to earnings
- Immediate dilution of EPS
- Executive may incur tax liability before shares are sold
- If stock depreciates, company's fixed-earnings charge exceeds tax deduction

(1) Assumes 83(b) election is not made. If an 83(b) is made, executive recognizes income on the date the restricted stock was issued, and the company receives an immediate tax deduction for the initial value of the shares (but not for subsequent appreciation during the restriction period); dividends paid during the restriction period are not deductible.

# 2

# The Time Is Right

## History of Restricted Stock Awards

Restricted stock plans were the most prevalent form of long-term incentive (LTI) compensation programs among executive ranks from the 1930s to 1969. However, the tax law changes of 1969 drastically changed the favorability of the plans' tax advantages. Consequently, the popularity of restricted stock plans dropped dramatically, and subsequently they were replaced with stock option programs.

Restricted stock plans made a resurgence in 1977 when the stock market continued to remain flat. As the stock market stalled in the early and late 1970s, companies became concerned with the large number of executives with underwater stock options. Retention of these executives became a key issue. Over the next several years under the bear market of the late 1970s, restricted stock again became one of the most prevalent forms of equity compensation among executive ranks.

Over the following two decades, restricted stock continued to be utilized among the executive ranks, especially among industries notorious for paying dividends, such as utilities, oil and gas, and real estate investment trusts. However, the period from the late 1980s to the early 2000s was documented widely as the stock option era, where stock options were the most predominant form of equity compensation throughout the United States. Figure 5, as reported in *WorldatWork Journal*, third quarter 2000, highlights the prevalence of long-term incentive award practices in U.S. companies in 2000.

**Figure 5: Percentage of Companies Utilizing LTI Vehicle**

| | Stock Options | Restricted Stock | Performance Shares/Units |
|---|---|---|---|
| **Fortune 50** | 100% | 44% | 19% |
| **Total Shareholder Return 50** | 98% | 18% | 0% |
| **Fastest Growing 50** | 89% | 13% | 2% |

## Unprecedented Times and Reasons for Granting Restricted Stock Awards

Times have changed. The new millennium has delivered unprecedented times from the perspective of legislation and the economy, along with an exposé on corporate corruption, which is further discussed below. Since 2000, each of these elements has risen to a crescendo where a "perfect storm" has been created for companies to make sweeping changes in the areas of corporate governance and executive compensation. Most notably is the sweeping change in LTI award practices.

## Stock Option Expensing

Stock options began in 1952 with Pfizer pioneering the practice to grant broad-based stock options. In 1972, the Accounting Principles Board (APB) announced the previously mentioned landmark decision, Opinion 25 (APB 25), Accounting for Stock Compensation. APB 25 introduced the measurement date principle stating that compensation expense should be measured when the number of shares and the price per share are known. Thus, expenses would either be fixed or variable depending on when the variables were known. The fixed, no charge expense associated with a fair market value (FMV) stock option gave way to the tremendous increase in using stock options over the following 30 years. In fact, the National Center for Employee Ownership (NCEO) reported that by 2001, approximately seven to 10 million employees held stock options in the United States, indicating that stock options were not just awarded to the upper echelon, but had been incorporated into the overall culture of many publicly traded companies across the United States, especially in the high-tech sector.

Over the years, legislators and shareholder activists criticized the appropriateness of no expense charge for FMV stock options. However, the first real shot against stock options did not occur until 2001 with the demise of Enron. The largest corporate corruption scandal to date led many employees, shareholders, legislators and media to believe that much of the demise of Enron was motivated by mega stock option awards to top executives. Many critics cried foul — there was no control on the number of stock options awarded because there was no respective charge to earnings. Consequently, the slightest upward movement in the stock price translated into multi-million dollar gains. As a result, many believed executives were motivated to artificially inflate earnings that in turn, increased to the value of the stock to achieve greater wealth at the expense of ethical practices.

Further, with board members reaping option gains as well, there wasn't the due diligence neded to protect shareholders. Subsequently, the exposed corporate corruption in the following years led many to support the movement for the Financial Accounting Standards Board (FASB) to mandate that all FMV stock options carry a charge to earnings.

While there has been much debate surrounding the concept of applying an earnings charge to equity that does not have readily ascertainable value from a tax perspective, FASB recently announced its intentions to expense in the March 31, 2004 exposure draft. FASB tentatively decided that publicly traded companies in the United States would be required to adopt the new standard using a "modified prospective" method, meaning all equity-based compensation cost would be recognized for all employee awards granted, modified or settled after Dec. 15, 2004, plus the nonvested portion of the awards granted or modified in fiscal years beginning after Dec. 15, 2004. Nonvested awards at the effective date would be valued in accordance with the original provisions of FASB statement No. 123, as opposed to any differing provisions under the final new standard.

Since July 2002, approximately 500 public U.S. companies have determined that FASB's decision was all but complete, and decided to voluntarily elect FAS 123 and expense the value associated with stock options. While the remaining U.S. companies will be slower to adopt as mandated by FASB, this recent announcement has changed the playing field for LTI alternatives — especially with respect to the associated accounting charges for each alternative. Figures 6 and 7 exemplify the difference in accounting for long-term incentive alternatives before and after FASB's 2003 announcement.

As evidenced by the charts, the LTI playing field from an accounting perspective has gone from three alternatives — no charge to earnings, fixed charge to earnings, and variable charge to earnings — to two alternatives: fixed charge to earnings and variable charge to earnings. Since many chief financial officers do not like to lie awake at night with the unknown variable charge to earnings, a majority of companies are trying to identify which fixed charge to earnings alternatives is the best. While other variables are forcing companies to identify better ways to attract, retain and motivate key employees through LTIs, FASB's recent announcement (to apply a charge to earnings to the historically, almighty stock option) is the primary force for driving change in long-term incentive award practices across publicly traded companies in the United States.

**FIGURE 6: Before FASB's Announcement — Before APB25**

**LTI Accounting Continuum**

| **Variable Charge to Earnings**<br>Open-ended liability | Budgeted **Charge** to Earnings<br>Closed liability | **No charge to earnings***<br>Footnote disclosure |
|---|---|---|
| Stock Appreciation Rights<br>Phantom Stock Plans<br>Performance Share Plans<br>Book Value Plans<br>Formula Plans | Restricted Stock Awards<br>Discounted Stock Options<br>Performance Units<br>Founders Stock | Stock Options*<br>(Granted at FMV)<br>*possibly subject to change |

**Which long-term incentive alternative would your CFO prefer?**

**FIGURE 7: After FASB's Oct. 29, 2003, Announcement — Under Modified Prospective**

**LTI Accounting Continuum**

| **Variable Charge to Earnings**<br>Open-ended liability | **Budgeted Charge to Earnings**<br>Closed liability |
|---|---|
| Stock Appreciation Rights (SARS)*<br>Phantom Stock Plans<br>Performance Share Plans*<br>Book Value Plans<br>Formula Plans<br>Public Shares | Restricted Stock Awards*<br>Discounted Stock Options<br>Performance Units<br>Founders Stock<br>Performance Share Plans* |

?

Stock Options Granted at FMV

* If the SARs are payable in shares rather than cash, the compensation cost would be fixed rather than variable (Source: Pillsburg Winthrop LLP below).

* Under FASB 123, the performance shares may be valued using the option pricing model on the date of grant (Source: Pillsburg Wintrop LLP Tax Bulletin, August 2003).

**Restricted Stock Units (RSU)**

* As long as the RSU is payable only in shares of stock (and not cash), the award date inconsistency is accounted for the same as restricted stock. A fixed charge occurs at the date if grant is equal to the value of shares or units allocated to the recipient.

## Volatile Markets

The volatility of U.S. stock markets has increased drastically over the past several years. Plunkett's On-line Trading reported:

> Over 75 percent of the shares of the average U.S.-based firm listed on the NYSE changed hands last year. That is, if a company has 10 million shares outstanding, 7.5 million of them were bought and sold last year alone, on average. That percentage has soared from 46 percent in 1990, and 12 percent in 1960.

While the price and availability of online trading has drastically increased the number of investors and the volume of trading, numerous other variables are considered to be factors in the ever-increasing volatility of U.S. stock markets, such as:

- Increased sophistication of investors
- The growing number of investors outside of the United States
- The shrinking proximity of the global market that makes one national market more dependent upon another
- The fragile geopolitical climate.

Whatever the underlying forces are, that have significantly increased stock market volatility, one thing is for sure: Volatility is here to stay.

Realizing that stocks will rise and fall at the whiff of good or bad news puts companies and stockholders (inclusive of employees that are awarded stock as compensation) in an interesting position. Theoretically, volatility is good for employees holding company stock because it creates more peaks of opportunity to sell at high points. This theory is an underlying assumption in most stock option pricing models. However, the assumption is flawed from the stance that volatility creates opportunity as long the volatility trend is going upward. However, as most Americans have come to realize over the past three years, their company's stock has been volatile, but as a result of dropping significantly in price. The result is that as of 2003, it is estimated that over 90 percent of Americans who hold stock options have at least one underwater stock option.

Besides the volatility created by a downward trending stock over the past three years, increasing restrictions and pressure have been placed upon employees, especially executive officers, to hold company stock versus selling vested stock. These restrictions, whether imposed by the company in blackout periods or self-imposed due to negative shareholder perception, also work against a volatile stock market.

One additional ancillary issue that has not been widely considered is the impact of a volatile market on the associated earnings expense of stock options. Almost all methodologies that have been considered by FASB to determine the value of an FMV stock option, such as Black-Scholes, utilize volatility as a variable in the calculation. For example, the Black-Scholes methodology currently utilized for reporting in company financial statements (as prescribed by APB Opinion 25) is dependent upon volatility as a key variable for determining the value of a fair market value stock option. Under Black-Scholes assumptions, the higher the volatility rate, the higher the stock option value. Therefore, the tremendous volatility realized by U.S. stock markets over the past several years, as well as years to come, would punish companies awarding stock options with an artificially inflated stock option expense. Consequently, companies would be more reluctant to utilize FMV stock options as an award to employees and would identify viable alternatives.

## Dividend Environment

Under current laws, qualified dividends received after 2002 are taxed to individuals, estates and trusts at the new lower capital gains tax rates (5 percent or 15 percent), according to IRS Forms & Publications "Change to Rules for Qualified Dividends." While some companies that have historically not paid out appreciation in the form of a dividend have adopted the policy in 2003, many other companies are considering adopting such a policy in the future.

Realizing that companies are changing or considering changing how shareholders receive a return on investment should force companies to evaluate how employees are rewarded from an equity perspective as well, especially in light of the fact that equity-based compensation is intended to align shareholder interests with employees. When considering the appropriate form of equity compensation for companies that pay dividends, restricted stock becomes one of the most obvious alternatives. To date, RSAs are the only form of equity compensation that provides employees the opportunity to receive dividends. Companies within industries, such as real estate investment trusts (REITS), oil and gas, and utilities that have traditionally paid shareholders in the form of dividends, have been heavy users of RSAs.

While companies can provide a cash payment equivalent to a dividend, also known as a dividend equivalent right (DER), these payments are, in fact, cash and accounted for as such with an associated expense. Dividends provided through restricted stock, on the other hand, are not expensed.

One item (discussed in Chapter 6) regarding the difference between RSAs and RSUs is the payment of dividends. RSUs do not provide dividend payments until the employee owns the stock, where RSAs provide dividend payments upon vesting.

## Shareholders and Dilution

Since 2000, shareholders, employees, media and legislators have had a less favorable view of stock options and an increasingly favorable view of restricted stock. There are various reasons for stock options falling out of favor, depending upon who is asked. Employees claim there is no value, or relatively little value associated with a fair market value stock option. Shareholders, media and legislators claim that stock options given to top executives will tempt corruption. Companies complain that as more stock options go underwater for a longer period of time, there are fewer shares available to award employees while the overhang (number of shares awarded and reserved for award to employees as a percentage of total shares outstanding) becomes too large. Thus, stock options are much more dilutive in a bear market compared to other LTIs.

When considering shareholder impatience with dilutive impact of equity awards, the number of shares utilized with stock option awards versus RSAs is a large factor. In fact, while much time and energy have been spent trying to mathematically determine the tradeoff value for restricted stock versus stock options, the reality is that there is an additional premium perceived by employees with restricted stock beyond the math.

From a purely mathematical standpoint, computing the ratio of restricted stock-to-stock options is a function of the original stock price and the expected appreciation of the stock over the life of the long-term incentive award. For example, not accounting for the discounted present value and assuming the stock is appreciating, the value of a stock option grant (Ys) over time is the product of the dollar value change in stock price (X, if X >= 0) and the number of shares awarded (as).

$$Ys = (X)\ as$$

The value of a restricted stock grant (Yr) over time is the product of the number of shares awarded (ar) and the sum of the original stock price (b0) and the change in stock price.

$$Yr = (X + b0)\ ar$$

To deliver the same targeted dollar value in long-term incentive for both awards (Yr = Ys), simple algebra reveals the ratio of stock options to restricted stock (as/ar)

$$as/ar = [1 + (b0/X)]$$

Accordingly, for a company with a current stock price at $50 and expected $10 appreciation over the time period, the ratio would be 6-to-1. For a company with a stock price at $10, with expected appreciation of $20, the ratio would be 1.5-to-1.

However, actual perceived value by the employees would affect this ratio significantly, and the ratio is customized to specific company and employee issues, including:

- Market cycle of company
- Age of workforce
- Risk tolerance of employees
- Market volatility
- Shareholder perception
- Overhang concern.

Considering these variables that impact employee perception of restricted stock vs. stock options, a general rule of thumb utilized by compensation practitioners for trading off restricted for stock options is one restricted stock for two-to-six stock options. Consequently, companies have needed to award far fewer shares of restricted stock than stock options.

## Underwater Stock Options

As of 2001, *workspan* magazine reported more than 80 percent of companies surveyed stated that some portion of their outstanding stock options was underwater. Of those, more than one-third reported that in excess of 50 percent of their outstanding options was underwater. With the markets continuing to drop since 2001, it estimated that over 90 percent of U.S. companies report some portion of their outstanding stock options is currently underwater. There are several problems associated with large amounts of underwater stock options.

First, companies are left in a quandary on how to retain key employees. While employees have no in-the-money value with underwater stock options, the situation becomes worse with deeply underwater options, resulting in no hope for in-the-money value. The situation worsens with the company next door offering star performers large stock option grants at all-time stock price lows.

Secondly, stock option repricing has fallen out of favor for several reasons. The main argument against repricing is that shareholders cannot reprice investments that go bad, but employees can. Employees already have an advantage because they do not have to invest money until they know the stock has appreciated. The translation is: no downside risk for option holders.

Additionally, FASB Interpretation 44 requires companies that reprice to use the "mark-to-market" accounting method for recording their compensation expense. In effect, the company has to expense, over the outstanding term of the repriced option, the amount the repriced option is in the money (or the stock price exceeds the exercise price) until the date of exercise.

Lastly, the growing number of unexercised stock options places pressure on overhang as well as the number of shares available in a given plan. As employees hold on to stock option awards, but do not exercise vested grants because there is no value, companies become restrained in their ability to provide meaningful additional awards to reinstate wealth accumulation opportunities.

## Retention of Key Talent

Retaining key talent is critical to a company's success, whether the market is characterized by the high growth of the late 1990s or the bear market in the first part of the 21st century. Given the longest bear market in post World War II history, and the resulting number of underwater stock options, companies are searching for innovative ways to retain key talent that will position them for future. Additionally, companies are searching for ways to accomplish this with many variables in mind, including smaller charge to earnings, with less dilution to shareholders, with alignment to shareholders (including a dividend-paying environment), and weathering a volatile stock market. As a result, the stage has been set for companies to start determining the most appropriate long-term incentive vehicle available. While there is no single magic pill to cure all, to date, the leading stock option alternative has been restricted stock.

# 3

# Drafting in the Peloton of Other Companies

**Peloton m 1.** SPORT, POL, ECON pack; être dans le ~ de tête *to be in with the front-runners*; être dans le ~ de queue *to be trailing behind* 2. MIL *squad*; (de sapeurs-pompiers) *contingent*; ~ de gendarmerie *police squad*; ~ d'exécution *firing squad*

The sport of cycling, not unlike the business world, is highly competitive, complex and, at times, brutal. Teams competing in road races, such as the Tour de France, must rely on tactics and drafting to overcome air resistance and the forces associated with gravity. Maximizing efficiency over both flat and hilly terrain becomes a necessity for competitors.

Because air resistance increases exponentially with speed, the technique known as drafting is most important during flat portions of the race where riders are traveling at higher speeds. Generally riders group together in a tight pack known as the "peloton" to take advantage of aerodynamic efficiencies. At times traveling only inches apart, peloton riders can save up to 40 percent in energy expenditures over nonparticipating competitors. The peloton is less effective during climbs where increased gravitational forces demand slower speeds. The peloton eventually breaks up and stronger riders begin to outpace competitors who relied more heavily on drafting effects.

This chapter takes a brief look at companies setting the peloton's pace with regard to the utilization of restricted stock in compensation programs. In addition, a look at other companies moving toward restricted stock will help identify the types of companies who may benefit from the drafting effect of these industry leaders. Finally, this chapter will discuss the steps needed to create value and how to make sure your company is prepared to ensure long-term success in a post-peloton environment.

## Key Companies Using Restricted Stock

**Amazon.com** The company offers less cash compensation than peers in the form of base salary. Executives are awarded relatively larger stock grants based on company performance. In November 2002, Amazon.com implemented an RSU program as its primary equity-based compensation vehicle. The company feels the RSU program allows for greater flexibility, less dilution and more closely aligns employees and shareholders.

**American Bankers Insurance Group** The company uses a nonqualified stock option program with contingent awards of restricted stock. All options are immediately vested over a short three-year term. Upon exercise, executives are eligible to receive three corresponding shares of restricted stock for each option. Executives receive dividend and voting rights during a five-year restriction period subject to forfeit if options are not held after exercise or they leave the company.

**Circuit City Stores Inc.** The company grants options and restricted stock under a 1994 stock incentive plan. Options, with an eight-year term, are granted and vest ratably over a four-year period. During fiscal 2003, the company began granting RSUs to senior management. Each unit is granted contingent upon continued employment over a three-year period. In addition, senior managers were granted restricted stock under a 1998 performance accelerated restricted stock award program (PARSAP). The PARSAP provides accelerated vesting based on total shareholder return.

**Colgate-Palmolive Co.** A "Long-Term Global Growth Program" replaced annual discretionary grants of restricted shares. Awards were determined based on financial criteria including compounded global annual net sales and earnings per share during three-year measurement periods. Threshold, target and maximum award opportunities are set in dollars as a percentage of base salary. Awards are paid in time-lapse restricted stock and are forfeitable if terminated.

**General Mills Inc.** After implementing a broad-based stock option program in the late 1980s, the company moved toward a combination of stock options and restricted stock with a proposal in 2003. The company plans to reduce overhang under the new plan while remaining competitive with its peers. RSAs will have a four-year minimum vesting period and will be granted contingent on continued employment.

**Intuit Inc.** The company has reduced annual stock option grants over the last several years to appropriately balance shareholder dilution concern. A fiscal 2003 mandatory share ownership plan offers executives a matching RSU bonus award for every two shares purchased.

**Darden Restaurants Inc.** Executives participating in the Management and Professional Incentive Plan (MIP) can receive prospective RSA and RSU grants based on the potential future impact of the employee, criticality going forward, and performance. In June 2003, the company elected to discontinue its practice of tying grants of restricted stock to the annual bonus.

**Prudential Financial Inc.** In March 2003, the company requested approval of an omnibus plan providing for the use of certain equity-based compensation incentives including, stock options, stock appreciation rights, restricted stock, RSUs and dividend equivalents. Under the new plan, the company intends to replace a current performance unit plan (PUP) with performance shares or restricted stock.

**ExxonMobil** Restricted stock replaced the use of stock options in 2002. Retention was identified as a key concern and the compensation committee concluded that restricted stock more closely aligned the interests of employees with those of the shareholders. Executive officers and 5,300 other key employees were eligible. Current shares owned will not be used to determine the size of subsequent grants.

**Western Digital Corp.** Executives are eligible to receive both non-qualified and incentive stock options in combination with RSAs and RSUs. The company targets above-average total compensation levels but seeks to put an above-average portion of total compensation at-risk or performance-based.

**Xerox Corp.** A "Leveraged Executive Equity Plan" (LEEP) requires employees to invest and deposit one year's base salary. Participants are eligible to receive company matches in nonqualified stock options and performance-based restricted stock earned over a three-year period. Awards are linked directly to ROA.

Although it may appear that these plans have little in common, each has been customized to meet individual company needs. In addition, the prevalence of restricted stock demonstrates not only increasing popularity, but also the value and versatility of restricted stock as a long-term incentive tool.

## Case Study: Microsoft

### *Background*

On July 8, 2003, Microsoft announced that it would grant RSUs to more closely align interests of employees and shareholders. The company also revealed plans to voluntarily restate prior financials under FAS 123 and to expense stock-based compensation moving forward. The statement attracted enormous media attention and intensified the stock option debate. The use of equity compensation and, more specifically, option alternatives took center stage. Although specific details remain undisclosed at the time of this publication, this case study serves to address the broader industry implications of Microsoft's new plan and possible motives for the policy shift.

After going public in 1986, Microsoft was among the first companies to implement a broad-based stock option program. Stock options were granted to all employees and everyone — executives and secretaries alike — shared in enormous amounts of wealth creation. Similarly, the company's recent decision to grant broad-based restricted stock will put Microsoft among the first major technology companies to move completely away from option use.

There are three elements to Microsoft's new plan: RSU awards, performance stock and the sale of underwater options to JP Morgan. Under the plan, all employees are eligible to receive RSUs, which vest ratably over a five-year period. Because the employee is receiving the right to receive shares in the future, dividends cannot be paid on the units and employees will not be able to make an IRC 83(b) election.

In addition to RSUs, the top 1 percent of Microsoft employees will also receive shared-performance stock awards. This smaller group, representing about 600 executives, will be given significant awards of stock based on performance criteria, including the number and satisfaction level of Microsoft customers. During three-year non-overlapping performance periods, executives are guaranteed to receive at least a third of the target award with a cap at 150 percent.

In perhaps the most notably innovative move, Microsoft also made plans to allow employees to sell underwater options to JP Morgan for cash. Subject to approval of the SEC, the opportunity included vested and unvested options with an exercise price of $33 dollars or greater. Actual prices paid for the options depended on the grant price and fair market value at the time of the transaction. The voluntary program required that employees choose to sell all or none of their eligible options. Employees electing to participate were to receive a portion of the proceeds at the time of sale and the remainder at a later date. The company would not be able to take tax deductions for option gains or cash payments following the transfer.

### *Implications*

When economic prosperity and bull markets create easier times for companies, groups quickly pack together in peloton-like formations. Companies seem content on drafting together and keeping pace with competitive pay trends. Stock option programs work great and industries huddle together benchmarking their peers. While these trends can be expected during good economic conditions, market downturns can force the peloton-like packs to dissolve. Companies that achieve greater efficiency in linking compensation strategy and organization success can emerge as undeniable leaders.

A number of unique characteristics separate Microsoft from its peers. On a relative basis, the company is in a superior cash position and not only can "afford" the compensation expense, but can also move forward with its plans to pay a dividend. This gives the company a competitive edge, even under the efficient market hypothesis, which theorizes that accounting expense for stock option plans have already been factored into financials through proxy footnote disclosure.

Although restricted stock works extremely well as a retention device, it is hard to argue that it attracts the same type of risk-taking employees who value stock options. Empirical evidence has shown that restricted stock programs are much more efficient when used in combination with FMV stock options. Companies should, therefore, consider options — or option alternatives — to supplement and diversify their LTI programs. Microsoft has attempted to take this approach with the addition of shared-performance stock awards. It is imperative that key decisions makers are retained and motivated to perform. The long-term effects of reducing risk (and reward) for the lower level employees remains to be seen.

These more historical aspects of restricted stock may not entirely apply to Microsoft as bear markets have left many option-holders somewhat bitter. Microsoft can take advantage of the current climate and continue to let culture, history and reputation set the company apart from its competitors. Although few companies can match Microsoft's prowess, the move to reallocate emphasis on the various aspects of attraction, retention and motivation highlights the need for companies to take customized approaches that properly support business strategy and capitalize on individual competitive advantages.

## Microsoft's Plan

*Pros*

- Employees receive value from underwater options
- Run rate reduction
- Balance longtime and new employees
- Employees will have immediate value
- Increased retention
- Increase in diversification of LTI plan
- Reduced overhang
- Utilization of compensation vehicle that competitors may not be able to match

*Cons*

- Appropriate risk-taking may be reduced
- May send negative signal to investors about anticipated stock appreciation
- May reduce attraction of key talent
- Premature announcement to expense under FAS 123 may have adverse impact due to irrevocability

On Dec. 12, 2003, Microsoft filed with the SEC formalizing plans to allow employees to sell underwater options to JP Morgan, essentially creating a market-based alternative to the Black-Scholes formula. Although the approach lends credibility to the pricing problem, it can create additional problems for companies. Surely, employees selling equity compensation (used for retention) to the highest bidder cannot make investors happy. In such an environment, employees could essentially liquidate long-term positions at companies (albeit at reduced prices) and accept offers elsewhere. Should the SEC approve the Microsoft/JP Morgan proposal, it is unlikely that shareholders will agree to transferability rights in the future.

Microsoft is not alone; many companies are moving away from stock options as FASB continues to move toward mandating stock option expensing. Key considerations of option alternatives are:

- Charge to earnings
- Cash flow
- Dilution
- Overhang
- Expected stock growth
- Need for attraction, retention and motivation.

## Steps to Creating Value

The key factors in designing and implementing broad-based restricted stock plans that support both corporate strategy and culture can be summarized in the following six steps:

**Step One:** *Identify employee behaviors that are strategically important.*

Generally, an organization's strategy can be categorized into, or into a combination of, the following five generic categories:

- Service/quality
- Innovation
- Niche
- Cost
- Core temporary

These strategies have implications for employee behavior. While innovation demands employees who can generate creative ideas, service demands a knowledgeable workforce committed to portraying the company positively to customers. The isolation of these desired behaviors can drive compensation design decisions to encourage greater behavior frequency.

**Step Two:** *Link strategic behaviors to the design of restricted stock plans.*

Taking steps to identify and link proper strategic behavior can increase program success. Microsoft used stock options to become a market leader because risk was a part of the company's history of encouraging innovation among employees. The program's ability to drive important employee behavior was critical to the plan's success. Microsoft valued and benefited from the types of employees who were drawn to a risk-tolerant culture.

If restricted stock is inherently less risky because of its inability to sink below water, is Microsoft trying to attract risk adverse employees? Not necessarily. While the shift may signal certain policy changes, it is more likely Microsoft has reallocated emphasis on attraction, retention and motivation.

**Step Three:** *Determine if other compensation tools could better achieve these objectives.*

Certain compensation tools have a proven track record of helping organizations achieve specific objectives, for example:

- Well-designed gain-sharing plans are reasonably successful in motivating specific performance objectives.
- Base pay usually serves an attraction and retention function.
- Pay above the market and the recruitment pool is bigger and the odds of employees staying are higher.
- Pay below the market causes applicant pools to increase and turnover to rise.

If a company wants to consider restricted stock to serve any of these objectives, it should ask if there is an incremental value added. Why did Microsoft previously use broad-based stock options as a recruitment tool? The answer is to attract a specific segment of people — those attracted by risk.

If restricted stock can send a desired message, then restricted stock should be part of the compensation package. If the goal for implementing a restricted stock program is to follow a trend, the company should be prepared for disappointment or even failure.

**Step Four:** *Subject the restricted stock program to a cost/benefit analysis.* While some find it easier to focus on the benefits of equity-based compensation, companies incur real costs when implementing, utilizing and maintaining equity-based programs. It isn't enough for the benefits of using restricted stock to outweigh costs. Companies should choose the program with the greatest total return or risk losing pace with the competition.

A cost/benefit analysis also should factor in both rising and falling market conditions. It is well known that much of the enthusiasm surrounding popular equity compensation programs (e.g., stock options) coincides with arguably the longest bull market in history. When the market exhibits volatility — or drops — many employees will lose enthusiasm for stocks. In short, companies should have compelling strategic reasons for using broad-based equity programs.

**Step Five:** *Ensure the program is consistent with other HR practices.* Compensation tools are only one of a large array of HR components that need to be properly aligned. To attract and retain appropriate risk takers, companies should be prepared to hire people with an appropriate capacity for risk-taking and train them to interpret information and make suitable decisions based on that information. Then, it is necessary to compensate for achievements and provide performance feedback to maximize future performance.

**Step Six:** *Continuously communicate the restricted stock program to employees.* Although often overlooked, two-way communication is a key component in all effective compensation design programs. When implementing broad-based plans, it cannot be assumed that employees understand the most basic components of equity compensation. Two-way communication and the presence of employee participation in decision making will help the program achieve desired objectives.

## Is Your Company Ready?

Compensation and other HR professionals usually are responsible for designing broad-based restricted stock plans. However, a successful implementation requires more than a good plan design, including some things that are somewhat outside of HR's control. First and foremost, the company must need and be ready to implement a broad-based plan. Other factors that have a make-or-break influence on a plan's success include cost, communication to employees, how the plan evolves to meet changing business needs and the rise and fall of stock prices.

Broad-based restricted stock programs may be inappropriate for companies with great growth potential, or smaller, closely held companies that do not want to go public or be sold.

### *Determining Readiness*

To determine whether the company needs a broad-based restricted stock plan, the key questions are:

- What emphasis does management place on attraction, retention and motivation respectively?
- What value will employees receive from a restricted stock program?
- Does the current rewards system need to change to support this?

The answers to the first two questions will vary from company to company, but certainly the trend is that an increasing number of companies are asking employees to find new ways to add value. For many of these companies, the reward system will need to change to adequately support the desired behaviors. Research shows that employees who believe that they will share in the company's success are more likely to be motivated to help the company succeed.

When the company decides it needs a broad-based restricted stock plan, it should assess whether the timing is right or whether it needs to lay other groundwork first. Companies will vary in the speed at which they move forward with designing and implementing a restricted stock plan.

The rate of speed depends upon:

- Strength of the culture that needs to be changed
- The speed at which the workforce changes or grows
- Employees' trust level for management
- The degree of change in migrating from the current rewards systems to the new system.

The company's reason for using a broad-based plan will determine the right time to implement the plan. Circumstances at the company need to be favorable for communicating a new broad-based plan. For example, pay inequities in the wake of an acquisition will infringe on the company's effort to communicate the new plan. In this case, the company should not implement a plan until it can communicate the new plan effectively.

If your company is considering implementing a restricted stock plan, it should keep the following in mind throughout the design process:

- Is restricted stock the best way for the company to attract and retain employees, and will the plan be effective in linking employee and shareholder interests?
- Can your restricted stock plan retain its attractiveness in the face of variable markets?
- Should RSAs be on top or carved out of other pay elements, such as salary?
- Should the plan be designed to include exceptions for downside catastrophes?

- How can restricted stock programs, their long-term nature, and the inherent risks be effectively communicated as more employees become eligible?

One attraction of broad-based restricted stock plans is the contribution they can make to the objective of creating an ownership culture. Whether stock is granted to executives only or to a much broader cadre of employees, striving to align worker interests with company interests is fundamental. Success obviously is dependent on knowing and understanding company interests. If problems exist after granting stock to top employees only, the company could be suffering from additional problems that cannot be solved by restricted stock. Decisions at the executive level are regularly made with an intimate understanding of corporate objectives, environmental obstacles and opportunities, and a wealth of financial and human resources information of which lower-level employees are unaware.

## Summary

Where do you want to be? Do you want to be in the peloton? Do you want to break away or lag behind? Whatever the decision, the key is to determine the path that is best for your company's long-term success. There will be sprints and there will be hills, but like the great Lance Armstrong, it is possible to overcome with the right planning, drive and determination.

# 4

# Restricted Stock vs. Other Long-Term Incentives

A thorough understanding of an organization's corporate vision and mission is the foundation of a discussion on compensation. The HR philosophy builds on the business strategy and serves as a guiding light in the design of all HR programs, including RSAs.

HR philosophy and strategy comprise the big picture. Total rewards philosophy and strategy narrow HR philosophy and strategy into three facets: compensation, benefits and work experience. (See Figure 8: Total Rewards Cycle.)

The circular process, surrounding the Total Rewards Cycle, indicates that any program should not become too far removed from the corporate mission.

FIGURE 8: **Total Rewards Cycle**

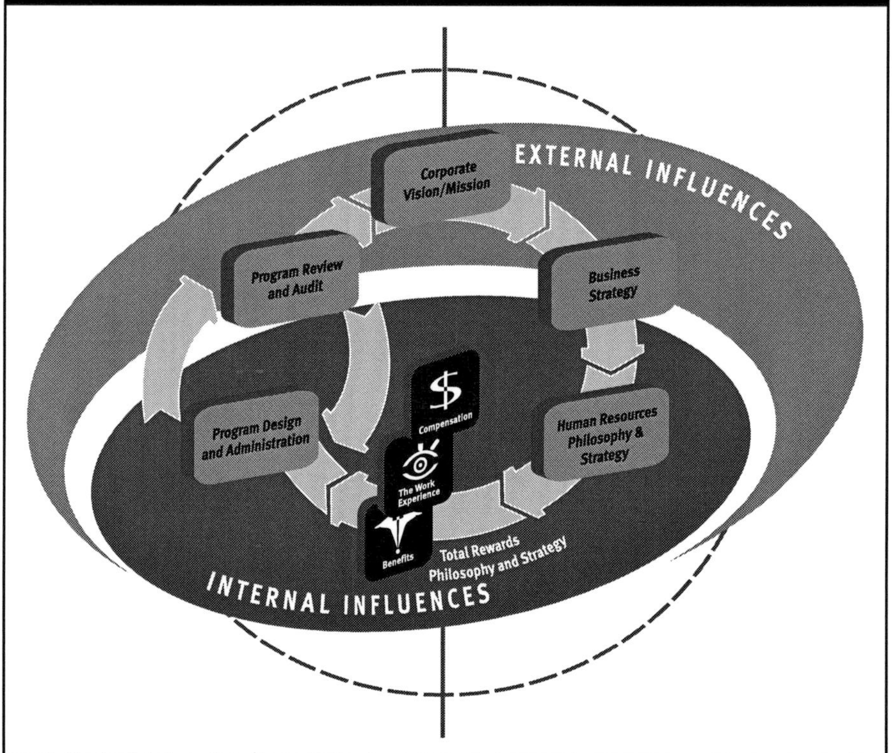

The organization's mission should be as clearly represented at the end of the process as it is at the outset.

## Influences on the Total Rewards Design Process

When designing a Total Rewards program, external and internal factors need to be considered. (See Figure 9: Influences on the Total Rewards Design Process.)

The key external influence that has precipitated the need to consider option alternatives — accounting change — is complex. However, the economy, politics, new corporate governance initiatives plus regulatory reform also are key drivers.

FIGURE 9: **Influences on the Total Rewards Design Process**

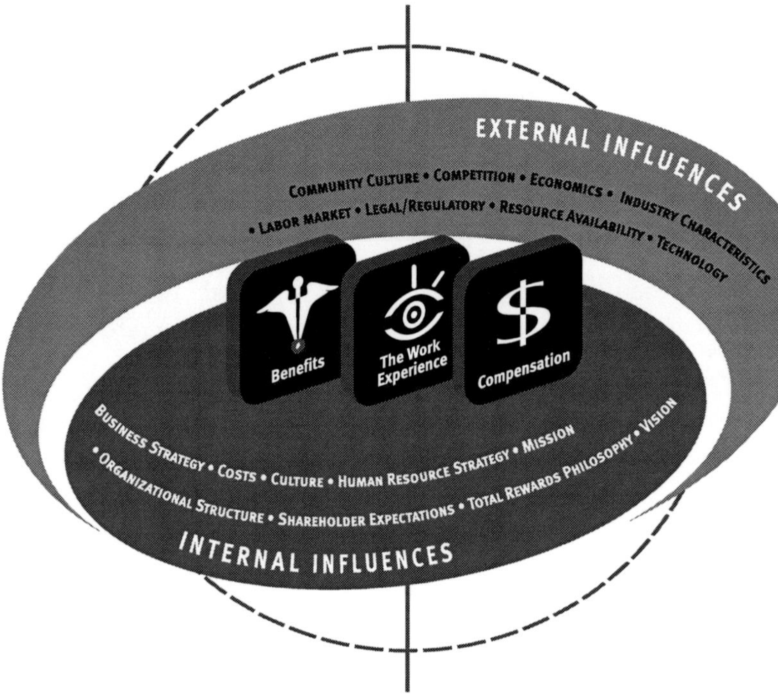

There will be several additional considerations in selecting LTIs that need to align with the company's HR philosophy and total remuneration strategy. In his book, *Executive Compensation Answer Book*, Bruce Overton lists these considerations:

1. **Executive investment.** Will the executive be required to make an investment, or will the executive participate in the plan without an investment?
2. **Ownership.** Is the program's objective to create ownership of the stock by the executive, or is the intent to reward the executive for improvement in stock price or some other financial measure?
3. **Company impact.** What are the long-term factors in the company business plan? What company goals should a long-term incentive plan support? How will the company change in the next three to five years, and what long-term incentive plan can best support this anticipated change?
4. **Performance measure.** What performance measures are indicative of company success? Is it stock price, earnings per share (EPS), or return on equity (ROE)? Is it important for executives to be rewarded based on a company performance measure that they can directly influence, rather than based on stock price — which is subject to outside factors such as stock market performance and the state of the economy?
5. **Tax and accounting impact.** What are the tax and accounting impacts on the company and the executives? When will the taxable event occur for the executive, which entitles the company to a corresponding compensation deduction in calculating its taxes? What is the plan's effect on the executive's tax situation? Will compensation be subject to ordinary or capital gains tax? Will the executive be subject to the alternative minimum tax? Is the payout chargeable as an expense against the company's income statement? Are there IRC 162(m) issues? Must the payout be accrued as a liability on the company's balance sheet? How important are income statement costs to the company? What percentage of the shares outstanding will be required for the plan, and how much dilutive effect will the plan have on EPS?
6. **Payout levels.** What payout level should the executive receive when long-term objectives are achieved? How much capital accumulation is appropriate and fair to the company, to the shareholders and to the

executives? What mix of short-term incentive and long-term incentive is desirable?

7. **Grant frequency.** How often should long-term grants and/or awards be made?
8. **Corporate and legal restrictions.** What corporate and/or legal restrictions might affect the company and the executive? What is the impact of federal and state securities laws on the plan, if any?
9. **Estate building.** Is the long-term incentive plan intended to supplement the retirement plan? How long will most participants be in the plan and how does this affect the amount of potential capital accumulation? If stock prices advance in the future as they have in the past, will the amount of capital accumulation be excessive?
10. **Eligibility.** Which executives have a direct effect on long-term performance?

What is the eligibility in competitor companies? What will be the impact if eligibility is increased or decreased?

As companies move away from the use of stock options and begin identifying possible alternatives, it may be a good time for HR executives to step backward and reevaluate the company's overall compensation philosophy to ensure its alignment with the HR philosophy and, ultimately, the corporate vision and mission. Once completed, HR executives and compensation committees will be in a position to prioritize the many considerations for selecting the best long-term incentive.

What's best for you? Let's take a look.

## The Contenders

### *Options*

Stock options give employees the right, but not the obligation, to purchase a predetermined number of shares in the company at a fixed price within a specified time period. Options can be deceptively complex, but they basically have value only if the stock price rises above the grant or strike price. They have been the predominant LTI vehicle since the mid '80s when the bull market was in full gear.

There are two basic types of options: incentive stock options (ISOs) and nonqualified stock options (NQSOs). These two broad categories are differentiated on the issue of whether the tax treatment favors the employee (ISOs) or the employer (NQSOs). Illustratively, they can be contrasted as follows:

> **Example:** XYZ Company awards 100 incentive stock options (ISOs) at $5 per share to employee Q on Jan. 1, 2004 (employee pays no tax). Employee exercises options at $10 per share on Jan. 2, 2005 (employee pays no tax except possible alternative minimum tax [AMT]). Employee then disposes/sells shares on Jan. 3, 2006 at $12 per share. The employee will pay capital gains on the $7 ($12 – $5). For the employer, there is no tax deduction unless the employee makes a disqualifying disposition. (See Figure 10.)

**FIGURE 10: Incentive Stock Options**

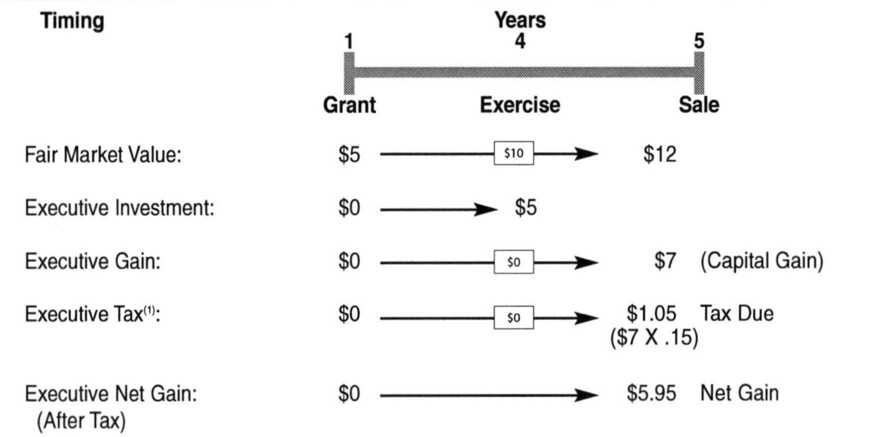


(1) Assumes the executive is subject to an ordinary income tax rate of 38.5%.

> **Example:** Mr. Middle Manager of Tsunami Corporation was granted 5,000 non-qualified stock options (NQSOs) on Aug. 5, 2003. The strike price of the options is $15, the fair market value (FMV) of the stock at grant. The options vest ratable over four years. By May 2008, the stock has risen to $22, and Mr. Manager exercises the options with a $7 in-the-money value. With the 5,000 options, Mr. Manager receives $35,000 in value and is taxed at ordinary income rates. The company receives a tax deduction equal to the employee's taxable income of $35,000. (See Figure 11.)

In addition there are many limitations on ISOs (eligibility, holding period, pricing, etc.) that do not apply to NQSOs. Summaries of each (Figures 12 and 13) are as follows.

FIGURE 11: Nonqualified Stock Options

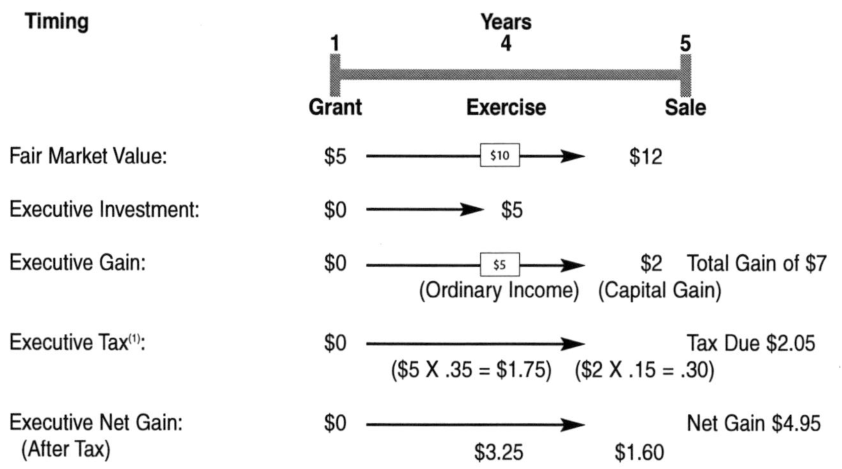


(1) Assumes the executive is subject to an ordinary income tax rate of 38.5%.

## *Performance Plans*

Since the mid 1980s, options have been the compensation incentive of choice. However, changes over the last 20 years have detracted from these programs making several other long-term incentive counterparts more attractive — the least of which are RSAs.

## *Performance Share Plans*

A performance share plan is a stock (or stock unit) grant award plan contingently granted upon the achievement of certain predetermined external or internal performance goals. These goals must be met during a specified period (e.g., three to five years) before the recipient has rights to the stock. Further, the share value is linked to either the fair market value of the employer's stock or a specific book/formula value. Thus, there is a double incentive for the grantee: Achieve the goals established and work toward a higher stock price.

> **Example:** Company provides Executive A with 1,000 performance shares, which have a five-year performance period and will be payable if certain performance metrics are met. The stock price at grant is $5. At the end of the five-year performance period, the stock has risen to $10. Executive A will be entitled to the 1,000 shares, now valued at $10, or $10,000. He will be taxed on the $10,000 and the company will receive a corresponding $10,000 tax deduction. (See Figures 14 and 15.)

**FIGURE 12: Incentive Stock Options — ISO(s)**

**Key Provisions**

- Executive may buy stock at a specified price (not less than 100% of fair market value) for a given period of time (ten-year maximum)
- Options may be exercised in any sequence
- The annual value of ISOs which become exercisable in any one year cannot exceed $100,000 per individual
- Appreciation from grant to sale qualifies for capital gain treatment provided holding period requirements are met
    - stock must be held at least two years after grant and one year after exercise

**Tax Impact on Executive**

- At grant — no tax
- At exercise — no tax assuming holding period requirements are met
- At sale — appreciation from grant price taxed at capital gains rate

**Tax Impact on Company**

- At grant — no tax deduction
- At exercise — no tax deduction
- At sale — no tax deduction unless executive fails to meet holding period requirements

**Earnings Impact**

- With FASB Statement 123 used to account for stock options, a charge to earnings will be calculated based on fair value at grant date using an option-pricing model
- Dilutive EPS Through Common Stock Equivalents

**Advantages**

- No charge to earnings if APB Opinion 25 is used
- Executive's tax liability is deferred until stock is sold
- Long exercise period allows executive flexibility and can be retentive
- Aligns executive interests with shareholders' interests
- Executive may defer taxes or may sell the stock earlier in a disqualifying disposition

**Disadvantages**

- Charge to earnings with FASB Statement 123
- Executive investment is required
- Company loses tax deduction
- Spread at exercise is considered tax preference item for purposes of computing alternative min tax
- Limited flexibility in designing option programs
- Dilutes EPS through common stock equivalents

Performance share plans would have been used more if not for the open-ended, unpredictable charge to earnings. In addition, goal-setting can be challenging as well.

## *Performance Unit Plans*

A performance unit plan (PUP) is a unit award plan contingently granted on the achievement of certain predetermined external or internal performance goals over a specified period (typically three to five years) before the recipient has a right to the unit. Unlike a PSP, the unit value rarely has any tieback to stock price, and the actual award payment is typically paid in cash.

## Figure 13: Non-Qualified Stock Options (NQSOs)

**Key Provisions**

- Executive may buy stock at a specified price for a given period of time
- Appreciation from grant date to exercise date taxed at ordinary income tax rates

**Earnings Impact**

- With FASB Statement 123 used to account for stock options, a charge to earnings will be calculated based on fair value at grant date using an option-pricing model
- Dilutes EPS through common stock equivalents

**Tax Impact on Executive**

- At grant — no tax
- At exercise — appreciation from grant price taxed at ordinary income tax rates
- At sale — appreciation from exercise price to sale price is taxed at capital gains rate

**Tax Impact on Company**

- At grant — no tax deduction
- At exercise — company receives tax deduction equal to executive's ordinary income
- At sale — no tax deduction

**Advantages**

- Aligns executive interests with shareholders' interests
- Company receives tax deduction
- No limitations on the amount that may be exercised
- Less dilutive than incentive stock options
- Recognizable to most executives
- Offers potential for long-term appreciation as company grows

**Disadvantages**

- Executive investment is required
- Executive incurs tax liability at exercise
- Dilutes EPS through common stock equivalents
- Possible charge to earnings with FAS 123

Example: Executive 2 is awarded 10,000 performance units based on revenue growth. The value of the unit is pegged at $30. Company Q will pay out the 10,000 units if sales grow at an annual rate of 10 percent per year. Assuming the goal is reached and the executive is still in the employ of the company at the end of the five-year performance period, she will receive $300,000. The executive will pay ordinary income tax on these monies while the company gets the deduction for the $300,000 as well. (See Figures 16 and 17.)

PUPs are a great diversification tool — especially when they are structured around the accomplishment of strategic (non-stock) goals and objectives.

**FIGURE 14: How Performance Shares Work**

| Timing | Years 1 | | 5 |
|---|---|---|---|
| **Performance Share** | **Grant** | | **End of Performance Period** |
| Share Value: Stock | $5 | Targets Met — Yes → | $10 Paid in Cash or |
| | | No → | $0 Shares Lapse |
| Executive Investment: | $0 | → | $0 |
| Executive Gain: | $0 | → ($10 X .35) | $10.00 (Ordinary Income) |
| Executive Tax(1): | $0 | → | $3.50 Tax Due |
| Executive Net Gain: (After Tax) | $0 | → | $6.50 Net Gain |

(1) Assumes the executive is subject to an ordinary income tax rate of 35%.

**FIGURE 15: Performance Shares**

**Key Provisions**

- Executive is granted contingent shares of stock at beginning of performance period (usually three to five years)
- Executive earns portion, or multiple, of shares originally granted; to the extent performance targets are met, they may be paid in cash and/or stock
- Minimum performance threshold must be met

**Tax Impact on Executive**

- At grant — no tax
- At payment — payout taxed as ordinary income

**Tax Impact on Company**

- At grant — no tax deduction
- At payment — company receives tax deduction equal to executive's ordinary income

**Earnings Impact**

- Under FAS 123, the performance shares may be valued using the option pricing model on the date of grant. (Source: Pillsbury Winthrop LLP)

**Advantages**

- No executive investment required
- Company receives tax deduction
- Performance oriented
- Potential maximum charge to earnings is fixed at grant
- Executive's tax liability can be paid out of award
- Helps finance options
- No dilution of shares outstanding unless paid in stock

**Disadvantages**

- Charge to earnings
- Difficulty in setting performance targets

## Figure 16: How Performance Units Work

| Timing | Years: 1 | | Years: 5 | |
|---|---|---|---|---|
| **Performance Share** | **Grant** | | **End of Performance Period** | |
| Unit Value: | $30 | Targets Met — Yes → | $30 | Paid in Cash or Stock |
| | | Targets Met — No → | $0 | Units Lapse |
| Executive Investment: | $0 | → | $0 | |
| Executive Gain: | $0 | → | $30.00 | (Ordinary Income) |
| Executive Tax[(1)]: | $0 | → ($30 X .35) | $10.50 | Tax Due |
| Executive Net Gain: (After Tax) | $0 | → | $19.50 | Net Gain |

(1) Assumes the executive is subject to an ordinary income tax rate of 35%.

## Figure 17: Performance Units

### Key Provisions

- Grants of units with absolute dollar value (e.g., $30) with payout contingent on meeting stated performance targets over a specified period (usually three to five years)
- To the extent targets are met, the dollar value of units is payable in cash and/or stock
- If minimum performance threshold is not met, units are forfeited
- Frequently used as financing mechanism for equity plans

### Tax Impact on Executive

- At grant — no tax
- At payment — payout taxed as ordinary income

### Tax Impact on Company

- At grant — no tax deduction
- At payment — company receives tax deduction equal to executive's ordinary income

### Earnings Impact

- Value of performance units is charged to earnings to the degree goals are achieved over the performance period

### Advantages

- No executive investment required
- Company receives tax deduction
- Performance oriented
- Potential maximum charge to earnings is fixed at grant
- Executive's tax liability can be paid out of award
- Helps finance options
- No dilution of shares outstanding unless paid in stock

### Disadvantages

- Charge to earnings
- Difficulty in setting performance targets

## *Phantom Stock*

Phantom stock is an arrangement whereby the executive receives the appreciation in the book, fair-market or formula value over a set period of time. Phantom shareholders do not own actual stock and typically do not have voting rights; however, they are usually eligible to receive dividends or their equivalent. Phantom stock is used by privately held companies that want to be competitive, but cannot or do not want to grant actual stock to executives.

> **Example:** On May 1, 2004, Executive C of Jessie James Corp. (a privately-held company) receives an award of 1,000 shares of phantom stock at no cost. Vesting is five years, or on April 30, 2009, as long as the executive remains an employee with the company. The value of the stock is $30 per share at the time of the award. Once vesting is complete, the stock has appreciated to $80 per share, an increase of $50 per share. Therefore, the executive will receive $50,000 of income. Jesse James Corp. will get a corresponding deduction of $50,000. (See Figures 18 and19.)

Phantom stock typically is the LTI of choice in privately held companies where shareholders desire that key management be aligned and motivated with them to increase the company's value without diluting the ownership structure.

**FIGURE 18: How Phantom Stock Works**

| Timing | Years: 1 | | Years: 5 | |
|---|---|---|---|---|
| **Phantom Stock** | **Grant** | | **Payout** | |
| Fair Market Value: (Book Value or Formula Value) | $30 | → | $80 | |
| Executive Investment: | $0 | → | $0 | |
| Executive Gain: | $0 | → | $30.00 | (Ordinary Income) |
| Executive Tax[(1)]: | $0 | → ($50 X .35) | $17.50 | Tax Due |
| Executive Net Gain: (After Tax) | $0 | → | $32.50 | Net Gain |

(1) Assumes the executive is subject to an ordinary income tax rate of 35%.

**Figure 19: Phantom Stock**

**Key Provisions**

- An arrangement whereby executive receives the appreciation in the book, fair market or formula value of a specified number of shares over a set period of time (e.g., five to ten years)
- Payable in cash and/or stock
- Executive may receive dividend equivalents

**Tax Impact on Executive**

- At grant — no tax
- At payment — appreciation is taxed as ordinary income

**Tax Impact on Company**

- At grant — no tax deduction
- At payment — company receives tax deduction equal to executive's ordinary income

**Earnings Impact**

- Appreciation is charged to earnings each quarter
- Also dilutes EPS by increasing shares outstanding if paid in stock

**Advantages**

- Aligns executive interests with shareholders
- Does not dilute stock ownership (when paid in cash)
- No executive investment required
- Company receives tax deduction
- Can be retentive if value increases

**Disadvantages**

- Unpredictable charge to earnings if paid in cash earnings
- May result in substantial cash outflows. Does not lead to direct stock ownership unless paid in stock
- Less flexibility since valuation date is set in advance

## *Stock Appreciation Rights*

A stock appreciation right, more commonly referred to as SAR, is an LTI vehicle whereby the corporation grants an executive the right to receive a dollar amount of value equal to the future appreciation of its shares. Typically, a SAR is exercised by the grantee after a specific vesting period. U.S. companies operating in foreign countries where the tax and/or other local laws preclude the use of stock options have used SARs extensively.

> Example: Executive L of Bat Masterson, Inc., received an award of 1,000 SARs at no cost May 1, 2004. Vesting is five years, or on April 30, 2009, as long as the executive remains an employee of the company. At the time of the award, the value of the company stock was $30 per share. When vesting is complete, the stock's value has appreciated to $80 per share. The executive will receive the difference between the $80 and $30 or $50 — for total income of $50,000. Bat Masterson, Inc., will get a corresponding deduction of $50,000. (See Figures 20 and 21.)

### Figure 20: How a Stock Appreciation Right Works

| Timing | Years 1 | | Years 5 | |
|---|---|---|---|---|
| **Stock Appreciation Right** | **Grant** | | **Exercise** | |
| Fair Market Value: (Book Value or Formula Value) | $30 | → | $80 | |
| Executive Investment: | $0 | → | $0 | |
| Executive Gain: | $0 | → | $50.00 | Paid in Cash (Ordinary Income) |
| Executive Tax[(1)]: | $0 | → ($50 X .35) | $17.50 | Tax Due |
| Executive Net Gain: (After Tax) | $0 | → | $32.50 | Net Gain |

(1) Assumes the executive is subject to an ordinary income tax rate of 35%.

### Figure 21: Stock Appreciation Rights (SARs)

**Key Provisions**

- Normally granted in tandem with an option where the executive, in lieu of exercising the option, can receive a payment equal to the excess of the stock's market value at exercise over the option price
- SARs may be attached to an Incentive Stock Option or a Non-Qualified Stock Option or may be granted on a "stand alone" basis without an option
- Payment of rights may be in cash, stock or a combination

**Tax Impact on Executive**

- Value between fair market value at time of exercise and price indicated on SAR is taxable income in the year of exercise and subject to withholding

**Tax Impact on Company**

- Tax deduction in the amount of the executive's income from exercise is allowed in the year executive is taxed

**Earnings Impact**

- If paid in cash, the value of the right, i.e., the excess of the market value of the stock over the option price (at the close of each accounting period), is a compensation expense that is accrued over the period the SAR is outstanding
- If paid in shares, the compensation cost would be fixed using an option pricing model and expensed over the vesting period

**Advantages**

- Forces executive to think like a shareholder
- Avoids executive financing costs of options
- Gains may be capped by company

**Disadvantages**

- Stock price changes may not parallel executive performance
- Accounting expenses are unknown in advance

Traditional SARs are best when granted in tandem with other plans. Stock-only SARs — where any appreciation will be paid out in company stock — are very advantageous to companies not concerned with dilution.

## Other Contenders

Contenders include:

- **Performance-based Stock Options** Performance-based options are stock options that require certain performance criteria to be met before the options can vest and then be exercised. Both incentive stock options and nonqualified stock options can be designed to be performance-based. This could mean the options may expire worthless if performance targets aren't met and there is no resultant vesting. These plans could prove beneficial because adding performance criteria enhances the motivational value of the grants. This, coupled with the already existent retention aspects, makes these plans very powerful, as long as the charge to earnings is palatable. Under APB 25, the plan has an open-ended charge, whereas under FAS 123, the charge is the determined fair value over the vesting period.
- **Indexed Stock Options** Like performance-based options, indexed options are indexed to some sort of external performance measure like the NASDAQ or the DOW. Payment is based on the stock price outpacing the performance of the set index. The accounting treatment for indexed stock options is identical to that of performance-based options. As these indices rise, the exercise price rises — and vice-versa. These plans have had favorable write-ups over the years, since they are perceived as being in perfect alignment with shareholder interests — except the resultant P&L charge. However, true analysis reveals these programs aren't as beneficial as touted — especially when considering the earnings dilution issues surrounding them and the disconnect with shareholders. Because of the nature and complexity of these options, they require significantly more shares to deliver the same value as traditional options. Therefore, dilution could be the most serious concern when granting index stock options. Also, from the perspective of shareholder alignment, it is probable that if stock price increases, the executive would not earn as much as the shareholder. Additionally, if the stock price drops, the executive could earn more than the shareholder, depending on the performance of the index. Combined with the unfavorable accounting treatment, these reasons make indexed stock options impractical for use by business today.

- **Dividend Equivalent Rights** In light of proposed tax changes, dividends may become more prevalent in U.S. companies. This will mean that companies will take a portion of their earnings (that drives stock price appreciation) and will pay it out to shareholders as a dividend. If this is the case, a dividend equivalent right (DER) may be appropriate in keeping executives in alignment with their shareholders. The "equivalent right" is usually a unit; each unit entitles the executive to the quarterly payments declared on the common stock. The unit can be payable on only vested awards or on both vested and non-vested, depending on the LTI program goals and cost constraints.
- **Economic Value Plans** Economic value plans are plans designed around the cost of capital. Capital costs include the cost associated with both equity and debt and usually are easy to identify on a company's financial statement. To the extent executives can deliver more than this cost of capital, the plan begins to pay out. These plans often do not have maximums, thereby creating intense desire to perform.
- **Qualified Plans** Employee stock purchase plans (ESPPs), employee stock ownership Plans (ESOPs) and 401(k) plans shouldn't be forgotten either, especially for companies whose cultures want to drive "ownership mentality" throughout their firms. All have favorable tax treatment, provided they abide by the rules and regulations set out by IRS for their use.

## Two True Contenders: Discounted Stock Options and Nonqualified Deferred Compensation

In the business world, there is always someone else vying to be the next "sheriff." We believe discounted stock options (DSO), along with nonqualified deferred compensation (NQDC) plans could possibly be the next "marshals to rule."

## Discounted Stock Options

A DSO is a standard nonqualified stock option with a grant or exercise price lower than the fair market value on the date of grant. The "discounting" provides what is, in effect, immediate ownership — similar to an RSA. As a result, it protects its grantees from market volatility in an effort to enhance retention. As with other long-term plans, vesting requirements are typically attached.

**Example:** Executive M works for High Tech, Inc., where she is granted 5,000 shares of stock on May 1, 2003. The fair market value of the stock at grant is $5, but the grant/exercise price is $2. After four years of vesting, the value of the stock has risen to $10. M has ordinary income of $8,000, which is calculated as follows:

| | |
|---|---|
| Value of the stock at exercise | $10,000 |
| Purchase Price (Grant Value) | $ 2,000 |
| Ordinary Income | $ 8,000 |

High Tech, Inc., receives a corresponding tax deduction for $8,000 like a typical stock option. (See Figures 22 and 23.)

The true power of a DSO is best seen graphically. Figures 24 and 25 show a comparison between stock options, restricted stock and DSOs.

As the stock price appreciates away from zero, the most obvious difference in restricted stock — compared to stock options — is a decreased slope due to the grant ratio. Assuming both awards are granted at point "x," an employee would strictly prefer a grant of restricted stock over area "A" up until point "y"; not surprisingly, the probability that price movement will remain in area "A" is much higher. Conversely, employees who believe the stock price will move past point "y" will strictly prefer stock options. These

**Figure 22: How Discounted Stock Options (DSOs) Work**

| Timing | Years: 1 | 4 | | 6 | |
|---|---|---|---|---|---|
| **NonQualified Stock Option** | **Grant Price** | **FMV@Grant** | **Exercise** | **Sale** | |
| Fair Market Value: | $2 → | $5 → | $10 → | $12 | |
| Executive Investment: | $0 → | $0 → | $2 | | |
| Executive Gain: | $0 → | $0 → | $8 (Ordinary Income) → | $2 (Capital Gain) | Total Gain of $10 |
| Executive Tax[(1)]: | $0 → | $0 → | ($8 X .35 = $2.80) → | $2 X .15 = .30) | Tax Due $3.10 |
| Executive Net Gain: (After Tax) | $0 → | $0 → | $5.20 → | $1.70 | Total Net Gain $6.90 |

(1) Assumes the executive is subject to an ordinary income tax rate of 35%.

employees generally are less risk adverse, as the probability the stock price will move higher decreases over area "B."

The second major difference is brought into play if the stock price depreciates past point "x" towards zero. While RSAs retain some in-the-money value, stock awards fall underwater anywhere between the origin and point "x." Given that the probability function used in this example shows that slight depreciation below the grant price is most likely, it is not surprising that employees in this company would prefer restricted stock.

This example shows the trade-off that exists between stock options and restricted stock. Employees granted restricted stock benefit from increased security, but may lack appropriate incentives to ensure proper risk-taking. To remedy this situation, companies may choose to grant a combination of restricted stock and stock options. Figure 25 shows how discounted stock options may better solve the problem.

**FIGURE 23: Discounted Stock Options (DSOs)**

**Key Provisions**

- Executive may buy stock at a specified discounted price for a given period of time
- Discountable appreciation from grant date to exercise date taxed at ordinary income tax rates

**Earnings Impact**

- Under APB 25, a charge to earnings equal to the discount option price less than 100% of fair market value at grant
- If FAS 125 is used, the charge to earnings will be calculated based on the estimated fair value at grant using an option-pricing model
- Dilutes EPS through common stock equivalents

**Tax Impact on Executive**

- At grant — no tax
- At exercise — discount plus appreciation from grant price taxed at ordinary income tax rates
- At sale — appreciation from exercise price to sale price is taxed at capital gain

**Tax Impact on Company**

- At grant — no tax deduction
- At exercise — company receives tax deduction equal to executive's ordinary income
- At sale — no tax deduction

**Advantages**

- Immediate "in the money" value
- Aligns executive interests with shareholders' interests
- Company receives tax deduction
- No limitations on the amount that may be exercised
- Recognizable to most executives
- Offers potential for long-term appreciation as company grows

**Disadvantages**

- Charge to earnings
- Executive investment is required
- Executive incurs tax liability at exercise
- Dilutes EPS through common stock equivalents

FIGURE 24: **Comparison of Stock Options, Restricted Stock and Discounted Stock Options**

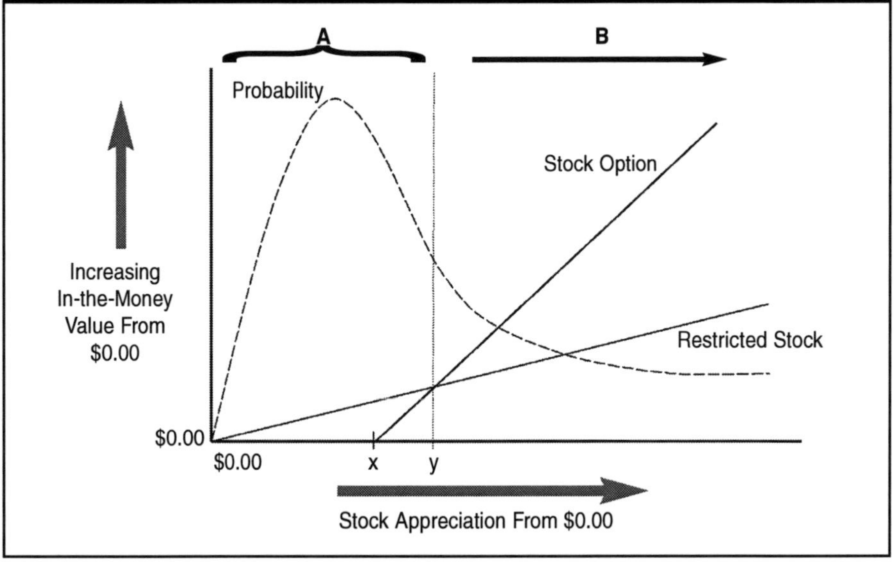


FIGURE 25: **Comparison of Stock Options, Restricted Stock and Discounted Stock Options**

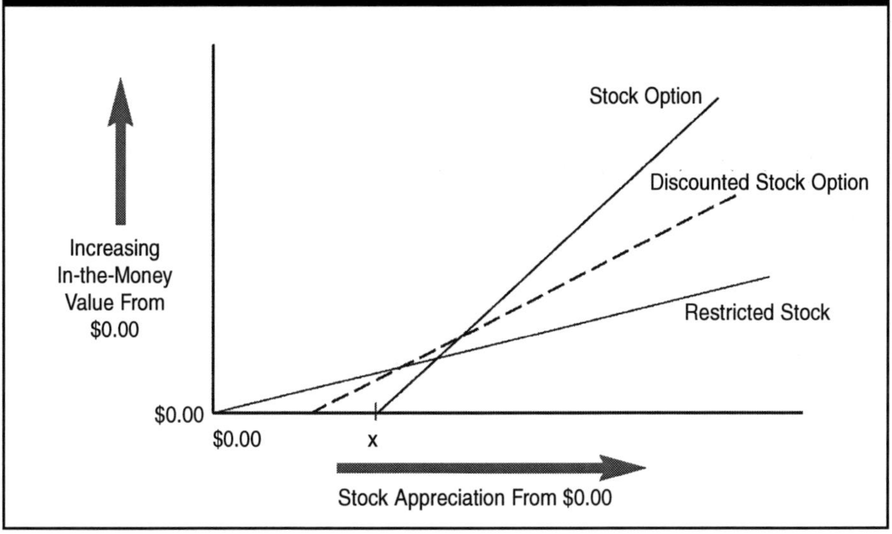


The discount associated with a DSO allows companies to incorporate appropriate levels of both downside protection and upside potential. This example shows a discounted stock option that has been awarded with roughly half of the downside protection of an RSA coupled with approximately half of the potential in-the-money value of a stock option. Thus, the DSO gives the employee both downside protection and an appropriate incentive to take warranted risk. Companies that take advantage of the ability to increase customization can gain efficiency and higher returns from their long-term incentive programs.

## Nonqualified Deferred Compensation Plans

Like restricted stock, nonqualified deferred compensation plans are an excellent, cost-effective tool for attracting and retaining quality executives and bolstering shareholder value.

### *What Are They?*

Nonqualified deferred compensation plans are usually extensions of qualified 401(k) plans that allow executives to defer a percentage of salary and, in some cases, defer bonus money and related taxation. The associated or prorated tax deduction is also deferred until payment is made to the participants.

As with qualified plans, these vehicles may be structured to provide tax-deferred growth, depending on the underlying investments. There may or may not be a company match, incentives for meeting performance goals and/or vesting schedules.

While companies are required to fund qualified plans, no such requirement exists for nonqualified deferred compensation plans. However, executive participation in these plans is much lower if a financing vehicle and trust are not in place to ensure the payouts.

Astute companies rely on "rabbi trusts," which usually guarantee that executives participating in a nonqualified plan will be paid even if the company is acquired, or future management tries to rescind the plan. In the event of bankruptcy, however, executives are unsecured general creditors.

### *Why Executives Like Them*

Nonqualified deferred compensation plans help executives accrue savings and investments so they can maintain their lifestyle upon retiring. Accounts grow on a tax-deferred basis and will be taxed at a presumably lower tax rate when the executive retires.

As the chart below shows, a middle-age employee earning $50,000 a year is typically able to receive 70 percent of his projected final salary from Social Security and qualified retirement plans alone. However, an executive earning more than $200,000 will usually receive barely over 20 percent of his final salary from these vehicles. This is due to the variety of IRS limits on what can be contributed to and received from qualified plans. Nonqualified deferred compensation plans help bridge this gap.

For example, a 55-year-old executive in 2004 whose annual compensation is $200,000 may have just finished paying off large college tuition bills and mortgage payments and want to defer $50,000 annually until retirement at age 62. However, the maximum amount that he can defer under qualified 401(k) rules in 2004 is $16,000. The nonqualified deferred compensation plan makes up the shortfall.

Executives also like the plans because they facilitate financial diversification. The return can be a fixed-rate or tied to a benchmark, such as the Moody's Corporate Bond Index. Other deferred compensation plans have returns that mirror mutual funds or other equity investments.

### *How They Serve Shareholders*

Unlike stock options, companies and their shareholders do not experience earnings dilution when they implement nonqualified deferred compensation plans. In fact, because executives are deferring their own compensation, plans can be structured so they have minimal or no cost to the company. Deferred compensation programs also can have company matches and even mirror the qualified 401(k) plan's provisions in this regard.

Some companies also will provide a higher match amount, or fixed-income crediting rate, tied to its return on equity or, for example, a division's performance.

In addition, these plans help give shareholders a "golden handcuff" on executives. There can be reductions on interest crediting and vesting provisions if executives take a job with a competitor, for example.

If a company does not have a deferred compensation plan, but simply chooses to pay a higher salary and bonus to retain an executive, it has absolutely no leverage once these monies are paid.

### *Fosters Managerial Stability*

In recent years, many executives became fixated on stock market trends and decided to liquidate stock options when a significant gain could be realized. This action undercuts the intention that many companies had when they designed these plans as long-term compensation vehicles that would focus executives' attention on sustained corporate profitability rather than stock market "pops."

With nonqualified deferred compensation plans, particularly those that have vesting provisions and financial incentive benchmarks, an executive's compensation can be more closely tied to actual corporate performance than with stock options.

Nonqualified deferred compensation plans are popular, though not yet universal. A recent study by The Todd Organization found that 59 percent of public companies with annual revenues over $250 million offer such plans. (See Figure 26.) That means four out of 10 companies have a competitive disadvantage when trying to attract and retain the best and brightest management talent.

Nearly all companies would be well served to adopt a nonqualified deferred compensation plan or review their existing plan. The benefits to executives and shareholders, coupled with the corporate stability nonqualified deferred compensation plans provide, are quite significant.

FIGURE 26: Importance of Qualified vs. Nonqualified Plans

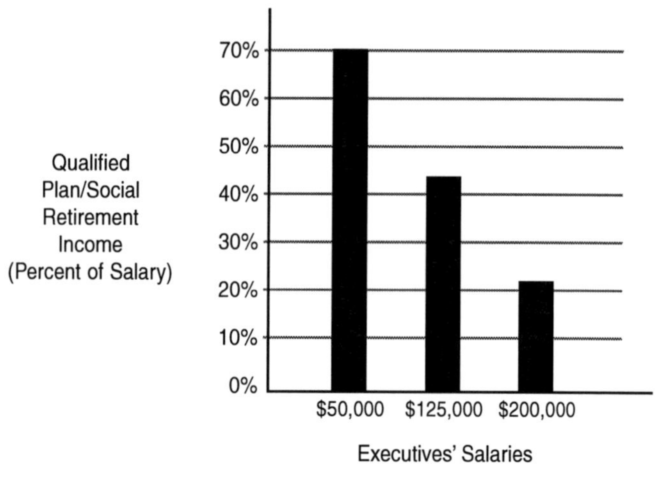


Source: The Todd Organization

## Comparison of RSAs to Other Key LTIs

### Restricted Stock Awards

**Key Provisions**

Whole value shares to employee/restrictions encourage retention

**Tax Impact**

Employee

- At grant — no tax (unless 83[b] election made)
- As restrictions lapse, ordinary income is taxable
- Dividends taxed as ordinary income

Employer

- Tax deduction on employees' ordinary income, including dividends paid

**Earnings Impact**

- Fixed charge to earnings equal to fair market value (FMV) of stock at grant date, amortized over vesting period

### Restricted Stock Unit

**Key Provisions**

Similar to RSAs except with units — an unfunded promise to pay

**Tax Impact**

Employee

- At grant — no tax
- Ordinary income when stock is issued
- Dividends taxed as ordinary income

Employer

- Tax deduction when employee has income

**Earnings Impact**

If payable in stock, fixed charge to earnings equal to FMV of stock at grant date, amortized over vesting period

### ISOs

**Key Provisions**

Qualified stock options / design restrictions

**Tax Impact**

Employee

- Capital gains at sale

Employer

- No tax deduction

**Earnings Impact**

APB 25

- No charge to earnings*

FAS 123

- Charge to earnings

* Could change soon

**Comparison of RSAs to Other Key LTIs (Continued)**

**NQSOs**

**Key Provisions**

Nonqualified stock options/design flexibility

**Tax Impact**

Employee

- Ordinary income at exercise
- Capital gains at sale

Employer

- Tax deduction on employees' ordinary income

**Earnings Impact**

APB 25

- No charge to earnings*

FAS 123

- Charge to earnings

**DSO**

**Key Provisions**

Nonqualified stock option granted below FMV

**Tax Impact**

Employee

- Ordinary income at exercise
- Capital gains at sale

Employer

- Tax deduction on employees' ordinary income

**Earnings Impact**

- Fixed charge equal to amount of discount below FMV

**Performance Shares**

**Key Provisions**

Employee earns portion of multiple of shares, paid in cash or stock, if targets are met.

**Tax Impact**

Employee

- At payment — ordinary income

Employer

- Tax deduction on employees' ordinary income

**Earnings Impact**

- Charge to earnings using option pricing model on grant date

* Could change soon

## Comparison of RSAs to Other Key LTIs (Continued)

### Performance Unit Plan

**Key Provisions**

Employee earns portion of units, paid in cash if targets are met

**Tax Impact**

Employee

- At payment — ordinary income

Employer

- Tax deduction on employees' ordinary income

**Earnings Impact**

- Charge to earnings base performance toward goal

### Phantom Stock

**Key Provisions**

Employee receives appreciation in book, formula or FMV of shares over a set time period. Paid in cash or stock.

**Tax Impact**

Employee

- At payment — ordinary income

Employer

- Tax deduction on employees' ordinary income

**Earnings Impact**

- Appreciation is charged to earnings each period

### SARS

**Key Provisions**

Granted stand alone or in tandem with stock options. Payment in cash or stock equal to stock's market value at exercise over the option price.

**Tax Impact**

Employee

- At payment — ordinary income

Employer

- Tax deduction on employees' ordinary income

**Earnings Impact**

The value of the right is a compensation expense accrued over period SAR is outstanding if paid in stock

## Comparison of RSAs to Other Key LTIs (Continued)

### ESOP

**Key Provisions**

Qualified defined contribution (DC) plan. Majority of shares in company stock

**Tax Impact**

Employee

- At distribution — ordinary income

Employer

- At payment contributions to fund ESOP and dividends paid on ESOP are deductible

**Earnings Impact**

Charge to earnings

### 401(k)

**Key Provisions**

Qualified DC plan. Employer match may be in company stock. No more than 10% of employee elective deferrals in company stock.

**Tax Impact**

Employee

- At distribution — ordinary income

Employer

- At contribution-tax deduction on contribution

**Earnings Impact**

Charge to earnings for any match

### NQDCs

**Key Provisions**

Flexible DC programs. Employer-sponsored retirement plan that does not meet requirements for a qualified plan under IRC 401(a).

**Tax Impact**

Employee

- Tax deferred until receipt

Employer

- Tax deduction deferred until employee is taxed

**Earnings Impact**

Charge to earnings for any match

# 5

# The Investment Required

## Are Restricted Stock Plans Worth the Cost?

RSAs can provide companies with many useful benefits. However, while they're becoming more common for a broader range of companies and employees, they're far from universal — primarily because they have significant economic and implementation costs.

## Economic Costs

There is great debate over the "right way" to evaluate and express the economic cost of equity grant to the company. FASB seemingly spends its entire life and energy on this issue. But, while there may be considerable debate about what is the right way to account for the cost of employee equity on a company's financial statements, few would argue that they have no economic cost. If equity did not have economic costs, it seems very likely that companies would grant far more than they do today.

The more equity the company grants, the greater the economic cost of the plan. Therefore, the key differentiating factors of RSA plans also are the key drivers of the plan's economic cost. The greater the participation, the more awards are granted and, hence, the higher the cost. Likewise, giving employees greater upside requires giving them larger grants, which again increases economic costs.

It is common practice to evaluate RSA grants, like options, as a percentage of shares outstanding. It's less effective than looking at the economic cost because this does not easily allow for plan comparison.

Consider a company looking to increase employee participation in business success. It is considering a gainsharing plan, which is expected to cost about $5 million per year. It also is considering a broad-based RSA plan. If the company knows that the RSA plan has an economic cost of $6 million a year, it can weigh the pros and cons of the RSA plan easily versus the gain-sharing plan. If the company knows only that the RSA plan would increase annual grants by .5 percent of shares outstanding, it is impossible to compare the costs of the two plans directly.

This does not imply that an RSA plan should only be implemented if the economic costs are lower than those of the alternatives. But without assigning a dollar cost to the RSA plan, decision makers cannot assess the balance of costs and benefits of the RSA plan appropriately relative to other program alternatives.

## Implementation Costs

Besides economic costs, there are at least three other categories of implementation costs that companies should consider before implementing an RSA plan: opportunity cost, communication cost and administration cost.

## Opportunity Costs

When a company considers implementing an RSA plan, it also should evaluate the alternative programs that could be implemented — either to address the same business issues that the broad-based option plan addresses or other issues that are important to the company. Specifically, while RSA plans can do much to support HR and business objectives, many other programs often can exceed RSAs with equal or less downside for the company (e.g., cost, risk, difficulty). These may include other forms of participatory compensation plans or programs that aren't compensation plans at all.



For example, an employee stock purchase plan (ESPP) and/or employee stock ownership plan (ESOP) may be worthwhile alternatives. An ESPP allows employees to purchase company stock at a discounted price (15 percent), often via payroll deduction.

An ESOP, on the other hand, is a qualified defined contribution plan that allows employees to receive company shares that accrue to plan participants and are payable upon retirement or separation from organization.

## Communication Costs

Communicating the stock option plan to employees is important and difficult. For global companies, communicating the plan to employees in locations worldwide is even more challenging. It is relevant for companies to view communication as a cost of plan implementation. Because these plans are strategic in nature, companies usually are willing to spend more time communicating them to employees. (See Chapter 8, "Final Considerations.")

## Administration Costs

An option plan with 100 anticipating employees can be managed with relative ease. However, when participation includes 10,000 employees, the administration costs take on a different scope. Administering a broad-based stock option plan to a large group of people requires full-time staff and sophisticated recordkeeping systems. The dollar cost of plan administration is not large compared to the economic cost of granting the options. The organization also may want to consider outsourcing plan administration, which incurs additional costs while saving others.

(See Chapter 8, "Final Considerations.")

# 6

# Restricted Stock with a Twist

## Restricted Stock Units (RSUs)

As highlighted in Chapter 3, RSUs are the newest version of restricted stock that has been widely publicized by Microsoft's 2003 announcement. RSUs are very similar to RSAs with a few key differences.

An RSU is an agreement to issue underlying stock at the time of vesting. No shares are delivered until the employee satisfies the vesting schedule. Once vested, the taxes owed are netted (deducted) out of the available units before the employee receives the units. By using units instead of the traditional RSA described in Chapter 1, a company secures additional advantages like:

- Eliminating the need for 83(b) elections and all the administrative and communication issues associated with this
- Facilitating the payment of taxes at vesting with an automatic withholding of shares
- Postponing shareholder dilution until vesting/payout
- For companies with multinational operations, RSUs often are better for participants then RSAs due to tax timing.

A summary of RSUs is highlighted in Figure 27.

## Performance-Accelerated Restricted Stock

A cool twist to the traditional time-vested restricted stock award is its "performance-vesting" counterpart known as a performance-accelerated restricted stock award plan (PARSAP). Under this type of plan, the restriction can be stretched over a longer period of time than usual (eight years versus three years) to add retention value and spread the P&L charges out, but with an enhanced motivational feature of accelerating or lifting of restrictions if certain pre-determined performance criteria are achieved.

## Figure 27: Restricted Stock Units

### Key Provisions

- Outright grant of shares to executives with restrictions as to sale, transfer and pledging
- Restrictions lapse over a period of time (e.g., three to five years)
- As restrictions lapse, executive has unrestricted shares which he or she may sell, transfer or pledge
- If executive terminates employment, all unvested shares are forfeited
- During restriction period, executive receives dividends and can vote the shares

### Earnings Impact

- Fair market value at grant charged to earnings over restriction period
- Subsequent appreciation not charged to earnings
- Immediate dilution of EPS for total shares granted

### Tax Impact on Executive [(1)]

- At grant — no tax
- As restrictions lapse — the current market value of vested shares taxed as ordinary income
- Dividends received during restriction period taxed as ordinary income

### Tax Impact on Company [(1)]

- At grant — no tax deduction
- As restrictions lapse — company receives tax deduction equal to executive's ordinary income
- At sale — no tax deduction
- Dividends paid during restriction period are deductible by company when paid

### Advantages

- No executive investment required
- Promotes immediate stock ownership
- Charge to earnings is fixed at time of grant
- If stock appreciates, company's tax deduction exceeds fixed charge to earnings
- Aligns executive's interests with shareholders
- Recognizable to most executives
- Offers executive potentially long-term appreciation as company grows

### Disadvantages

- Charge to earnings
- Immediate dilution of EPS
- Executive may incur tax liability before shares are sold
- If stock depreciates, company's fixed-earnings charge exceeds tax deduction

(1) Assumes 83(b) election is not made. If an 83(b) is made, executive recognizes income on the date the restricted stock was issued, and the company receives an immediate tax deduction for the initial value of the shares (but not for subsequent appreciation during the restriction period); dividends paid during the restriction period are not deductible.

**Example:** An Executive is awarded 40,000 restricted shares that vest ratably over an eight-year period. The current stock price is $10. The annual amortized charge to earnings is $50,000 per year (5,000 shares X $10). Each 30 percent appreciation in stock price accelerates vesting two years. In the event the stock appreciates to $13 at year 1, 15,000 shares become vested (5,000 for time+10,000 performance accelerated). If the stock appreciates to $29 in year 1, all 40,000 shares become vested. The company takes a charge to earnings matching the vested amount of shares, but the maximum charge to earnings is known and budgeted. Additionally, the company receives a matching tax deduction equal to the executive's recognized ordinary income — or the full amount of the stock appreciation times the number of shares — assuming no 83(b) election was taken.

There are several benefits of PARSAPS. First is the accounting and tax anomaly. The amortized charge to earnings for a PARSAP is spread over a longer period of time than a traditional RSA. Using the above illustration, 40,000 RSAs awarded at FMV of $10 with typical vesting of four years would equal a $100,000 annual charge to earnings. However, the above PARSAP is spread over an eight-year period, and the annual charge to earnings is $50,000. In the event the performance requirements are met, vesting is accelerated. At such time, the accelerated portion of the award is taken as an accelerated charge to earnings. However, the charge to earning is always capped at the grant date price, while the tax deduction equals the executive's taxable ordinary income, which is the number of shares vested times the appreciated stock price. In the above example, assuming the stock price appreciates to $30 in year one, all 40,000 shares become vested. The company takes the full charge to earnings of $400,000 (40,000 shares x $10); however, the company gets a full tax deduction equal to the executive's taxable income of $1,200,000. Assuming a corporate tax rate of 35 percent, the company would save $420,000 while taking a $400,000 charge to earnings. Simply stated, the company would have a net positive effect of $20,000. Companies can do their own math to match acceleration for performance with financial gain.

Second, this simple "twist" boosts the retentional and motivational aspects over a traditional RSA significantly. Boards, shareholders and HR executives tend to favor the additional performance wrinkle to quiet critics of restricted stock the so-called "payment for breathing." Combine the added retention and motivation with the better accounting consequences and the PARSAP may prove beneficial in a company's LTI program.

## Founder's Stock

Founders stock is stock granted very early in a company's business cycle whereby key employees (founders) purchase shares of common stock at a nominal value. Similar to restricted stock awards, there are usually restrictions attached, such as continued employment. In the event the employee (founder) does not meet the stated restrictions, the shares are forfeited. The idea behind founders stock is to provide an ownership opportunity for executives while the stock is at a deep discount.

**Example:** On May 1, 2003, Executive 2 is granted 10,000 shares of NEWCO stock at $1 per share. There is a five-year restriction on the plan. At the end of the five years, the company has gone public. Now the stock is trading at

$50 per share. Assuming no 83(b) election has been taken, (Note: Usually, they are in this situation since the amount of tax paid is nominal) the executive will receive $500,000 of income. On April 30, 2008, NEWCO will get a tax deduction for the same. However, in the event the 83(b) election was taken, then the executive recognizes long-term capital gains on the $490,000 and the company does not get the deduction. (See Figure 28.)

**FIGURE 28: How Founders Stock Works**

| Timing | Years 1 | | Years 5 | |
|---|---|---|---|---|
| **Restricted Stock** | **Grant** | | **Restrictions Lapse** | |
| Fair Market Value: | $5 | → | $10 | |
| Dividends: | $0 | → | $1.00 | |
| Executive Investment: | $0 | → | $0 | |
| Executive Gain: | $0 | → | $11.00 | (Ordinary Income) |
| Executive Tax[(1)]: | $0 | → ($11.00 X .35) | $3.85 | Tax Due |
| Executive Net Gain: (After Tax) | $0 | → | $7.15 | Net Gain |

(1) Assumes the executive is subject to an ordinary income tax rate of 35%. If an 83(b) election was made within 30 days of the award, the executive would be taxed on the fair value of the stock at grant as ordinary income, with subsequent appreciation treated as a capital gain. 83(b) elections are not typically made because the executive cannot recover taxes paid at grant if he or she forfeits the shares or if the shares decrease in value.

## *Uses of Founders Stock and Why*

The uses of founders stock are identical to those of RSAs discussed earlier. However, the positive psychological ramifications that go along with being a "founder" are substantial and should not be overlooked. In addition, early on when a company is strapped for cash, this type of award and its upside potential can aid in bridging any cash discrepancies for a while.

## *Tax Implications for the Employee*

Under current federal income tax rules, an RSA recipient is not taxed at the time the award is granted, but rather when the restrictions lapse (when vesting occurs) unless an 83(b) election is made. (See Chapter 7.) The amount of income subject to tax is the FMV of the shares at the time of vesting less any amount paid for the shares. In the event the employee holds the stock for one year and a day after the date of vesting (and after paying the initial ordinary income tax on the value of the stock upon vesting less any amount paid to purchase the stock), the employee qualifies for long-term capital gains treatment for any subsequent stock price appreciation between the vesting date and sell date.

### *83(b) Election*

See Chapter 7 for a detailed discussion on 83(b) elections.

### *Tax Implications for the Company*

The company only receives a matching tax deduction when an employee recognizes ordinary income and is taxed accordingly. Therefore, the company does not receive a tax deduction at the time of grant, but does receive a tax deduction equal to the employee's ordinary income at the time the restrictions lapse. In the event the employee does not meet the holding requirements to qualify for long-term capital gains treatment at the sale of the stock, the company receives a tax deduction equal to the ordinary income received by the employee. If the employee makes an 83(b) election and pays the required taxes in the year of the award, the company receives a matching tax deduction for the income recognized by the employee.

### *Accounting Treatment*

Like an RSA, a company must elect to utilize either FAS 123 or APB 25 to calculate the appropriate earnings charge of a founder stock award. Under APB 25, founders stock is a full value award and subsequently carries a charge to earnings. The charge to earnings is fixed on the date of grant and is equal to the fair market value on the date of grant times the number of shares awarded. This charge to earnings is spread over the vesting period. However, in the event the shares are purchased, not granted, the company records the cash received as capital, and no compensation expense is recognized.

### *Advantages vs. Disadvantages*

**Advantages:**

- Founders may take advantage of an 83 (b) election and receive capital gains treatment on significant stock price appreciation
- No executive investment required
- Promotes immediate stock ownership
- Can provide significant wealth opportunity for the executives

- Strong motivational and retention characteristics
- Great psychological boost by being referred to as a "founder."

**Disadvantages:**

- Founders stock generally is only available to start-ups, or relatively young companies.
- Founders could lose their right to the stock if they don't meet vesting requirements.
- Valuation of the stock may prove difficult.
- If the company is not successful, other constituencies, like debt holders and preferred shareholders, may obtain advantages in voting and dividend rights over the common (founders) shareholders. (See Figure 29.)

## Deferrals into Restricted Stock

One twist companies commonly use with restricted stock is deferrals. Whether mandatory or elective, companies use restricted stock deferrals as a retention tool and for financial planning.

### *Base Salaries*

One form of deferral into restricted stock is the use of base salaries. Companies may allow a mandatory or elective deferral of base salary into restricted stock for a premium. For example, a start-up company may provide additional founder's stock in lieu of market competitive base salaries to conserve cash and provide employees with upside potential. Additionally, employees that receive founder's stock at nominal prices have the eligibility to take 83(b) elections and recognize capital gains treatment on the appreciation of the stock price.

### *Annual Incentives*

The most common form of deferrals into restricted stock is annual incentives. Companies often provide employees the opportunity to defer incentive payments so the employee can defer taxes. Deferrals into restricted stock allow the company to amortize the charge over the restriction period. Additionally, companies often provide a premium for deferring cash into restricted stock. Longer restriction periods usually translate into higher premiums. For example, if an employee is provided a bonus for $100,000, but elects to defer $50,000 into restricted stock over a two-year period, the

**FIGURE 29: Founders Stock**

**Key Provisions**

- Outright grant of shares to executives with restrictions as to sale, transfer and pledging
- Restrictions lapse over a period of time (e.g., three to five years)
- As restrictions lapse, executive has unrestricted shares which he or she may sell, transfer or pledge
- If executive terminates employment, all unvested shares are forfeited
- During restriction period, executive receives dividends and can vote the shares

**Earnings Impact**

- Fair market value at grant charged to earnings over restriction period
- Subsequent appreciation not charged to earnings
- Immediate dilution of EPS for total shares granted

**Tax Impact on Executive** (1)

- At grant — no tax
- As restrictions lapse — the current market value of vested shares taxed as ordinary income
- Dividends received during restriction period taxed as ordinary income

**Tax Impact on Company** (1)

- At grant — no tax deduction
- As restrictions lapse — company receives tax deduction equal to executive's ordinary income
- At sale — no tax deduction
- Dividends paid during restriction period are deductible by company when paid

**Advantages**

- No executive investment required
- Promotes immediate stock ownership
- Charge to earnings is fixed at time of grant
- If stock appreciates, company's tax deduction exceeds fixed charge to earnings
- Aligns executives' interests with shareholders
- Recognizable to most executives
- Offers executive potentially long-term appreciation as company grows

**Disadvantages**

- Charge to earnings
- Immediate dilution of EPS
- Executive may incur tax liability before shares are sold
- If stock depreciates, company's fixed-earnings charge exceeds tax deduction

(1) Assumes 83(b) election is not made. If an 83(b) is made, executive recognizes income on the date the restricted stock was issued, and the company receives an immediate tax deduction for the initial value of the shares (but not for subsequent appreciation during the restriction period); dividends paid during the restriction period are not deductible.

company may provide a 10 percent premium for the deferral. The employee would receive $55,000 worth of stock, but the company would amortize that charge over the two-year period.

### *Sales Incentives*

While sales employees hail cash as king, some innovative sales incentive programs incorporate the use of restricted stock on windfall payouts. For example, a sales employee makes a mega-sale that would constitute a large, one-time windfall payment. The company could defer the additional windfall payment beyond a typical sale utilizing restricted stock to help retain the employee over time. The restricted stock deferral also would conserve cash, amortize the charge to earnings over time, as well as diffuse a potential internal conflict of payment equity often created by windfall payments.

### *Sign-on Bonuses*

Post Sarbanes-Oxley, sign-on bonuses increasingly have been provided in the form of restricted stock. Before the 2002 Sarbanes-Oxley Act, many companies utilized loans to attract and retain employees. However, the Sarbanes-Oxley Act prohibited the use of loans in publicly traded companies for senior executives. Consequently, public companies have turned more to restricted stock to attract and retain key talent.

### *Private Company Version*

Private companies can also use restricted stock in actual form or via a phantom stock plan. Restricted stock in a private company mirrors restricted stock in a public company except that when the restrictions lapse, there is not a readily available market to sell the stock.

Restricted stock inside a phantom stock plan has a unique twist in that it is a full-value award like restricted stock, but it is a cash-based plan like phantom stock. A company may establish a restricted stock plan that simply gives a percentage of the company expressed in units. For example, a company may establish 10,000,000 units equal to 100 percent of the company's market value and then award units on this basis. The units are easy to understand and have meaningful value. However, because there is no market to sell the stock once the units vest, the employee may not value the stock as highly as an employee with stock in a public company. Companies can address this through loan provisions on vested value or establishing liquidity events such as change in control or retirement. Also, dividend equivalent rights may be provided as an additional payout for phantom restricted stock.

## FIGURE 30: Phantom Restricted Stock

**Key Provisions**

- Grant of units, that vest as restrictions lapse
- Restrictions lapse over a period of time (e.g., three to five years)
- As restrictions lapse, executive receives unrestricted shares which he or she may sell, transfer or pledge upon stated liquidity events
- If executive terminates employment, all unvested units are forfeited and vested units are paid out at a discount to the Company value
- During restriction period, executive can receive dividend equivalents and cannot vote the shares
- IRC 83(b) election unavailable

**Earnings Impact**

- Subject to auditor review and depending on the amount of restrictions, a portion of the vested value, depending on a market valuation, is charged to earnings on an annual basis
- Immediate dilution of EPS for total shares granted

**Tax Impact on Executive**

- At grant -- no tax
- At payment upon termination– vested value plus any outstanding loans are taxed as ordinary income upon payment
- Dividend equivalents received during restriction period taxed as ordinary income

**Tax Impact on Company**

- At grant -- no tax deduction
- At payment upon termination or liquidity event -- company receives tax deduction equal to executive's ordinary income
- Dividend equivalents paid during restriction period are deductible by company when paid

**Advantages**

- No executive investment required
- Liquidity may be provided through loan provision
- No dilution
- Aligns executive's interests with shareholders
- Recognizable to most employees
- Offers potential for long-term appreciation as company grows
- As company grows in value, fewer phantom units are needed to attract and retain talent

**Disadvantages**

- Variable charge to earnings; however, should not be full value depending upon restrictions
- 83(b) election unavailable
- Employees may not feel like true owners
- Lack of liquidity may have lower retention value

# Summary

Restricted stock can come in many shapes and sizes. This is critical when trying to customize to one's culture. The key is knowing what's available and being able to implement and communicate accordingly.

# 7

# Getting Technical

When choosing an LTI vehicle to properly attract, retain and motivate key employees, it becomes vitally important for the human resources department to work in conjunction with the finance and legal departments. This ensures that the long-term incentive programs accomplish their goals, while being fiscally responsible for the company and its employees. This chapter will provide an in-depth analysis of the tax, accounting and legal considerations of restricted stock — for the company and the employee. While laws, tax codes and accounting standards change at a fast clip, these issues are key components for consideration in LTI planning. These elements are also basic to the understanding of the technicalities of restricted stock.

## Tax Considerations

There are serious tax code considerations when implementing a restricted stock program for both the employee and the employer.

### *Employee*

To the employee, the tax effects of receiving restricted stock can create difficulties. The timing of the employee's tax obligation occurs at vesting, based on the fair market value of the vested amount of stock. The employee pays ordinary income tax rates based on this value in the first taxable year in which they are not subject to a substantial risk of forfeiture, or when they can transfer the stock free of the substantial forfeiture risk, whichever comes first. In addition, the employee pays tax on any dividends received while unvested. (For example, see Figure 31.)

Herein lies the negative aspect to employees because, unlike stock options and other vehicles, the employee has no control over the timing of the tax for a typical RSA. Many times, the employee will have to sell vested shares to simply cover his tax obligation, and critics of restricted stock point to this as reducing the employee's ownership stake and interest in the company's long-term performance. Additionally,

**Figure 31: How Restricted Stock Works**

| Timing | Years: 1 | | Years: 5 | |
|---|---|---|---|---|
| **Restricted Stock** | **Grant** | | **Restrictions Lapse** | |
| Fair Market Value: | $5 | → | $10 | |
| Dividends: | $0 | → | $1.00 | |
| Executive Investment: | $0 | → | $0 | |
| Executive Gain: | $0 | → | $11.00 | (Ordinary Income) |
| Executive Tax[(1)]: | $0 | → ($11.00 X .35) | $3.85 | Tax Due |
| Executive Net Gain: (After Tax) | $0 | → | $7.15 | Net Gain |

(1) Assumes the executive is subject to an ordinary income tax rate of 35%. If an 83(b) election was made within 30 days of the award, the executive would be taxed on the fair value of the stock at grant as ordinary income, with subsequent appreciation treated as a capital gain. 83(b) elections are not typically made because the executive cannot recover taxes paid at grant if he or she forfeits the shares or if the shares decrease in value.

executives filing Form 144 cannot explain on the form that they are selling shares to cover a tax bill. Therefore, all shareholders and investors could perceive that the executive is selling off stock at a high. In the case of RSUs, however, the tax obligation does not occur until the units are converted to actual shares. Therefore, an employee with RSUs can time the tax because he/she chooses when the units are converted.

Once the employee has vested in the restricted stock, he or she may still wish to hold the stock in hopes of additional appreciation. After the vesting date and ordinary income has been paid on the compensation, the tax treatment for shares held is identical to any equity position. If the stock is sold after one year holding, the preferable long-term capital gains rates apply to the appreciation over the value at vesting. If held for less than one year, short-term capital gains equal to ordinary income rates apply to that appreciation.

Thankfully, the Jobs and Growth Tax Relief Reconciliation Act of 2003 reduced not only the rates in the income tax brackets, but also significantly reduced the tax rate for dividends received. Although it does not directly affect dividends paid on unvested restricted stock, the change in tax rate for dividends may be another key factor in the increased use of restricted stock. Many have predicted dividends will become more attractive with their lower tax rate, more companies will begin paying out dividends to their shareholders as a result and, therefore, more restricted stock programs will ensure employees are aligned with shareholders by participating in these dividend payouts.

### *83(b) Election*

The IRC Section 83(b) provides a little twist from the ordinary income tax treatment described above, as well as a key decision for the employee. (See Figure 32.) If the employee makes an 83(b) election *within 30 days of the grant,* he/she can recognize income in the year the restricted stock was granted based on the fair market value at grant (no discount allowed for the restrictions on the stock). The advantage of accelerating the income is that any future appreciation in the stock would be taxed as capital gains when the stock is *sold.*

**FIGURE 32: IRC Section 83**

IRC Section 83:

(b)

Election to include in gross income in year of transfer

(1) In general

Any person who performs services in connection with which property is transferred to any person may elect to include in his gross income for the taxable year in which such property is transferred, the excess of

(A) the fair market value of such property at the time of transfer (determined without regard to any restriction other than a restriction which by its terms will never lapse), over

(B) the amount (if any) paid for such property. If such election is made, subsection (a) shall not apply with respect to the transfer of such property, and if such property is subsequently forfeited, no deduction shall be allowed in respect of such forfeiture.

For example, an employee granted 100,000 restricted shares valued at $0.01 per share makes an 83(b) election within 30 days of the grant. In that tax year, the employee pays ordinary income tax (assumed 35 percent) on the fair market value of the grant ($1,000) for a tax obligation of $350. Seven years later, the restrictions have lapsed, the company has gone public, and the employee sells his shares of stock now worth $10 each. Due to the election, instead of paying 35 percent of $1,000,000 ($350,000) *when the stock vests,* the employee pays capital gains rates (15 percent) on the appreciation over the grant value. The tax obligation *when the stock is sold* is $149,850 ($999,000 x 15 percent). Adding that to his original tax payment of $350 results in a savings of $199,800 ($350,000 – $150,200). (See Figure 33.)

Unfortunately, an 83(b) election is irrevocable and does have downside risk, making the decision a little tougher. First, if the election is made and the stock declines in value from the grant date, the employee will have paid ordinary income tax rates on the stock that may only produce a capital loss at sale. Second, if the employee forfeits the right to the stock before vesting, he/she is not entitled to a refund of the ordinary income tax; at best, one can claim a capital loss on the stock. Also, after making the election, the tax bill comes at a time when the employee is restricted from selling the shares to help cover the tax obligation, resulting in a potentially onerous cash outlay.

Clearly the decision regarding an 83(b) election takes serious thought and careful tax planning. Although not a guarantee, Figure 34 gives some general guidance on scenarios of an 83(b) election.

Another point to note is that due to the nature of RSUs, granting them eliminates the opportunity for an 83(b) election because shares are not transferred, but units are converted to shares at a later date. Thus, by granting RSUs in a broad-based program, companies such as Microsoft have eliminated an employee's opportunity to take an 83(b) election.

### *Company*

To the company granting restricted stock, the tax considerations can be quite advantageous. Due to restricted stock's characteristics — including their risk of forfeiture — the accounting charge taken at grant (discussed in the following pages) is an after-tax charge that is not calculated for the company tax filings. However, the tax-deductible compensation expense occurs later, as the awards vest and value is transferred to the employee. Additionally, dividends paid during the restriction period are deductible (unless the

**Figure 33: IRC Section 83**

**Election Under Section 83(b) of the Internal Revenue Code of 1986**

(To Be Filed No Later Than 30 Days Following the Property Transfer Date With the Internal Revenue Office With Which the Person Rendering Services Files His or Her Income Tax Return)

I hereby elect under section 83(b) of the Internal Revenue Code of 1986 to include in gross income any excess of fair market value over purchase price with respect to the transfer of the property described below:

1. **Taxpayer Information:**

   Employee Name
   123 Anywhere Street

   **Social Security Number:** xxx-xx-xxxx

2. **Tax Year of Election:** Calendar year 2003.
3. **Description of Property:** 10,000 shares of XYZ Corp.
4. **Date of Property Transfer:** December 1, 2003.
5. **Nature of Property Restrictions:** The shares are subject to time lapsing restrictions.
6. **Fair Market Value at the Time of Transfer:** $100. The fair market value at the time of transfer was determined without regard to any lapse restrictions as defined in section 1.83-3(i) of the Income Tax Regulations.
7. **Amount Paid for Property:** 0.
8. **Copies of Election:** In accordance with section 1.83-2(d) of the Income Tax Regulations, a copy of this election has been furnished to the person for whom the services are performed and to the recipient of the transferred property where that recipient is other than the person performing the services.

   Dated: December 20, 2003.

______________________________
Employee Name

**Source: Pillsbury Winthrop LLP

| Figure 34: General Guidance on 83(b) Election Scenarios | |
|---|---|
| **When to take an 83(b) election** | **When not to take an 83(b) election** |
| • Current value of stock is low, making ordinary income tax at grant nominal | • Current value of stock is high, triggering a significant tax obligation |
| • Anticipation of significant stock appreciation | • Unsure of future stock performance, with potential stock depreciation |
| • Start-up company with high growth potential | • Mature company with slow growth and stagnant stock performance |
| • Wide gap between ordinary income and capital gains tax rates (i.e., higher tax bracket) | • Narrow gap between ordinary income and capital gains tax rates (i.e., lower tax bracket) |
| • Cash outlay upfront is feasible | • Limited cash resources (cannot sell restricted shares to pay tax) |

employee makes an 83[b] election, in which case the company tax deduction occurs when the employee recognizes ordinary income and dividends are not deductible).

The deduction amount is equal to the amount of ordinary income recognized by the employee. Therefore, depending on the stock appreciation between grant and vesting, *the company deduction potentially can exceed the charge to earnings.* For example, a company grants 1 million shares of restricted stock to its employees with the share price at $1. The company takes a $1 million earnings charge, but when the shares vest, they have appreciated to $5. As the shares vest, the company would be looking at an unfavorable Schedule M, showing the difference between the accounting expense and the tax deduction. At the time the shares vest, the company receives a tax deduction equal to the ordinary income to its employees of $5 million. Assuming a 35 percent corporate tax rate, the company would save $1,750,000 in taxes. With the original accounting cost for the award of $1 million, the restricted stock grant would have a net positive effect of $750,000.

An additional consideration for the company is that restricted stock generally is not exempt from the $1 million limitation on tax-deductible compensation per IRC 162(m). In this regard, the IRS does not view restricted stock as a "performance-based" payment due to its typical time-lapse restrictions; therefore, for highly compensated executives, the company may lose the tax deduction on annual compensation above $1 million including the value of restricted stock grants. However, if the grant or the vesting of the shares is performance-based, the exemption may be available.

## Accounting Considerations

Currently, with regard to stock compensation, accounting for employee stock grants falls under two methods for reporting. As the debate heats up between the two methods for stock options, accounting for a typical restricted stock grant is nearly the same under Accounting Principles Board Opinion 25, Accounting for Stock Issued to Employees ("APB 25") and FASB Statement No. 123, Accounting for Stock-Based Compensation ("FAS 123"). As 2004 gets underway, it appears unlikely that FASB will include changes to accounting for restricted stock when it makes its sweeping changes to stock option accounting.

The total charge to earnings for a typical grant of restricted stock is a straightforward calculation — *the product of the number of shares in the award and the price of the stock at the grant date.* Any subsequent appreciation of the shares is not charged to earnings. This total earnings charge is fixed at grant, thus making restricted stock easily budgeted and a friend of the finance department. (See Figure 35.) The big picture of the accounting is consistent for the various types of restricted stock grants discussed in this book, including RSAs, RSUs and performance-accelerated RSAs. However, where they differ is in the amortization of the total charge over the vesting period.

**FIGURE 35: LTI Accounting Continuum**

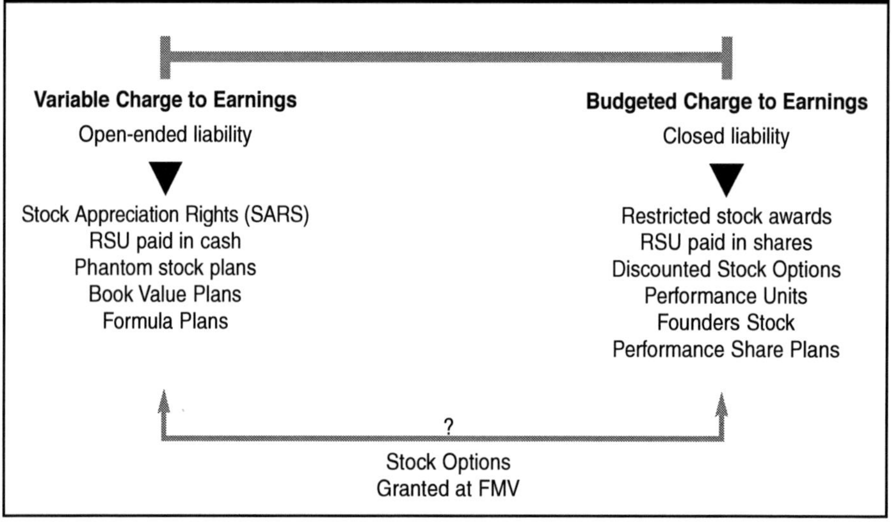

### *Vesting*

Assuming the restrictions lapse over a period of time longer than one year (hence "long-term" incentive), the total charge to earnings for a restricted stock grant does not need to hit the books all at once in the same year. The charge can be spread over a period of several years using an amortization schedule corresponding with the vesting requirements on the restrictions. Note: The expense should be 100 percent amortized by the time the awards are 100 percent vested.

For example, a company grants $10 million in restricted stock to its employees, which vests ratably over four years. The $10 million charge to earnings can be amortized in a number of ways, depending on the expected rate of forfeiture and the conservative or liberal accounting practices of the company. One generally accepted approach is highlighted in Figure 36. However, if the vesting is a four-year cliff, the typical approach in this scenario would be 25 percent amortization per year. As a general rule, the more conservative the approach, the greater portion of the award is amortized in the earlier years of the grant.

**FIGURE 36: LTI Generally Accepted Approach**

| | | Aggregate Cumulative Percentage of Compensation Accrued by the End of Each Year of Vesting Period | | | |
|---|---|---|---|---|---|
| | | Year | | | |
| For Rights Vested in | Service Period (Years) | 1 | 2 | 3 | 4 |
| Year 1 | 1 | 25.00% | 25.00% | 25.00% | 25.00% |
| Year 2 | 2 | 12.50% | 25.00% | 25.00% | 25.00% |
| Year 3 | 3 | 8.33% | 16.67% | 25.00% | 25.00% |
| Year 4 | 4 | 6.25% | 12.50% | 18.75% | 25.00% |
| Aggregate percentage accrued at end of each year | | 52.08% | 79.17% | 93.75% | 100.00% |
| Rounded | | 52% | 79% | 94% | 100% |

Because one-fourth of the rights vest each year, the service period over which compensation is accrued as a charge to expense is determined separately for each one-fourth portion.

### *Dilution*

A potential downside of restricted stock to both the company and shareholders is its impact on earnings per share. Because the restricted stock is an outright grant of shares, it requires a reduction of shares from treasury stock, an increase of shares issued, but not an increase in shares outstanding. Shareholders sometimes take issue with this, as it results in potential dilution (the decrease in the ownership percentage of current owners when additional shares of stock are issued). However, because the number of shares used is significantly smaller when compared to stock options, dilution can be less of an issue to shareholders. Although restricted stock does not appear in basic earnings per share (EPS) calculations until vesting, at grant diluted EPS must be adjusted for the increase in the number of shares based on the number of shares granted as restricted stock. The increase of shares outstanding (denominator), combined with the reduction of earnings for the cost of the grant (numerator), results in a double impact on diluted EPS. Figure 37 is an example of the dilution calculation.

**FIGURE 37: Dilution Calculation Example**

| | |
|---|---|
| **Existing:** | |
| Average Shares Outstanding | 28,650,000 |
| Net Income | $73,090,000 |
| Basic EPS | $2.55 |
| **Restricted Stock granted at $10:** | |
| Additional shares issued | 1,000,000 |
| Reduction of earnings | $10,000,000 |
| Diluted EPS = $63,090,000 / 29,650,000 = | $2.13 |

### *Forfeiture*

When an employee leaves and forfeits the right to the restricted shares, the shares return back to treasury, and become available to be awarded to another employee or a new hire.

### *Booking*

Several methods exist for the accounting of a typical restricted stock grant and account names may vary, but Figure 38 highlights a common method, including the debits and credits associated with the grant, the vesting and forfeiture. Figure 39 highlights excerpts of sample financial statements, including the line items influenced by restricted stock. As a side note, when the tax deduction exceeds the expense recognized (as it would for restricted stock with significant appreciation over the grant price or as it has in the past for FMV stock options with no expense), the permanent difference would most likely roll through "paid in capital" to account for the tax advantage.

### *Performance Issues*

Many times, institutional shareholders encourage grants subject to performance vesting. In other words, if certain criteria (i.e., specific financial goals) are not met, the shares are forfeited. In this case, because the shares are not guaranteed, the earnings impact is a variable charge under APB 25, but fixed under FAS 123. Due to the APB measurement date principle, under APB 25, the charge to earnings is adjusted periodically based on expectations of the performance goals being met and the shares vesting. Because the price per share and/or the number of shares in an award are not known, there has not been a measurement date according to APB 25. In contrast, under FAS 123, compensation cost is estimated at the grant date for the number of instruments based on the likelihood of the performance-related conditions being met. However, the company would make periodic adjustments until the vesting date as performance expectations change.

In contrast to performance vesting, some restricted stock programs are designed to have accelerated vesting schedules based on achieving specific performance goals. The accounting for the PARSAP program is consistent under both APB 25 and FAS 123, since only the vesting of the awards is subject to performance criteria and not the receiving of the awards. The charge to earnings is fixed at grant, but the amortization schedule of the charge is customized to match the actual vesting of the awards. Again, the expense should be 100 percent amortized by the time the awards are 100 percent vested. (See Figure 38.)

### *Stock Option Cancellations*

Accounting treatment for the cancellation of stock options is covered by FASB Interpretation No. 44 ("FIN 44") and EITF 11-23. Issues 39(a) and 39(b) of EITF 00-23 address accounting consequence of restricted stock. (See Figure 40.) The EITF concluded that variable accounting is required for all existing stock option awards subject to the offer when the offer is made and, for those stock option awards that are retained by employees because the offer is declined, variable accounting should continue until the awards are exercised, are forfeited, or expire unexercised. Under variable accounting, compensation

### FIGURE 38: LTI Common Methods

A company grants 1,000,000 shares of restricted stock at $5 per share. The vesting period is five years cliff vesting, so the earnings charge is spread evenly at 20% per year.

At grant, shares are deducted out of the treasury stock account at the par value per share — in this case, $0.01 per share. The difference between market value at grant and the par value is recorded in a paid-in-capital type account as follows:

| Deferred Compensation | |
|---|---|
| $5,000,000 | |

| Treasury Stock | |
|---|---|
| | $10,000 |

| Additional Paid-in-Capital | |
|---|---|
| | $4,990,000 |

As vested, compensation expense is recognized ratably over the vesting period — in this case, $1,000,000 per year. The year-end entry for each year of the five- year vesting period is as follows:

| Compensation Expense | |
|---|---|
| $1,000,000 | |

| Deferred Compensation | |
|---|---|
| | $1,000,000 |

After five years at the time the awards are vested, the company has recognized the full expense for the grant of $5,000,000.

If an employee terminates and shares are forfeited, a reversal entry is required to back out the compensation expense and the shares return back to treasury. In this case, an employee terminates in year five after the company has recognized $40,000 compensation expense for the employee's grant — thus forfeiting 10,000 shares. The reversal entries would be as follows:

| Additional Paid-in-Capital | |
|---|---|
| $49,900 | |

| Compensation Expense | |
|---|---|
| | $40,000 |

| Treasury Stock | |
|---|---|
| $100 | |

| Deferred Compensation | |
|---|---|
| | $10,000 |

cost is adjusted each period for increases or decreases in the value of the stock. All of the company's outstanding options currently are accounted for under 25; therefore, no compensation expense is recognized. However, if variable accounting is triggered for any options, those options identified will

**FIGURE 39: Excerpts of Sample Financial Statements**

| **Excerpt from Balance Sheet (financials reported in thousands)** | |
|---|---|
| Shareholders' equity: | 2003 |
| Preferred stock—no par value: | |
| Authorized — 2,000,000 shares; Issued and outstanding — none | $– |
| Common stock—par value $1 a share: | |
| Authorized — 750,000,000 shares; Issued — 416,879,000 shares | $416,879 |
| Capital surplus | $712,286 |
| Retained earnings | $3,155,397 |
| Cost of common stock in treasury — 66,257,000 shares | $(1,102,503) |
| Deferred compensation on restricted stock | $(15,340) |
| Accumulated other comprehensive (loss)/income | $(13,885) |
| **Total shareholders' equity** | **$3,152,834** |

| **Excerpt of Statement of Cash Flows (financials in thousands)** | |
|---|---|
| Cash flows from operating activities: | 2003 |
| Net earnings and comprehensive income | $19,728 |
| Adjustments to reconcile net earnings to cash provided by (used in) operating activities | |
| Depreciation and amortization | $5,456 |
| LIFO charge (credit) | $(1,525) |
| Deferred income taxes | $3,728 |
| Amortization of deferred compensation on restricted stock incentive plan | $2,241 |
| Closed stores reserve charges (credits) | $(284) |
| (Gain) loss on disposition of property and equipment | $(660) |
| Imputed interest expense on closed stores reserve | $159 |
| Issuance of shares as compensation for professional services | $25 |

As vested and expensed, it appears in the income statement under SG&A expenses.

| Excerpt of Consolidate Statement of Income (dollars in thousands) | |
|---|---|
| | 2003 |
| Revenues | $508,544 |
| Cost of goods sold | $345,721 |
| Selling, general and administrative expenses | $139,394 |
| Operating income | $23,429 |

**Figure 39: Excerpts of Sample Financial Statements (Continued)**

Also, the restricted stock grant affects many of the line items in statement of shareholder's equity.

Excerpt from Statement of Shareholder's Equity (in thousands except number of shares)

| | *Common Stock* Shares | Amount | Additional Paid-in-Capital | Retained Earnings | *Treasury Stock* Shares | Amount | Deferred Compensation | Total Share-holders' Equity |
|---|---|---|---|---|---|---|---|---|
| Balance January 31, 2002 | 29,139,726 | $291 | $39,142 | $174,507 | (10,487,738) | $(130,086) | $(7,295) | $76,559 |
| Net earnings and comprehensive income | | | | $10,670 | | | | $10,670 |
| Cash dividends ($.10 per share) | | | | $(1,765) | | | | $(1,765) |
| Issuance of restricted stock | 21,500 | | $64 | | | | $(64) | |
| Cancellation of restricted stock | (2,700) | | $(18) | | | | $18 | |
| Amortization and vesting of deferred compensation on restricted stock incentive plan | | | $ (224) | | | | $2,173 | $1,949 |
| Issuance of shares under directors' stock plan | 9,521 | | $36 | | | | | $36 |
| Issuance of shares as compensation for professional services | 22,288 | $1 | $94 | | | | | 95 |
| Purchase of treasury stock | | | | | (1,418,000) | $(5,497) | | $ (5,497) |
| Balance January 31, 2003 | 29,190,335 | $292 | $39,094 | $183,412 | (11,905,738) | $(135,583) | $(5,168) | $82,047 |

be subject to future compensation expense. In issue 39(b) of EITF 00-23, the EITF clarified that an offer to cancel an existing fixed stock option for a promise to grant restricted stock more than six months from the cancellation date is an offer to re-price the existing award that results in variable award accounting. The six-month waiting period is irrelevant because the grantee will participate in increases in the stock price after the cancellation, but before the new grant is made.

Paragraph 51 of FIN 44 provides that if an employee accepts the offer, but the grant of new stock is for fewer shares than canceled, then the six-month look-back, look-forward provisions should be applied (by individual) to the remaining canceled options that were not replaced. Therefore, if options were granted within six months before or after the options were cancelled at an exercise price below the cancelled options, variable accounting will be required for the options granted within six months (up to the number of options cancelled). It is important to realize that the *look-back, look-forward provisions mean a replacement award is identified even when the company did not intend the award to be a replacement.*

### *The Future*

One school of thought with regards to FASB changes to stock options accounting suggests that changes eventually will have to be made to restricted stock accounting as well. Up until now, there has actually been consistency in accounting treatment for FMV options, DSOs and RSAs. The earnings charge has been fixed equal to the current award value on the grant date. (See Figure 41.) For example, for a $10 stock price, on the grant date:

- RSA charge = $10 — difference between current stock price and a "strike price" of $0
- 20 percent DSO charge = $2 — difference between current stock price and a strike price of $8
- FMV option charge = $0 — difference between current stock price and a strike price of $10

Because restricted stock is based on the same underlying security as a stock option, it follows logically that if FASB mandates an earnings charge on the "potential future appreciation value" for a stock option, that same potential appreciation would apply to restricted stock of the same company. Therefore, this potential appreciation value would need to be added to the value at grant in order for a consistent compensation expense for both stock options and restricted stock. This development may be years down the road, or never happen at all; however, it must be taken into consideration as FASB begins to pick up on the inconsistencies they will have created.

**FIGURE 40: Accounting Consequence of Restricted Stock**

On Oct. 1, 2003, Company A cancels an employees stock option award for 100 shares. At the date of cancellation, company A issues the employee an RSA of 60 shares which vests 100% after one year. The quoted market price on Oct. 1, 2003, of A's stock is $10 per share. The total compensation expense of $600 (60 shares * $10/share) would be recorded straight-line over the one-year vesting period. Sixty of the 100 stock options cancelled are considered to be replaces by the 60 restricted shares issued. The remaining 40 cancelled stock options are subject to the "look-forward, look-back" provisions. First, would look back six months from the date of cancellation. If any options were issued with a lower exercise price than the 40 cancelled shares, those outstanding options would be accounted for as variable beginning on Oct. 1, 2003. Assuming the options have an exercise price of $7 and a market price of $12 on Dec. 31, 2003, compensation expense of $200 would be recorded for the 2003 fourth quarter ($12 market price less $7 exercise price times 40 shares). If at least 40 replacement shares were not identified during the six-month look-back period, A would look-forward six months. Compensation expense would continue to be recorded quarterly for the 40 stock options identified, based on changes in A's stock price, until the options are exercised or forfeited.

**FIGURE 41: Three Forms of Employee Stock Programs**

Three forms of employee stock programs

Stock price at grant = $10

| Restricted Stock Awards (RSAs) | Discounted Stock Options (DSOs) | FMV Stock Options |
|---|---|---|
| *Full value stock award or Strike price = $0** | *Strike price < $10** | *Strike price = $10* |

* A restricted stock award essentially is a discounted stock option discounted 100 percent or a stock price of $0.

# Legal Requirements

As with any compensation program, and especially long-term incentive plans, the legal department must be involved to ensure compliance on a number of levels. Several parties have an interest in the reporting of restricted stock by both the employee and employer, including the SEC, IRS and shareholders. Obviously, for a private company, the reporting requirements are not as stringent due to the limited SEC involvement.

## *Employee*

Aside from the IRS, the employee has limited reporting requirements for restricted stock. The employee may be required to file a Form 144 with a broker at the time the shares are sold. A sample Form 144 is highlighted in Figure 42. This form must be filed as notice of the proposed sale of restricted securities or securities held by an affiliate of the issuer in reliance on Rule 144, when the amount to be sold during any three-month period exceeds 500 shares or units or have an aggregate sales price in excess of $10,000.

### *Employer*

The company granting restricted stock will have a number of legal obligations and reporting as a result. First, to implement a restricted stock program, the company needs to develop a plan document and gain shareholder (including board of directors) approval of the plan and the number of shares to be reserved for the plan. Some omnibus plans already allow for restricted stock to be granted under the plan, so no additional approval is needed. A sample plan document for restricted stock, as well as an omnibus plan document is included in the Appendix. Additionally, some companies require an officer or director to pre-announce at the opening of the employee trading window the intention to sell company stock, including the maximum number of shares to be sold.

Once the plan is in place, three key events require special reporting steps by the company: grant, sale and forfeiture.

1. Grant — The SEC requires a Form 4 filing *within two business days* of grant (per Sarbanes-Oxley Act of 2002), and it is the company's responsibility to file on behalf of the employee. The Form 4 Statement of Changes in Beneficial Ownership information (highlighted in Figure 43) is used for disclosing the transactions and holdings of directors, officers and beneficial owners of public companies. Also, at grant the company may contact its transfer agent to produce actual stock certificates for the issuance, either as one certificate showing all the shares in the award or as separate certificates showing groups of shares based on vesting period. The transfer agent adds a ledger to the back of the certificates describing the restrictions on the shares, and the company typically holds the certificate until the restrictions lapse. Additionally, the company discloses the restricted stock in proxy reporting to shareholders per SEC S-1 and S-8 requirements.
2. Sale — The company must again file a Form 4 on behalf of the employee disclosing the sale of company stock. This filing is critical; as analysts and investors are very interested anytime an officer or a director is selling the company stock.

3. Forfeiture — The company returns to the transfer agent the certificate for the forfeited shares, with a request to cancel the shares and put the stock back into the treasury stock of the company.

Finally, it is important to note in the design of restricted stock plans that loans are prohibited under Sarbanes-Oxley. In the past, executive loans with forgiveness provisions were incorporated into many of these programs to help alleviate tax obligations or to buy additional shares of stock. Now, these practices have been eliminated due to several instances of abuse.

## ERISA Considerations

Section 3(2)(A) of ERISA defines an employee pension benefit plan as "any plan, fund, or program ... established or maintained by an employer" which (i) "provides retirement income to employees, or (ii) results in a deferral of income by employees for periods extending to the termination of covered employment or beyond, regardless of the method of calculating the contributions made to the plan."

The breadth of this definition may catch many employers by surprise,[1] but in considering whether a plan or program maintained by an employer for the benefit of its employees is a pension plan under ERISA, two questions must be answered: First, does the program provide retirement income? Second, does it result in the deferral of income to termination of employment or beyond? If either condition is satisfied, then the plan is an "employee pension plan" and is covered by ERISA. It is the second prong of this definition that is most often difficult to overcome in a program in which the employer is attempting to stay out of ERISA's grasp. Furthermore, a program need not satisfy these tests by its express terms, but may be a pension plan if "as a result of surrounding circumstances," it has either effect.

In a typical restricted stock, stock appreciation right or other stock incentive plan, ERISA usually is not a problem. An award is made to employees who will vest over a period of service, such as five years, as the restrictions on the stock lapse or, in the case of a plan where the form of payment is cash; a cash payment is made to the employee. In the meantime, the employee generally enjoys the right to vote the stock and to receive dividends paid by the employer during the restricted period. Since the right to receive the stock free of any restriction arises, or a cash payment — measured by the stock's value — becomes due during the employee's employment, it is neither intended to provide retirement income nor to defer income to or beyond termination of employment.

## Figure 42: Sample Form 144

**UNITED STATES**
**SECURITIES AND EXCHANGE COMMISSION**
**Washington, D.C. 20549**

| OMB APPROVAL |
|---|
| OMB Number: 3235-0101 |
| Expires: August 31, 2000 |
| Estimated average burden hours per response ....... 2.0 |

| SEC USE ONLY |
|---|
| DOCUMENT SEQUENCE NO. |
| CUSIP NUMBER |
| WORK LOCATION |

# FORM 144

## NOTICE OF PROPOSED SALE OF SECURITIES PURSUANT TO RULE 144 UNDER THE SECURITIES ACT OF 1933

**ATTENTION:** *Transmit for filing 3 copies of this form concurrently with either placing an order with a broker to execute sale or executing a sale directly with a market maker.*

| 1 (a) NAME OF ISSUER *(Please type or print)* | (b) IRS IDENT. NO. | (c) S.E.C. FILE NO. | |
|---|---|---|---|
| 1 (d) ADDRESS OF ISSUER STREET CITY STATE ZIP CODE | | | (e) TELEPHONE NO. AREA CODE NUMBER |
| 2 (a) NAME OF PERSON FOR WHOSE ACCOUNT THE SECURITIES ARE TO BE SOLD | (b) IRS IDENT. NO. | (c) RELATIONSHIP TO ISSUER | (d) ADDRESS STREET CITY STATE ZIP CODE |

*INSTRUCTION: The person filing this notice should contact the issuer to obtain the I.R.S. Identification Number and the S.E.C. File Number.*

| 3 (a) Title of the Class of Securities To Be Sold | (b) Name and Address of Each Broker Through Whom the Securities are to be Offered or Each Market Maker who is Acquiring the Securities | SEC USE ONLY Broker-Dealer File Number | (c) Number of Shares or Other Units To Be Sold *(See instr. 3(c))* | (d) Aggregate Market Value *(See instr. 3(d))* | (e) Number of Shares or Other Units Outstanding *(See instr. 3(e))* | (f) Approximate Date of Sale *(See instr. 3(f))* (MO. DAY YR.) | (g) Name of Each Securities Exchange *(See instr. 3(g))* |
|---|---|---|---|---|---|---|---|
| | | | | | | | |
| | | | | | | | |
| | | | | | | | |

**INSTRUCTIONS:**

1. (a) Name of issuer
   (b) Issuer's I.R.S. Identification Number
   (c) Issuer's S.E.C. file number, if any
   (d) Issuer's address, including zip code
   (e) Issuer's telephone number, including area code
2. (a) Name of person for whose account the securities are to be sold
   (b) Such person's I.R.S. identification number, if such person is an entity
   (c) Such person's relationship to the issuer (e.g., officer, director, 10% stockholder, or member of immediate family of any of the foregoing)
   (d) Such person's address, including zip code
3. (a) Title of the class of securities to be sold
   (b) Name and address of each broker through whom the securities are intended to be sold
   (c) Number of shares or other units to be sold (if debt securities, give the aggregate face amount)
   (d) Aggregate market value of the securities to be sold as of a specified date within 10 days prior to the filing of this notice
   (e) Number of shares or other units of the class outstanding, or if debt securities the face amount thereof outstanding, as shown by the most recent report or statement published by the issuer
   (f) Approximate date on which the securities are to be sold
   (g) Name of each securities exchange, if any, on which the securities are intended to be sold

**Potential persons who are to respond to the collection of information contained in this form are not required to respond unless the form displays a currently valid OMB control number.**

SEC 1147 (6-00)

## TABLE I — SECURITIES TO BE SOLD

*Furnish the following information with respect to the acquisition of the securities to be sold and with respect to the payment of all or any part of the purchase price or other consideration therefor:*

| Title of the Class | Date you Acquired | Nature of Acquisition Transaction | Name of Person from Whom Acquired *(If gift, also give date donor acquired)* | Amount of Securities Acquired | Date of Payment | Nature of Payment |
|---|---|---|---|---|---|---|
| | | | | | | |

**INSTRUCTIONS:** 1. If the securities were purchased and full payment therefor was not made in cash at the time of purchase, explain in the table or in a note thereto the nature of the consideration given. If the consideration consisted of any note or other obligation, or if payment was made in installments describe the arrangement and state when the note or other obligation was discharged in full or the last installment paid.

2. If within two years after the acquisition of the securities the person for whose account they are to be sold had any short positions, put or other option to dispose of securities referred to in paragraph (d)(3) of Rule 144, furnish full information with respect thereto.

## TABLE II — SECURITIES SOLD DURING THE PAST 3 MONTHS

*Furnish the following information as to all securities of the issuer sold during the past 3 months by the person for whose account the securities are to be sold.*

| Name and Address of Seller | Title of Securities Sold | Date of Sale | Amount of Securities Sold | Gross Proceeds |
|---|---|---|---|---|
| | | | | |

**REMARKS:**

**INSTRUCTIONS:**
See the definition of "person" in paragraph (a) of Rule 144. Information is to be given not only as to the person for whose account the securities are to be sold but also as to all other persons included in that definition. In addition, information shall be given as to sales by all persons whose sales are required by paragraph (e) of Rule 144 to be aggregated with sales for the account of the person filing this notice.

**ATTENTION:**
*The person for whose account the securities to which this notice relates are to be sold hereby represents by signing this notice that he does not know any material adverse information in regard to the current and prospective operations of the Issuer of the securities to be sold which has not been publicly disclosed.*

____________________
DATE OF NOTICE

____________________
(SIGNATURE)

*The notice shall be signed by the person for whose account the securities are to be sold. At least one copy of the notice shall be manually signed. Any copies not manually signed shall bear typed or printed signatures.*

**ATTENTION: Intentional misstatements or omission of facts constitute Federal Criminal Violations (See 18 U.S.C. 1001)**

SEC 1147 (6-00)

## FIGURE 43: Form 4 — Statement of Changes in Beneficial Ownership

**FORM 4**

☐ Check this box if no longer subject to Section 16. Form 4 or Form 5 obligations may continue. *See* Instruction 1(b).

(Print or Type Responses)

**UNITED STATES SECURITIES AND EXCHANGE COMMISSION**
**Washington, D.C. 20549**

**STATEMENT OF CHANGES IN BENEFICIAL OWNERSHIP**

Filed pursuant to Section 16(a) of the Securities Exchange Act of 1934, Section 17(a) of the Public Utility Holding Company Act of 1935 or Section 30(h) of the Investment Company Act of 1940

| OMB APPROVAL | |
|---|---|
| OMB Number: | 3235-0287 |
| Expires: | January 31, 2005 |
| Estimated average burden hours per response. . . . . . | 0.5 |

1. Name and Address of Reporting Person*

(Last) (First) (Middle)

(Street)

(City) (State) (Zip)

2. Issuer Name and Ticker or Trading Symbol

3. Date of Earliest Transaction Required to be Reported (Month/Day/Year)

4. If Amendment, Date Original Filed(Month/Day/Year)

5. Relationship of Reporting Person(s) to Issuer (Check all applicable)
_____ Director _____ 10% Owner
_____ Officer (give title below) _____ Other (specify below)

6. Individual or Joint/Group Filing (Check Applicable Line)
___ Form filed by One Reporting Person
___ Form filed by More than One Reporting Person

**Table I — Non-Derivative Securities Acquired, Disposed of, or Beneficially Owned**

| 1. Title of Security (Instr. 3) | 2. Transaction Date (Month/Day/Year) | 2A. Deemed Execution Date, if any (Month/Day/Year) | 3. Transaction Code (Instr. 8) | | 4. Securities Acquired (A) or Disposed of (D) (Instr. 3, 4 and 5) | | | 5. Amount of Securities Beneficially Owned Following Reported Transaction (s) (Instr. 3 and 4) | 6. Ownership Form: Direct (D) or Indirect (I) (Instr. 4) | 7. Nature of Indirect Beneficial Ownership (Instr. 4) |
|---|---|---|---|---|---|---|---|---|---|---|
| | | | Code | V | Amount | (A) or (D) | Price | | | |
| | | | | | | | | | | |
| | | | | | | | | | | |
| | | | | | | | | | | |
| | | | | | | | | | | |
| | | | | | | | | | | |
| | | | | | | | | | | |

Reminder: Report on a separate line for each class of securities beneficially owned directly or indirectly.
* If the form is filed by more than one reporting person, *see* Instruction 4(b)(v).

**Potential persons who are to respond to the collection of information contained in this form are not required to respond unless the form displays a currently valid OMB control number.**

(Over)
SEC 1474 (06-03)

**FORM 4 (continued)**

**Table II — Derivative Securities Acquired, Disposed of, or Beneficially Owned**
**(*e.g.*, puts, calls, warrants, options, convertible securities)**

| 1. Title of Derivative Security (Instr. 3) | 2. Conversion or Exercise Price of Derivative Security | 3. Transaction Date (Month/Day/Year) | 3A. Deemed Execution Date, if any (Month/Day/Year) | 4. Transaction Code (Instr. 8) | | 5. Number of Derivative Securities Acquired (A) or Disposed of (D) (Instr. 3, 4, and 5) | | 6. Date Exercisable and Expiration Date (Month/Day/Year) | | 7. Title and Amount of Underlying Securities (Instr. 3 and 4) | | 8. Price of Derivative Security (Instr. 5) | 9. Number of derivative Securities Beneficially Owned following Reported Transaction (s) (Instr. 4) | 10. Ownership Form of Derivative Security: Direct (D) or Indirect (I) (Instr. 4) | 11. Nature of Indirect Beneficial Ownership (Instr. 4) |
|---|---|---|---|---|---|---|---|---|---|---|---|---|---|---|---|
| | | | | Code | V | (A) | (D) | Date Exercisable | Expiration Date | Title | Amount or Number of Shares | | | | |
| | | | | | | | | | | | | | | | |
| | | | | | | | | | | | | | | | |
| | | | | | | | | | | | | | | | |
| | | | | | | | | | | | | | | | |
| | | | | | | | | | | | | | | | |
| | | | | | | | | | | | | | | | |
| | | | | | | | | | | | | | | | |
| | | | | | | | | | | | | | | | |
| | | | | | | | | | | | | | | | |
| | | | | | | | | | | | | | | | |

Explanation of Responses:

** Intentional misstatements or omissions of facts constitute Federal Criminal Violations.
*See* 18 U.S.C. 1001 and 15 U.S.C. 78ff(a).

______________________ **Signature of Reporting Person ______________ Date

Note: File three copies of this Form, one of which must be manually signed. If space is insufficient, *see* Instruction 6 for procedure.

Potential persons who are to respond to the collection of information contained in this form are not required to respond unless the form displays a currently valid OMB Number.

Page 2

However, if a restricted stock, stock appreciation right or other stock incentive plan systematically delays payment or vesting until retirement or termination of employment, then it is likely a "pension plan." If it is not an unfunded "top-hat plan," it probably will be subject to the substantive pension benefit provisions of ERISA.[2]

There are two important exceptions to this rule: The payment could be a payroll practice involving incentive or bonus payments that are only incidentally related to termination of employment.[3] A plan satisfying this "bonus payment" exception generally would be designed so that payment or vesting only incidentally extends to termination. For example, payment or vesting may extend a long period of time, such as 10 to 20 years, but not be contingent on termination or retirement. The case law in this area is not sufficiently developed to definitively state where a plan may cross the line and provide for a vesting or payment period that is so long that a court would find it to be merely a proxy for retirement. However, if a plan is designed in such a way that many of the participants will receive payment or vest prior to termination or retirement, the plan should not be subject to ERISA. However, a plan that systematically provides that a participant may delay payment into retirement or elect a payment method that begins with termination or retirement, and extends for several years beyond termination, is likely to be found to be a pension plan governed by ERISA.

Another possible exception is if the stock incentive plan can be designed to operate as a severance plan. It is still subject to ERISA, except that it is a welfare benefit plan. As such, it is subject to the reporting and disclosure, fiduciary, and enforcement provisions of ERISA, but is not subject to the substantive regulations governing pension plans.[4] The regulations provide a safe harbor under which a plan will be treated as a severance plan and not a pension. The conditions that the plan must meet are as follows: (1) the payments must not be contingent, directly or indirectly, upon retirement; (2) total payments must not exceed twice the employee's annual compensation during the year immediately preceding the termination; and (3) payments must be completed within 24 months of termination of employment (unless the plan is a limited program of terminations).[5]

The importance of designing a stock incentive plan in a manner that avoids coverage by ERISA cannot be overemphasized, because of what happens if the plan is determined to be a pension plan subject to ERISA. If it is an unfunded top-hat plan, it is subject to the reporting and disclosure provisions of ERISA. As a consequence, an employer must either file an annual report or make a one-time filing with the U.S. Department of Labor (DOL).[6] If a plan is not a top-hat plan, it is subject to both the reporting and disclosure and substantive provisions of ERISA. As a result, the plan sponsor will need to, among other things: prepare and distribute summary plan descriptions; file annual reports; comply with the vesting, spousal rights, distribution and fiduciary provisions of ERISA; and provide for a claims procedure.

If the plan provides for a deferral of income through elections to defer a portion of an employee's compensation into the plan, then failure to satisfy ERISA's trust requirements can become a serious problem. Under current regulations, employee contributions must be contributed to a trust as soon as feasible after the payroll date the compensation would otherwise be paid, but in any event no later than the fifteenth business day after the end of month in which the compensation would have otherwise been paid.[2] An employer's failure to comply with these rules represents a fiduciary breach, and possible personal civil and criminal liability could be imposed on those fiduciaries that fail to timely deposit the plan money into a trust. It is also possible that the trust requirement can be violated even if no employee contributions are made to the plan, if the company grants shares of stock to an employee, but retains possession of the certificate until the stock fully vests.

When designing a stock incentive plan, it is important that the employer carefully consider the reach and ramifications of ERISA. The long-arm of ERISA can be a trap for the unwary. Because of its stringent compliance requirements and costly penalties, the results of ignoring ERISA are potentially disastrous for both the employer and the individuals who administer stock incentive plans.

## Conclusion

In today's complicated world of executive pay, getting technical is a necessity. Figure 44 shows the "four cornerstones of executive pay." To get the best bang for the buck for one's shareholders, the synergies of several different disciplines are required. If left compartmentalized (where one discipline isn't talking to the other), it not only affects the ROI intended for the recipient, but also might lead to a visit from our friends from the SEC, IRS, DOL or even — as we've seen lately — much, much worse.

FIGURE 44: Four Cornerstones of Executive Pay

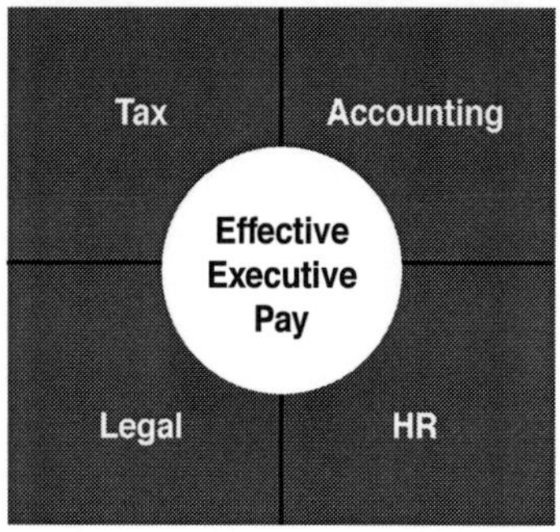

## *Endnotes*

1 See, e.g., Modzelewski v. Resolution Trust Corp., 14 F.3d 1374, 1377, 17 EBC (BNA) 2298 (9th Cir. 1994) where the court stated: "[b]ecause ERISA's definition of a pension plan is so broad, virtually any contract that provides for some type of deferred compensation will also establish a de facto pension plan, whether or not the parties, intended so."

2 29 C.F.R. 2510.2-3(c) provides that "[f]or purposes of title I of the Act and this chapter, the terms 'employee pension benefit plan' and 'pension plan' shall not include payments made by an employer to some or all of its employees as bonuses for work performed, unless such payments are systematically deferred to the termination of covered employment or beyond, or so as to provide retirement income to employees."

3 For employers this could be the best of all worlds. There are no substantive rules governing the provisions of the plan, but since the participant is limited to ERISA's enforcement provisions, the employer is not exposed to possible consequential or punitive damages. Also, if the plan is properly designed, the employer's determination of claims for benefits and interpretation of the plan, when acting as plan administrator, will normally be given deference by a court in any dispute over entitlement to benefits.

4 29 C.F.R. 2510.3-2(b).

5 29 C.F.R. 2520.104-23.

6 29 C.F.R. 2510.3-102.

# 8

# Final Considerations

RSA plans will accomplish the key objectives of attracting, motivating and retaining key employees only when they are administered and communicated properly.

With FASB requiring companies to expense stock options, the new corporate governance rules, a volatile market and greater scrutiny of equity compensation packages than ever before, companies will need to develop well-structured and well-communicated initiatives to promote and ensure the success of their long-term incentive programs. And, since perception of pay deteriorates as the distance from the CEO increases, programs will need to be customized to all organizational levels to gain maximum return on investment.

When a company decides to implement an RSA program, management typically will arrange for the preparation of an appropriate plan document. The plan's structure, as well as its specific terms and conditions, will be determined in consultation with the company's legal counsel, accountants, and the human resources compensation or benefits specialists. On the most basic level, the LTI record keeping and reporting system's purpose is to store all the data related to a corporation's LTI program. However, within a constantly changing competitive marketplace, the system should be used as more than just an administrative database to track awards and exercises. It can and should be used as a decision-making tool like any other management information system, such as an accounting or inventory system.

As a critical tool, the LTI system should be able to respond quickly to the many complicated inquiries senior management or the board of directors might have. It should be able to serve diverse administrative objectives — from determining the effectiveness of LTI-based compensation, to developing guidelines and policies for future awards.

The LTI administration process is governed by a strict regulatory and legal structure created by the SEC, FASB and the IRS.

Shareholders, particularly institutional investors, have become diligent in challenging LTI plan resolutions at annual shareholder meetings. Although the IRS and various stock exchanges issue regulations that impact LTI awards, a well-designed LTI record keeping and reporting system will efficiently and accurately respond to these important issues and insure that the reporting tools remain current with regulatory compliance issues as well as accounting principals. To maximize the motivational effectiveness of the LTI program, companies are adopting practices that continually communicate the objectives and value of the LTI awards to all participants.

## Designing the RSA Plan

The corporate board of directors usually creates a committee responsible for the oversight of LTI compensation programs, including RSA plans. The committee frequently is called the compensation committee or the human resources committee. This committee should approve all plan documents, share authorizations, awards and any substantive changes to plans or grant features. It has the final authority on all plan matters, although most administrative responsibilities are delegated to company management. It should be noted that the shareholders have final approval authority on the actual plan or share numbers allocated.

The departments usually responsible for managing LTIs are HR, payroll, accounting or treasury. Determining the appropriate department depends upon the corporate culture, staffing and organization.

The plan's day-to-day operation usually is the HR office's responsibility, since HR typically has the responsibility of designing and implementing programs to attract, retain and motivate employees.

However, regardless of which department is responsible for the management of the LTI programs, the HR department should always be involved in the strategic planning of LTI-based compensation issues. HR responsibilities should include plan reporting and analysis for senior management and the board of directors.

The planning process for the LTI record keeping and reporting system implementation should begin as early as possible, because the mechanics, in terms of the dataflow, are very complex. The departments usually involved in the planning process include:

- HR — for plan design, implementation, reporting, evaluation and administration
- Finance — for accounting treatment to balance sheet, profit and loss (P&L) statements and cash flow

- Payroll — to report taxable income and impact on company costs.
- Legal — to manage the many legal documents, filings and corporate insider issues
- Tax — for corporate tax filings
- Treasury — to manage the relationship with the transfer agent.
- Information technology — to manage the internal data and system for record keeping and reporting
- Internal audit — to ensure data and process accuracy.

All these departments play a critical role in the implementation process, but the department that is ultimately responsible for stock plan administration usually spearheads the project. When a company does not have an official HR department, finance usually takes charge.

At the initial meeting, department representatives should discuss the data flow, assign responsibilities and set timelines. The meeting's purpose is to ensure that all the areas involved understand the big-picture goals of RSA programs, know their roles and are familiar with their contacts in other departments. Although preferable, it is not necessary for record keeping and reporting to be fully functional before the first RSA grant date, except in the case of record keeping for Section 16 — that reporting must be done within two days of grant. It should, however, be at least partially implemented before the first quarterly earnings release after the initial grant, because RSA grants may affect this release.

Before the first post-grant earning release, the grant information should be entered on the LTI software. This is necessary for any earnings per share (EPS) dilution calculations to be performed and its impact disclosed.

## Recordkeeping: Measuring for Accuracy

Government regulations require publicly held corporations to continually inform shareholders of their business operations, financial conditions and management. Additionally, an LTI administrative system serves as a vital link between key employees and a program that is designed to motivate them to achieve the company's long-term goals. LTI programs will carry certain administrative requirements such as data collection and record keeping for:

- Plans
    - Plan name and date

- Number of authorized shares/units
- Term of the plan as authorized
- Type of grants allowed

- Participants
  - Name
  - Social Security number
  - Home address
  - Interoffice address
  - Officer/insider status
  - Department
  - Job code
- Provisions
  - Grant: Grant date, number of shares/units, restriction period, expiration date, termination grace period
  - Restriction lapsing: Restriction lapsing date, number of shares/units vested, market price when restrictions lapse date, W-2 income realized, taxes paid

Figure 45 offers examples of some of the record keeping requirements for LTI plans.

## Reporting

Reporting to shareholders, the IRS, DOL, SEC and to stock plan participants can be a daunting requirement without the appropriate administrative system. Whether requirements are accomplished in-house or via a third-party administrator, the employer must provide full and fair disclosure of all material information about the company and LTI operations to all the concerned parties.

Some reporting requirements for RSA plans include:

- IRS
  - Employee taxable earnings
  - Corporate tax deductions

**FIGURE 45: Record Keeping — RSA Plans**

| Process | Overview | Timeframe |
|---|---|---|
| Share/unit price input | The high, low closing and average price for the RSA must be entered into the LTI software. The prices can come from the business section of a newspaper and should be verified at the end of every month against another source. | For every stock market trading day / once a year if private |
| Vesting notification | RSAs usually are granted with a multiyear vesting provision. Thus, only a portion of the RSA grant will become exercisable per year, usually on the anniversary of the grant (e.g., 25 percent per year). | Usually annually |
| Exercises | As employees vest their RSA, they will receive a form from the HR department. | Daily or as vesting occurs |
| Transmittal letter | For each exercise, instructions are sent to the transfer agent to issue shares and send the certificates to the grantee. | Daily, or as exercises occur |
| Confirmation of exercise | Verifies to the grantee that the exercise has been processed and gives the cost basis of the shares/units that will be issued | Daily, or as exercises occur |
| Inquiries | A telephone number for the HR office should be set up and put on most grantees communi-cations. Participants may call for RSA plan information such as statement of RSA account balances or procedural instructions. | Daily |
| Dividends | All exercise forms that are received on or before the record date for a dividend payment will be entitled to such dividend and should be expedited to the transfer agent. | Quarterly, if applicable |
| Expirations | RSAs usually have a maximum life. The grantee should be notified of any impending expiration. | Three months before the RSA expiration date and again two weeks before expiration |
| Terminations | All severances from the company (whether voluntary, involuntary, death, disability or retirement) should be processed on the software and a notice sent to the grantee regarding any post-employment exercise grace period for vesting options, if appropriate. | Monthly |
| Cancellations | Any grant that expires unexercised (most will be due to terminations) should be cancelled. | Monthly |

- SEC
  - SEC Form 3 — Disclosure of corporate officer stock holdings
  - SEC Form 4 — Disclosure of corporate officer stock transactions
  - SEC Form 5 — End of year summary of Form 4 disclosures
  - SEC Form 10-k — Annual report of public company financials
  - SEC Forms S-1, S-8
- Shareholders
  - Annual Report — Disclosure of corporate information to shareholders
- Participants
  - Summary Annual Report — Summary of information included in the Annual Report

Figures 46 and 47 are lists of internal and external reports and disclosures that normally are generated through the reporting system for the LTI plan.

## How Does All This Get Done?

Managing all the processes in a coordinated fashion is likely the biggest challenge in implementing an LTI record keeping and reporting system. There are many options to managing the process, such as developing the system in-house, buying software from a vendor or outsourcing the entire function to a third-party administrator. The decision centers around issues such as cost, the company's capabilities, staffing levels and internal IT resources.

When thinking about in-house administration requirements of RSA plans, consider what type of demands will be set upon internal resources. The departments involved in in-house administration should include:

- Human resources
- Accounting
- Payroll
- Legal
- Tax
- Treasury
- Information technology
- Internal audit.

**FIGURE 46: Internal Department Reports — RSA Plans**

| Department | Data Received | Timeframe | Use of Data |
| --- | --- | --- | --- |
| Payroll | Taxable compensation realized by grantee when restrictions lapse | Monthly | Update of pay stub and W-2 |
| | Taxes paid by grantee when restrictions lapse | Monthly | Update of pay stub and W-2 |
| Tax | Total taxable compensation realized by all grantees | Quarterly | Corporate tax deduction |
| Accounting | Grants, exercises and cancellations | Monthly | Track grants outstanding |
| | Earnings per share dilution report | Monthly | Footnote to earnings release |
| Legal | Notification of restricted person exercise | As appropriate | Reminder of insider trading and window period rules |
| | Notification of any executive officer activity (e.g., grant, exercise) | As appropriate | SEC filing |
| Treasury | Total number of shares issued from RSA grants | Monthly | Track shares issuances and decide how to fund shares |

There also will be some technological demands. An organization's IT department may be able to develop a software system internally or purchase a software specifically designed for corporate stock option record keeping and reporting.

Many corporations within various revenue sizes, life-cycle stages and industry categories use off-the-shelf software programs. These programs can be customized to meet the needs of the company's specific administrative procedures and communication design. Whenever possible, though, administrative software should be integrated with the broader HRIS or payroll system.

## Outsourcing as an Option

Some companies may think that purchasing software and training an administrator are burdens they do not want to undertake, or the LTI plan's size is large enough that it is difficult to manage. Several independent

**Figure 47: External Disclosures**

| Department | Data | Disclosure |
|---|---|---|
| Accounting | The earnings per share dilution is a complex calculation performed by the software | Quarterly and annual earnings releases |
| | Overall plan balances and activity for a given year are summarized in the annual report's statistics report | LTI plan section of annual report |
| Legal | Grant table vesting RSA | Proxy statement |
| | Vesting/holdings table RSA | Proxy statement |
| | RSA grant column for summary compensation table | Proxy statement |
| | Awards and strategy for the compensation committee on executive compensation | Proxy statement |
| | Grantee statements for director and officer beneficial ownership table | Proxy statement |
| | Executive officer stock activity | SEC Form 3,4, or 5 |
| | Plan share authorizations | SEC Form S-8 |
| | Plan share authorizations | Stock exchanges |

vendors, software companies and stockbrokers provide an outsourcing alternative service.

Corporations can outsource the entire plan operation or retain certain strategic components. The plan data are generally stored at the outsourcing firm. The outsource provider should be able to generate computer files that can be used to integrate option plan data onto the payroll, accounting or HRIS. Companies choose to outsource LTI administration for several reasons, including:

- It allows management to focus on growth and profits.
- It provides consistent, high-level service to employees.
- It increases employee productivity.
- Administrative responsibilities can be demanding especially during peak market times.

- The responsibility of insuring that current legal/accounting guidelines are followed and housed outside the company.

The decision of whether to administer the plan internally or to outsource this function should be based on a company's staffing levels, expertise, costs and willingness to forego a majority of the control over the LTI plan data. When analyzing the cost versus benefits to outsourcing, it is important to consider the total cost of the number of employees involved and the cost of the software, training and hardware. Many companies do not realize they will still need people to provide the information (e.g., shares granted, terminations, payroll information, personnel information, etc.) to the outsourcing firm. This should be included in the analysis.

## Communication

The successful implementation and ongoing administration of an RSA program requires effective, continuous communication. Though the use of stock options has increased in recent years, many employees holding stock options know little or nothing about how they actually work. If that is the case, then understanding stock option equivalents will be even more difficult. Employees need to understand the potential of these plans in order for them to act and feel like company shareholders.

The primary key to effective communication is to ensure all RSA plan participants understand their grant and are able to gain access to the information quickly and easily. There are many communication methods that can be used to achieve these results, including e-mail, Internet access, Web sites, voice mail, faxes, pamphlets and informational meetings.

Another equally important reason to communicate to RSA plan participants regularly is the issue of litigation. The tax implications are of "key" importance to RSA recipients. Recently, there has been an increase in the number of lawsuits filed in the United States focusing on stock ownership and what has — and has not — been communicated to employees and participants. Company communications have been a key issue in determining whether the plan provisions were portrayed appropriately in these cases. Figure 48 offers several communication tips to consider.

Provide all eligible employees with as much information as possible. Employees should know everything about the RSA plan except, of course, how many stock options their co-workers are receiving. Continued communication is important in ensuring that employees do not lose sight of the plan.

Here are examples of the type of information that should be communicated:

- Why the company has granted RSAs/RSUs
- Values, number of shares/units
- Who is eligible
- Vesting/restriction periods
- Voting rights of the shares (if applicable)
- Ownership rights of the shares
- Employee obligations concerning costs
- When transactions are prohibited (if applicable).

**FIGURE 48: Communicating Tips**

- Convey a consistent message.
- Align communications with the corporate mission, vision, strategic business plans and organizational objectives.
- Use caution to avoid inadvertently creating conflict between stock option program communications and any other equity-based rewards programs and messages sent to employees.
- Recognize the difference between giving "advice" and meeting a standard communication requirement.
- Maintain confidentiality and communicate the organization's sensitivity and policy on the issue
- Encourage feedback by providing a way to receive employee feedback and questions.
- Communicate frequently about the plan rather than limiting communications to milestones, such as when grants are made or when options vest.

## Risks and Rewards

The risk associated with LTI awards should be communicated clearly and effectively. The fundamentals of equity ownership, tax implications and termination applications are key pieces of the RSA plan provisions. It is important to understand the tax implications of owning and selling grants, particularly with plans that create a tax liability. Participants should have enough information to make educated decisions about investment diversification, risk assessment and future planning to enable them to assess and administer their investments. The company should provide enough communication on a regular basis to allow participants to make informed decisions about their company RSA plans.

Figure 49 is a list of sample forms and communications that should be used to keep participants informed. Also, sample documents are provided in the Appendix.

## Electronic Communications

The company intranet is an efficient way of keeping employees well informed. Both e-mail messages and information pages on the employee intranet or HR Web site are extremely useful in informing employees about

| Figure 49: Sample Forms and Communication | | |
|---|---|---|
| **Form Name** | **Description/Purpose** | **Timing** |
| Grantee statement | Provides grantee with overall account balances as of certain date | Annually. Can be sent to grantee with other communications, such as the vesting notification |
| Grant letter, plan document and prospectus | Drafted by the legal department or outside counsel. Gives grantee terms and features of the RSA | At grant |
| Vesting notification | Notifies grantee that grants are available for exercise | At vesting |
| Tax schedules | Used by grantee. Drafted by payroll department. Gives grantee the rates for tax withholdings due on Vesting | Vesting |
| Confirmation of exercise form | Notifies grantee of date of exercise, taxable compensation and basis of cost shares | Shortly after exercise |
| Termination grace period notice | Notifies grantee of date of post-employment exercise period | At severance of employment, if appropriate |
| Expiration notice form | Warns grantee of pending expiration of award | Before the expiration date |

RSAs and their plan specifics, providing an accessible platform for giving feedback, asking questions and accessing individual accounts.

## The Importance of Getting it Right

Equity compensation is among the most comprehensively regulated forms of compensation. A multitude of tax, corporate and securities legal provisions and conditions affect their adoption, implementation, operation and administration. A well-designed and well-managed record keeping and reporting system can help a company deal with the complications. If strategically implemented, the system minimizes costs and time associated with the administrative requirements. It will reduce the company's potential exposure to liabilities, while maximizing the impact of the equity compensation plan.

The challenge of implementing an RSA record keeping and reporting system is managing all processes in a coordinated fashion. All departments involved should provide feedback on how best to structure the system to meet all the administrative objectives within the corporate culture.

When implementing a record keeping and reporting system, the issues in Figure 51 should be addressed.

In the end, a great plan is not "great" unless it is administered and communicated appropriately. Without these two final pieces of the puzzle, a

FIGURE 50: **LTI Plan Administration**

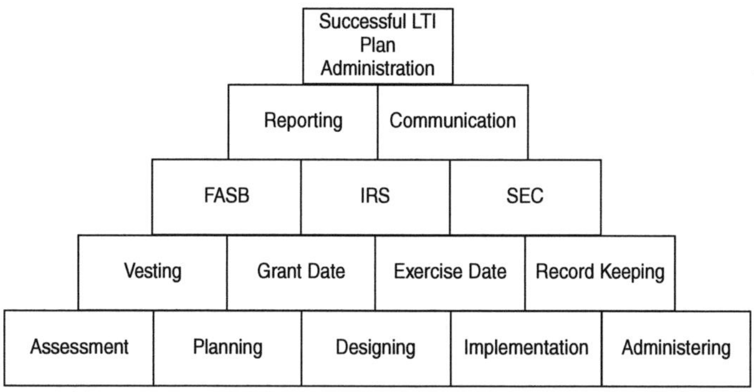


company's attempt to use RSA to attract, retain and motivate it's key people could likely fail.

## Plan, Review and Audit

An occasional program audit is recommended to assess the program's effectiveness in supporting the organization's mission, objectives and values. Specifically:

- Is the RSA program effective in aligning pay with the organization's other compensation and performance objectives?
- Is the program integrated with the established organization structure, career path and career progression?
- Is the program reinforcing the type of behaviors that are critical to the company's success?
- Have the appropriate policies, procedures and guidelines been put in

place, which allow the organization to administer and maintain the program as efficiently and effectively as possible?

- Do people understand the program and is it being communicated effectively?

Once the review is complete, the key findings should be reported. These findings will need to be shared with the compensation committee, the CEO and other executive officers as appropriate. There should be an executive summary that is concise and to the point. Other areas that may be addressed include:

**Figure 51: Final Issues to Consider**

- Board of directors/compensation committee approved plan document
- Total number of shares/units approved prior to grants
- Identified 16(b) participants and have them separated from all other participants
- Record keeping system is integrated with HRIS and payroll
- Process to report taxable income to payroll at the time a participant exercises options
- Distribute the Summary Annual Report to participants annually
- Communicate all plan provisions to participants
- Educate participants on the issues surrounding options to maximize their effectiveness

- Summary of project objectives, approach and methodology
- Predominant themes emerging from executive interview feedback and their implications
- Results of external competitive direct compensation analyses
- Results of internal reviews of the RSA.

An active plan should be developed where appropriate, to ensure modifications or improvements are implemented. The action plan should specify:

- Action plan objectives, or a summary of what needs to be accomplished
- Work steps required
- Individual roles and responsibilities
- Deliverables, or the end results of work steps
- Estimated costs associated with accomplishing work steps
- The specific dates by which essential work steps and deliverables need to be completed.

Bottom line: Without good ongoing reviews, it's impossible to know what, if anything, your compensation programs are achieving. It's the best way to give a board and your shareholders the assurance that your programs are competitive and reasonable — which is key in today's world.

## Summary

The "devil is in the details" axiom rings true when it comes to the importance of administration, communication and review. Successful companies realize that a sound investment here is a great investment toward their future. Companies like Dell Computer make the necessary investment into these areas to ensure they are maximizing their return while enhancing the utility afforded its most important asset — its people.

# Appendix

## Frequently Asked Questions

## Sample Forms

## Glossary

## Selected References

## Frequently Asked Questions

### What is a restricted stock award?

A restricted stock award is stock given (or sold at a discount) to an employee, who is restricted from selling or transferring it for a specified period of time — usually three to five years. The executive receives dividends and typically has voting rights, but must forfeit the stock if he/she terminates employment before the restriction period ends. If the employee remains in the employ of the company through the restricted period, the shares vest, usually irrespective of employment or company performance.

### Is it what some term a "full value plan?"

Yes. Full value plans are plans under which the participant receives "full value" of the employer's capital share or equivalent; e.g., restricted stock, phantom share without any investment or purchase required. Value may be based on market price (typical), book value (private companies) or a formula.

### What kind of "restrictions" are there?

Typically it's length of service. Sometimes performance criteria are added, but that is still rare.

### How is a restricted stock unit plan (RSU) different?

An RSU is an agreement by the employer to deliver/issue stock to the employee at time of vesting. However, no shares are delivered until the employee satisfies their vesting requirements. Once vested, taxes owed will be taken out prior to the employee receiving the units. By using units versus awards an employer can gain several advantages — especially administratively.

### Which plan is better?

It depends on your company, its mission, value and HR philosophy. No "one size" will fit all. It is important to explore all the factors, internally and externally, before putting either plan (or both) in place.

**Is Microsoft the only company granting RSUs?**

No. Other companies like Hewlett Packard, Raytheon, Lucent and United Technologies Corporation have also utilized this program.

**What, in your opinion, is the key issue?**

In our opinion, the principal advantage of an RSU over an RSA is the ability for the executive to defer taxation. With an RSA this cannot occur. However, since an RSU is, in essence, an unfunded promise to pay at a later date, the unit is not "property" for tax purposes and the ability to defer results.

**What is vesting? How long is it typically with either of these plans?**

The vesting period is the time it takes before the restrictions lapse or are lifted. Typical vesting is between three and four years.

**Is there a preference as to what type of vesting is used?**

Yes. Most companies prefer "cliff" vesting over graded. This is probably due to the fact cliff vesting is more "retention oriented" than graded.

**What is cliff vesting?**

Cliff vesting is where 100 percent of a plan is vested at the end of a term. Graded vesting is where vesting occurs through the term; e.g., 25 percent per year.

**What happens to my award if I voluntarily leave the employ of my company before I vest?**

You forfeit the part of your award that is not vested.

**Are there other considerations?**

Absolutely. The tax, legal and accounting issues are key, but so are issues surrounding economic environment, corporate culture, market cycle, etc. It's key that significant thought and analysis go into any compensation decision that effects a company's #1 asset/investment — its people.

# Sample Forms

# Formula Stock Option Plan

## STOCK OPTION PLAN

THIS INDENTURE is made as of the_________ day of ___________ year, by ______________________________company, a corporation organized and doing business under the laws of the State of ____________________ (the "Company").

1. Purpose. The Company is adopting the _________________________ Stock Option Plan (the "Plan") to secure and retain the services of directors and key employees of the Company and any of its subsidiaries by giving them an opportunity to invest in the future success of the Company. The Board of Directors of the Company (the "Board") believes this Plan will promote personal interest in the welfare of the Company by, and provide incentive to, the individuals who are primarily responsible both for the regular operations, and for shaping and carrying out the long-term plans, of the Company, thus facilitating the continued growth and financial success of the Company.

2. Administration. The Board shall appoint at least two of its members to a committee (the "Committee") that will administer this Plan on behalf of the Company. The Committee may be the Compensation Committee of the Board if the Board so chooses. Each member of the Committee shall be both a "Non-employee Director" within the meaning of Rule 16b-3 ("Rule 16b-3") of the Securities Exchange Act of 1934, as amended (the "Exchange Act"), and an "Outside Director" as defined for purposes of Section 162(m) of the Internal Revenue Code of 1986, as amended (the "Code").

   Each member of the Committee shall serve at the discretion of the Board, which may fill any vacancy, however caused, in the Committee. The Committee shall select one of its members as a chairman and shall hold meetings at the times and in the places as it may deem advisable. All actions the Committee takes shall be made by majority decision. Any action evidenced by a written instrument signed by all of the members of the Committee shall be as fully effective as if the Committee had taken the action by majority vote at a meeting duly called and held.

Subject to the express provisions of this Plan, the Committee shall have complete authority, in its discretion, to determine with respect to all options other than options granted to directors pursuant to Section 7 hereof (the "Formula Options"):

(a) the directors and key employees of the Company and any subsidiaries to whom, the times when, and the prices at which it shall grant options;

(b) the type of options to be granted; i.e., either incentive stock options as defined in Section 422 of the Code ("Incentive Stock Options") or non-qualified stock options ("Non-Qualified Stock Options") (collectively, the "Options");

(c) the total number of Options to grant to an optionee;

(d) the time and duration of the period of exercise of each Option;

(e) the number of shares of the common stock, no par value per share, of the Company (the "Common Stock") subject to each Option; and

(f) the terms and conditions for payment.

The Committee shall also have complete and conclusive authority to (i) interpret this Plan, (ii) prescribe, amend and rescind rules and regulations relating to it, (iii) determine the terms and provisions of the stock option agreements the Company makes with optionees who are granted Options (the "Agreement"), the terms of which need not be identical, and (iv) make all other determinations necessary or advisable for the administration of this Plan. The Committee's determinations on these matters shall be conclusive.

In addition to any other rights of indemnification that they may have as directors of the Company or as members of the Committee, the directors of the Company and members of the Committee shall be indemnified by the Company against the reasonable expenses, including attorneys' fees, actually and necessarily incurred in connection with the defense of any action, suit or proceeding, or in connection with any appeal therein, to which they or any of them may be a party by reason of action taken or failure to act under or in connection with this Plan or any Option or Formula Option granted hereunder, and against all amounts paid by them in settlement thereof or paid by them in satisfaction of a judgment in any action, suit or proceeding, except in relation to matters as to which it shall be adjudged in the action, suit or proceeding that such director is liable for gross negligence or misconduct in the performance of his duties; provided that within 60 days after institution of any action, suit or proceeding, a director shall in writing offer the Company the opportunity, at its own expense, to handle and defend the same.

3. Eligibility. The Committee shall grant Options only to directors and key employees of the Company or its subsidiary corporations within the meaning of Code Section 424 (f) (each, a "Subsidiary"); provided, however, that an Incentive Stock Option may only be granted if such individual is an employee of the Company or a Subsidiary and that only Formula Options may be granted to directors who are not also employees or officers of the Company. Subject to the limits set forth in this Plan, the Committee at any time may grant additional Options to directors or key employees to whom the Committee had previously granted Options, so that an optionee may hold more than one Option at the same time.

4. Stock Subject to Plan. The Company has authorized and reserved for issuance upon the exercise of Options and Formula Options pursuant to this Plan an aggregate of __________ shares of Common Stock (the "Shares"), each of which may be the subject of an Incentive Stock Option or a Non-Qualified Stock Option, in the sole discretion of the Committee. Any one optionee may not be granted Options, including Formula Options, to purchase in excess of __________ Shares during any fiscal year of the Company or in excess of __________ Shares. If any Option or Formula Option is canceled, expires or terminates without the respective optionee exercising it in full, the Committee may grant Options with respect to those unpurchased Shares to that same optionee or to another eligible individual or individuals; provided, however, that in the case of an Option which is canceled in the same fiscal year in which it is granted, in determining whether an optionee

has received the maximum number of Shares he is entitled to receive during such fiscal year, both the canceled Option and any other Option issued to such optionee during such fiscal year shall be treated as outstanding, and, in the case of an Option canceled at any time, in determining whether an optionee has received the maximum number of Shares he is entitled to receive during the term of the Plan, both the canceled Option and any other Option issued to such optionee during the term of the Plan shall be treated as outstanding.

The Committee shall adjust the total number of Shares and any outstanding Options and Formula Options, both as to the number of Shares and the exercise price, and the number of Shares to be issued pursuant to Formula Options granted under Section 7 hereof, for any increase or decrease in the number of outstanding Shares resulting from a stock split or a payment of a stock dividend on the Shares, a subdivision or combination of the Shares, a reclassification of the Shares in accordance with the provisions of the next paragraph, a merger or consolidation of the Shares or any other like changes in the Shares or in their value. The Committee shall not issue fractional Shares as a result of any of these changes and shall eliminate from the outstanding Options and Formula Options any fractional Shares that result from such a change. The Committee shall not adjust outstanding Options and Formula Options for cash dividends or the issuance of rights to subscribe for additional stock or securities of the Company.

Except as provided in the following paragraph, after any merger of one or more corporations into the Company, any merger of the Company into another corporation, any consolidation of the Company and one or more other corporations, or any other corporate reorganization to which the Company is a party that involves any exchange, conversion, adjustment or other modification of the outstanding Options and Formula Options, each optionee shall receive at no additional cost upon the exercise of his Option or Formula Option, as applicable, subject to any required action by shareholders and in lieu of the number of Shares as to which he would otherwise exercise the Option or Formula Option, as applicable, the number and class of shares of stock or other securities or any other property (including cash) to which the terms of the agreement of merger, consolidation or other reorganization would entitle the optionee to receive, if, at the time of the merger, consolidation or other reorganization, the optionee had been a holder of record of the number of Shares as to which he could exercise the Option or Formula Option, as applicable. Comparable rights shall accrue to each optionee in the event of successive mergers, consolidations or other reorganizations.

In the event of a Sale of the Company (as hereinafter defined) in which the purchaser of the Company does not agree to the assumption of the Options or Formula Options, provisions shall be made to cause each outstanding Option and Formula Option to become exercisable prior to the Sale of the Company and to terminate upon the consummation of the Sale of the Company. "Sale of the Company" shall mean (i) the approval by the shareholders of the Company of a reorganization, merger or consolidation, or substantially all of the individuals and entities who were the beneficial owners, respectively, of the Common Stock and the Company's voting securities outstanding immediately prior to such reorganization, merger or consolidation do not, following such reorganization, merger or consolidation, beneficially own, directly or indirectly, a majority or more of, respectively, the then outstanding shares of common stock and the combined voting power of the then outstanding voting securities entitled to vote generally in the election of directors, of the corporation resulting from such reorganization, merger or consolidation, in substantially the same proportions as their ownership, immediately prior to such reorganization, merger or consolidation, of the Common Stock and the Company's voting securities, respectively; or (ii) the approval by the shareholders of the Company of (a) a complete liquidation or dissolution of the Company or (b) the sale or other disposition of all or substantially all of the assets of the Company, other than to a corporation with respect to which following such sale or other disposition, a majority or more of, respectively, the then outstanding shares of common stock of such corporation and the combined voting power of the then outstanding voting securities of such corporation in each case with respect to which all entitled to vote generally in the election of directors is then beneficially owned, directly or indirectly, by all or substantially all of the individuals and entities who were the beneficial owners, respectively, of the Common Stock and the Company's voting securities outstanding immediately prior to such sale or other disposition, in substantially the same proportion as their ownership, immediately prior to such sale or other disposition, of the Common Stock and the Company's voting securities, respectively.

The foregoing adjustments and the manner of application of the foregoing provisions shall be determined by the Committee in its sole discretion. Any adjustment may provide for the elimination of any fractional Share, which might otherwise become subject to an Option or Formula Option.

The grant of an Option or Formula Option by the Committee shall not affect in any way the right or power of the Company to make adjustments, reclassifications, reorganizations or changes in its capital or business structure, or to merge, consolidate, dissolve, liquidate, sell or transfer all or any part of its business or assets.

5. Terms and Conditions of Options and Formula Options. Each Option and Formula Option granted pursuant to this Plan shall be authorized by the Committee and shall be evidenced by an Agreement, or a Formula Option Agreement (as defined in Section 7 hereof) in the case of a Formula Option, in the form and containing the terms and conditions as the Committee from time to time may determine, provided that each Agreement or Formula Option Agreement, as the case may be, shall:

   (a) state the number of Shares to which it pertains;

   (b) state that the price at which each Share may be purchased shall not be less than the "Fair Market Value" (as defined below) of a Share on the date of grant of the Option;

   (c) state the terms and conditions or payment, except as otherwise provided by Section 11 hereof;

   (d) state the term of the Option or Formula Option, as the case may be, and the period or periods during the term in which the optionee may exercise the Option or Formula Option, as the case may be, or portions thereof

   (e) provide that the Option or Formula Option, as the case may be, is not transferable by the grantee other than by will or the laws of lineal descent and, in the case of an Option or Formula Option other than an Incentive Stock Option (i) to the spouse or any lineal ancestor or descendant of the grantee, (ii) to any trust, the sole beneficiaries of which are any one or all of such grantee, such grantee's spouse or any lineal ancestors or descendants of such grantee, and (iii) to any other person or entity as the

Committee may approve. A holder of an Option or Formula Option other than the grantee thereof may not transfer such option other than by will or the laws of lineal descent;

(f) provide that, with respect to any Options or Formula Options granted to an employee and/or director, the Option or Formula Option, as the case may be, shall terminate 30 days following the date the grantee ceases to be an employee and/or director of the Company or a Subsidiary, other than by reason of death or disability (as defined in Code Section 22 [e] [3]);

(g) provide that, if a grantee dies or becomes disabled (as defined in Code Section 22[e][3]) while he is an employee and/or director of the Company or a Subsidiary, as applicable, any Options or Formula Options, as the case may be, granted to such grantee may be exercised by the then holder thereof at any time within one year after the grantee's death or disability or, if earlier, the expiration of the term of such Option or Formula Option, as the case may be; and

(h) specify whether the Option is an Incentive Stock Option or a Non-Qualified Stock Option.

The Committee may provide in any Option or Formula Option, as the case may be, which it grants that a condition to the exercise of such Option or Formula Option, as the case may be, shall be the grantee's agreement to remain an employee of and/or to otherwise render services to the Company or any of its Subsidiaries for a specified period of time following the date of grant. This condition shall not impose on the Company or any Subsidiary any obligation to employ the grantee or otherwise retain the grantee as a director for any period of time or otherwise constitute a contract of employment.

The "Fair Market Value" of a Share on a given date shall be (a) if the Common Stock is then listed or admitted for trading on any national securities exchange or included in The Nasdaq National Market or The Nasdaq SmallCap Market, the last reported sales price of a Share for the trading day immediately preceding such date as reported on such exchange or such market, as the case may be; (b) if the Common Stock is not then listed or admitted for trading on any national securities exchange or included in The Nasdaq National Market or The Nasdaq SmallCap Market, the average of the last reported closing bid and asked quotation for a Share as reported on the

Automated Quotation System of NASDAQ or a similar service if NASDAQ is not reporting such information for the trading day immediately preceding such date; (c) if the Common Stock is not then listed or admitted for trading on any national securities exchange or included in The Nasdaq National Market or The Nasdaq SmallCap Market or quoted by NASDAQ or a similar service, the average of the last reported bid and asked quotation for a Share as quoted by a market maker in the Common Stock for the trading day immediately preceding such date(or if there is more than one market maker, the bid and asked quotation shall be obtained from two market makers and the average of the lowest bid and highest asked quotation shall be the "Fair Market Value"); or (d) if the Common Stock is not then listed or admitted for trading on any national securities exchange or included in The Nasdaq National Market or The Nasdaq SmallCap Market or quoted by NASDAQ and there is no market maker in the Common Stock, the fair market value of a Share as determined by the Committee in good faith.

6. Additional Terms and Conditions of Incentive Stock Options. In addition to the terms and conditions set forth in Section 5 hereof, each Agreement evidencing the grant of an Incentive Stock Option shall:

   (a) provide for an exercise price that shall not be less than 100% of the Fair Market Value (as defined above in Section 5 hereof) of the Shares on the date of grant of the Option, provided that: if the optionee owns (subject to applicable ownership attribution rules of Code Section 424[d] and the regulations promulgated thereunder by the Department of Treasury) stock possessing more than 10% of the total combined voting power of all Shares or of shares of any parent corporation within the meaning of Code Section 424(e) (a "Parent") or Subsidiary of the Company at the time the Option is granted (assuming the immediate exercise of such Option), the exercise price shall not be less than 110% of the Fair Market Value of the pertinent number of Shares of the Company on the date the Option is granted; and subject to the foregoing, the Committee, in determining the Fair Market Value, shall have full authority and discretion and be fully protected in doing so;

   (b) provide that the Option is not exercisable after the expiration of ten (10) years (or such lesser period as is specified in the Agreement) from the date the Option is granted, except that, if the optionee owns (subject to applicable ownership attribution rules of Code Section 424[d] and the regulations promulgated thereunder by the Department of the Treasury) more than 10% of the total combined voting power of all Shares or of shares of any Parent or Subsidiary at the time the Option is granted (assuming the immediate exercise of such Option), the Option is not exercisable after the expiration of five (5) years (or such lesser period as is specified in the Agreement) from the date the Option is granted; and

(c) provide that during the optionee's lifetime, the Option is exercisable only by the optionee.

7. Formula Grants to Directors. Each person who is first elected as a non-employee director of the Company after ____________ shall be granted a non-qualified stock option as of the date he or she first commences services as a director to acquire _________ Shares at a per share exercise price equal to the Fair Market Value (as defined above in Section 5 hereof) of a Share. Each non-employee director of the Company shall be granted a non-qualified stock option pursuant to this Section each year on the date of the first Board meeting following each annual meeting of shareholders, commencing with the annual meeting of shareholders of the Company first held after the date hereof, to acquire __________Shares at a per share exercise price equal to the Fair Market Value of a Share, provided such individual is a director of the Company on such date. Formula Options shall be subject to such additional terms as may be set forth in a Non-Qualified Formula Stock Option Agreement (the "Formula Option Agreement") complying with Section 5 hereof, approved by the Committee and used to evidence the grant of a Formula Option. Notwithstanding any other provision of this Plan, the provisions of this Section 7 and of the Formula Option Agreement may not be amended more than once every six months, other than to conform it with changes in the Code, the Employee Retirement Income Security Act of 1974, or any rules promulgated under either of the foregoing.

8. Compliance with Code for Incentive Stock Options. All Incentive Stock Options are intended to comply with Code Section 422, and all provisions of this Plan and all Incentive Stock Options granted hereunder shall be construed in such manner as to effectuate that intent.

9. Limitation on Incentive Stock Option Amounts. An Incentive Stock Option may not be granted to an optionee to the extent the aggregate Fair Market Value, determined at the time the Committee grants the Option, of Common Stock with respect to which stock options intended to meet the requirements of Section 422 of the Code are exercisable for the first time by such optionee during any calendar year under all plans of the Company and any Parent or Subsidiary exceeds $100,000.

10. Term of Plan. The Company shall submit this Plan to its shareholders for approval within 12 months of the adoption of this Plan by the Board. No Option or Formula Option shall be exercisable prior to the receipt of such shareholder approval. Unless shareholder approval is obtained within said twelve-month period, both this Plan and all outstanding Options and Formula Options shall be rendered immediately void and of no effect.

    The effective date of this Plan shall be the earlier of the date on which the shareholders of the Company or the Board approve this Plan (the "Effective Date"). This Plan shall terminate 10 years after that date. The Committee may grant Options and Formula Options pursuant to this Plan at any time on or between the Effective Date and that termination date, subject to the other provisions contained herein.

11. Exercise of Option by Optionee. A holder of an Option or Formula Option may purchase Shares pursuant thereto only upon receipt by the Company of a notice in writing from such holder of his intent to purchase a specific number of Shares, which notice contains such representations regarding compliance with the federal and state securities laws as the Committee may reasonably request. The exercise price shall be paid in full upon the exercise of an Option or Formula Option, and no Shares shall be issued or delivered until full payment thereof has been made. Payment of the exercise price for all Shares purchased pursuant to the exercise of an Option or Formula Option shall be made in cash or by certified check or, alternatively, if the applicable Agreement so allows, as follows:

    (a) by delivery to the Company of a number of shares of Common Stock which have been owned by the holder for at least six months prior to the date of exercise, having a fair market value on the date of exercise, as determined by the Committee in its sole discretion, either equal to the exercise price or in combination with cash in a sufficient amount to equal the purchase price; or

(b) by receipt of the exercise price in cash from a broker, dealer or other "creditor" as defined by Regulation T issued by the Board of Governors of the Federal Reserve System following delivery by the holder to the Committee of instructions in a form acceptable to the Committee regarding delivery to such broker, dealer or other creditor of that number of shares of Common Stock with respect to which the Option or Formula Option is exercised.

Until the Option or Formula Option has been exercised and payment of the exercise price for, and any withholding tax obligations with respect to, all Shares purchased pursuant to the exercise of the Option or Formula Option has been received by the Company in accordance with the terms of the applicable Agreement or Formula Option Agreement, the holder shall have no rights as a shareholder with respect to the Shares the Option or Formula Option covers. The Company shall make no adjustment to the Shares for any dividends or distributions or other rights for which the record date is prior to the issuance of that stock certificate, except as this Plan otherwise provides.

12. Withholding Taxes. Whenever the Company proposes or is required to issue Shares to a holder of an Option or Formula Option, pursuant to the exercise of a Non-Qualified Stock Option or Formula Option granted under this Plan, or the holder makes a disqualifying disposition (within the meaning of Code Section 421[b]) of Shares acquired upon the exercise of an Incentive Stock Option, the Company shall have the right to require the grantee to remit to the Company an amount sufficient to satisfy any federal, state and local withholding tax requirement prior to the delivery of any certificate or certificates for such Shares. A grantee may pay the withholding tax (a) by making payment in cash or by certified check, (b) if the applicable Agreement or Formula Option Agreement so provides, by electing to tender to the Company the smallest number of whole Shares that have been owned by such grantee for at least six months prior to the Tax Date (defined below) that, when multiplied by the Fair Market Value of the Shares determined as of the Tax Date, is sufficient to satisfy federal, state and local, if any, withholding taxes arising from exercise of the Option or Formula Option if the applicable Agreement or Formula Option Agreement so provides, or (c)

by electing to have the number of Shares which the holder is to receive upon exercise reduced by the number of Shares determined in (b) above (a grantee's election to tender or offset as described in [b] or [c] above is referred to as a "Withholding Election"). A grantee may make a Withholding Election only if the following conditions are met:

(a) the Withholding Election must be made no later than the date on which the amount of tax required to be withheld is determined (the "Tax Date") by executing and delivering to the Company a properly completed notice of Withholding Election in the form prescribed by the Committee;

(b) any Withholding Election is irrevocably given in a manner that satisfies the requirements of the exemption provided under Rule 16b-3, if any; and

(c) if the grantee is considered by the Committee to be subject to Section 16 of the Exchange Act, the Withholding Election is delivered to the Company sufficiently in advance of the Tax Date as the Committee determines is necessary or appropriate to satisfy the conditions of the exemption from Section 16(b) of the Exchange Act provided under Rule 16b-3.

Notwithstanding anything to the contrary herein, the Committee may in its sole discretion disapprove and give no effect to any Withholding Election for an Option or Formula Option and no Option or Formula Option to which any Withholding Election relates may be exercised prior to one year after the Company has been subject to the reporting requirements of Section 13 of the Exchange Act and has filed all reports and statements required to be filed pursuant to that Section during that year.

13. Assignability. Except as Section 5 of this Plan permits or the terms of the Option or Formula Option Agreement permit, no Option or Formula Option or any of the rights and privileges thereof accruing to an optionee shall be transferred, assigned, pledged or hypothecated in any way whether by operation of law or otherwise, and no Option or Formula Option, or right or privilege shall be subject to execution, attachment or similar process.

14. The Right of the Company to Terminate Employment. No provision in this Plan or any Option or Formula Option shall confer upon any

grantee any right to continue in the employment of the Company or any Subsidiary or to continue performing services for or to interfere in any way with the right of the Company or any Subsidiary to terminate his employment or of the right of shareholders of the Company to remove such grantee as a director at any time for any reason.

15. Amendment and Termination. Except as set forth in Section I hereof, the Board at any time may amend or terminate this Plan without shareholder approval; provided, however, that the Board may condition any amendment on the approval of the shareholders of the Company if such approval is necessary or advisable with respect to tax (including Code Sections 162[m] and 422), securities or other applicable laws and rules and regulations to which the Company, this Plan, optionees or eligible employees and/or directors are subject. No amendment or termination of this Plan shall adversely affect the rights of an optionee with regard to his Options or Formula Options without his consent.

16. General Restriction. Notwithstanding anything contained herein or in any of the Agreements to the contrary, no purported exercise of any Option or Formula Option granted pursuant to this Plan shall be effective without the approval of the Committee, which may be withheld to the extent that the exercise, either individually or in the aggregate together with the exercise of other previously exercised stock options and/or offers and sales pursuant to any prior or contemplated offering of securities, would, in the sole and absolute judgment of the Committee, require the filing of a registration statement with the United States Securities and Exchange Commission or with the securities commission of any state. The Company shall avail itself of any exemptions from registration contained in applicable federal and state securities laws that are reasonably available to the Company on terms, which, in the Committee's sole and absolute discretion, it deems reasonable and not unduly burdensome or costly. Each holder shall, prior to the exercise of an Option or Formula Option, deliver to the Company such information, representations and warranties as the Committee may reasonably request in order for the Committee to be able to satisfy itself that the Shares to be acquired pursuant to the exercise of an Option or Formula Option are being acquired in accordance with the terms of an applicable exemption from the securities registration requirements of applicable federal and state securities laws.

17. Choice of Law. The laws of the State of __________ shall govern this Plan.

IN WITNESS WHEREOF, the Company has caused this Plan to be executed in the form and as of the date set forth above.

Attest: ____________________________________.

Title: ________________________________

[CORPORATE SEAL]

Title: ________________________________

## Sample Omnibus Incentive Stock Plan

1. Purpose of the Plan. The Incentive Stock Plan (Stock Plan) has been established to attract and retain individuals eligible to participate in the plan and to further the growth, development and financial success of the Company by aligning the personal interests of Participants, through the ownership of shares of the Company's Common Stock and other incentives, with those of the Company and the Company's shareholders. Awards granted under the Plan may be Incentive Stock Options, Nonstatutory Stock Options, Restricted Stock, Stock Appreciation Rights, Stock Purchase Rights, or Other Stock Based Awards.

2. Definitions. As used herein, the following definitions shall apply:

   (a) "Administrator" means the Board or any of its Committees as shall be administering the Plan in accordance with Section 4 hereof.

   (b) "Applicable Laws" means the requirements relating to the administration of stock option plans under U.S. State corporate laws, U.S. Federal and state securities laws, the Code, any stock exchange or quotation system on which the Common Stock is listed or quoted and the applicable laws of any other country or jurisdiction where Options or Stock Purchase Rights are granted under the Plan.

   (c) "Award" means a grant under this Plan of Stock Options, Restricted Stock, Stock Appreciation Rights, Stock Purchase Rights, or Other Stock-Based Awards.

   (d) "Award Agreement" means the document which evidences an Award and which sets forth the terms, conditions, and limitations relating to such Award.

   (e) "Board" means the Board of Directors of the Company.

   (f) "Code" means the Internal Revenue Code of 1986, as amended.

(g) "Committee" means a committee of Directors appointed by the Board in accordance with Section 4 hereof.

(h) "Common Stock" means the Common Stock of the Company.

(i) "Company" means________________________________.

(j) "Director" means a member of the Board of Directors of the Company.

(k) "Disability" means total and permanent disability as defined in Section 22(e)(3) of the Code.

(l) "Employee" means any person, including Officers, employed by the Company or any Parent or Subsidiary of the Company. An Employee shall not cease to be an Employee in the case of (i) any leave of absence approved by the Company or (ii) transfers between locations of the Company or between the Company, its Parent, any Subsidiary, or any successor. For purposes of Incentive Stock Options, no such leave may exceed ninety days, unless reemployment upon expiration of such leave is guaranteed by statute or contract. If reemployment upon expiration of a leave of absence approved by the Company is not so guaranteed, on the 181st day of such leave any Incentive Stock Option held by the Optionee shall cease to be treated as an Incentive Stock Option and shall be treated for tax purposes as a Nonstatutory Stock Option. Neither service as a Director nor payment of a director's fee by the Company shall be sufficient to constitute "employment" by the Company.

(m) "Exchange Act" means the Securities Exchange Act of 1934, as amended.

(n) "Fair Market Value" means, as of any date, the value of Common Stock determined as follows:

    (i) If the Common Stock is listed on any established stock exchange or a national market system, including without limitation the Nasdaq National Market or The Nasdaq SmallCap Market of The Nasdaq Stock Market, its Fair Market Value shall be the closing sales price for such stock (or the closing bid, if no sales were reported) as quoted on such exchange or system for the last market trading day prior to the time of determination, as reported in *The Wall*

*Street Journal* or such other source as the Administrator deems reliable;

(ii) If the Common Stock is regularly quoted by a recognized securities dealer but selling prices are not reported, its Fair Market Value shall be the mean between the high bid and low asked prices for the Common Stock on the last market trading day prior to the day of determination; or

(iii) In the absence of an established market for the Common Stock, the Fair Market Value thereof shall be determined in good faith by the Administrator.

(o) "Incentive Stock Option" means an Option intended to qualify as an incentive stock option within the meaning of Section 422 of the Code.

(p) "Nonstatutory Stock Option" means an Option not intended to qualify as an Incentive Stock Option.

(q) "Officer" means a person who is an officer of the Company within the meaning of Section 16 of the Exchange Act and the rules and regulations promulgated thereunder.

(r) "Option" means a stock option granted pursuant to Section 8.

(s) "Optioned Stock" means the Common Stock subject to an Option or a Stock Purchase Right.

(t) "Optionee" means the holder of an outstanding Option or Stock Purchase Right granted under the Plan.

(u) "Other Stock Based Award" means an Award granted pursuant to Section 12, other than a Stock Option, Restricted Stock, Stock Appreciation Right, or Stock Purchase Right, that is paid with, valued in whole or in part by reference to, or is otherwise based on Shares.

(v) "Parent" means a "parent corporation," whether now or hereafter existing, as defined in Section 424(e) of the Code.

(w) "Participant" means any person, including Employees and Directors selected by the Administrator to receive an Award under this Plan.

(x) "Plan" means this YEAR'S Stock Incentive Plan.

(y) "Restricted Stock" means an Award granted to a Participant pursuant to Section 10.

(z) "Section 16(b)" means Section 16(b) of the Securities Exchange Act of 1934, as amended.

(aa) "Share" means a share of the Common Stock, as adjusted in accordance with Section 12 below.

(bb) "Stock Appreciation Right" or "SAR" means the grant, pursuant to Section 9, of a right to receive payment from the Company, in the form of stock, cash or a combination of both, equal to the excess of the Fair Market Value of one or more Shares over the exercise price of such Shares under the terms of such Stock Appreciation Right.

(cc) "Stock Purchase Right" means a right to purchase Common Stock pursuant to Section 11.

(dd) "Subsidiary" means a "subsidiary corporation," whether now or hereafter existing, as defined in Section 424(f) of the Code.

2. Stock Subject to the Plan. Subject to the provisions of Section 12 of the Plan, the maximum aggregate number of Shares which may be issued or sold under the Plan is_____ Shares, plus an annual increase to be added on the first day of the Company's fiscal year beginning in year equal to the lesser of (i)___% of the outstanding shares on such date, or (ii) an amount determined by the Administrator, The Shares may be authorized but unissued, or reacquired Common Stock. The following limitations shall apply to all Awards granted under the Plan:

(i) No Participant in any calendar year shall be granted more than 1,000,000 shares of Stock or a Stock Appreciation Right with respect to more than 1,000,000 shares.

(ii) In connection with his or her initial service, a Participant may be granted up to an additional 1,000,000 shares of Stock which shall not count against the limit set forth in subsection (i) above.

If an Award expires or becomes unexercisable without having been exercised in full, the unpurchased Shares, which were subject thereto, shall become available for future grant or sale under the Plan (unless the Plan has terminated). However, Shares that have actually been issued under the Plan, upon exercise of an Award, shall not be returned to the Plan and shall not become available for future distribution under the Plan, except that if Shares of Restricted Stock are repurchased by the Company at their original purchase price, such Shares shall become available for future grant under the Plan.

3. Administration of the Plan.

(a) Administrator. The Board shall administer the Plan or a Committee appointed by the Board, which Committee shall be constituted to comply with Applicable Laws.

(b) Powers of the Administrator. Subject to the provisions of the Plan and, in the case of a Committee, the specific duties delegated by the Board to such Committee, and subject to the approval of any relevant authorities, the Administrator shall have the authority in its discretion:

(i) to determine the size and type of Awards;

(ii) to determine the Fair Market Value;

(iii) to select the Participants to whom may from time to time be granted hereunder;

(iv) to determine the number of Shares to be covered by each such Award granted hereunder;

(v) to approve forms of agreement for use under the Plan;

(vi) to determine the terms and conditions, of any Award granted hereunder. Such terms and conditions include, but are not limited to, the exercise price, the time or times when Awards may be exercised (which may be based on performance criteria), any vesting acceleration or waiver of forfeiture restrictions, and any restriction or limitation regarding any Award or the Common Stock relating thereto, based in each case on such factors as the Administrator, in its sole discretion, shall determine;

(vii) to determine whether and under what circumstances an Option may be settled in cash under subsection 9(e) instead of Common Stock;

(viii) to reduce the exercise price of any Option to the then current Fair Market Value if the Fair Market Value of the Common Stock covered by such Option has declined since the date the Option was granted;

(ix) to prescribe, amend and rescind rules and regulations relating to the Plan, including rules and regulations relating to sub-plans established for the purpose of qualifying for preferred tax treatment under foreign tax laws;

(x) to allow Participants to satisfy withholding tax obligations by electing to have the Company withhold from the Shares to be issued upon exercise of an Award that number of Shares having a Fair Market Value equal to the amount required to be withheld. The Fair Market Value of the Shares to be withheld shall be determined on the date that the amount of tax to be withheld is to be determined. All elections by Optionees to have Shares withheld for this purpose shall be made in such form and under such conditions as the Administrator may deem necessary or advisable; and

(xi) to construe and interpret the terms of the Plan and awards granted pursuant to the Plan.

(c) Effect of Administrator's Decision. All decisions, determinations and interpretations of the Administrator shall be final and binding on all Participants.

4. Eligibility.

(a) Subject to the provisions of the Plan, the Administrator may from time to time select, from all eligible Participants, those to whom Awards shall be granted and shall determine the nature and amount of each Award. No eligible Participant shall have the right to receive an Award under the Plan, or, if selected to receive an Award, the right to continue to receive Awards.

(b) Neither the Plan nor any Award granted under the Plan shall confer upon any Participant any right with respect to continued employment by the Company, nor shall it interfere in any way with his or her right or the Company's right to terminate such relationship at any time, with or without cause.

5. Term of Plan. The Plan shall become effective upon its adoption by the Board. It shall continue in effect for a term of ten (10) years unless sooner terminated under Section 14 of the Plan.

6. Award Agreement. Each Award granted under the Plan shall be evidenced by an Award Agreement that shall specify the terms, conditions, limitations and such other provisions applicable to the Award as the Committee shall determine.

7. Stock Options

   (a) Type of Option. Each Option shall be designated in the Award Agreement as either an Incentive Stock Option or a Nonstatutory Stock Option. However, notwithstanding such designation, to the extent that the aggregate Fair Market Value of the Shares with respect to which Incentive Stock Options are exercisable for the first time by the Optionee during any calendar year (under all plans of the Company and any Parent or Subsidiary) exceeds $100,000, such Options shall be treated as Nonstatutory Stock Options. For purposes of this Section 8(a), Incentive Stock Options shall be taken into account in the order in which they were granted. The Fair Market Value of the Shares shall be determined as of the time the Option with respect to such Shares is granted.

   (b) Term of Option. The term of each Option shall be stated in the Award Agreement; provided, however, that the term shall be no more than ten (10) years from the date of grant thereof. In the case of an Incentive Stock Option granted to an Optionee who, at the time the Option is granted, owns stock representing more than ten percent (10%) of the voting power of all classes of stock of the Company or any Parent or Subsidiary, the term of the Option shall be five (5) years from the date of grant or such shorter term as may be provided in the Award Agreement.

   (c) Option Exercise Price and Consideration,

      (i) The per share exercise price for the Shares to be issued upon exercise of an Option shall be such price as is determined by the Administrator, but shall be subject to the following:

      (ii) In the case of an Incentive Stock Option

         (A) granted to an Employee who, at the time of grant of such Option, owns stock representing more than ten percent (10%) of the voting power of all classes of stock of the Company or any Parent or Subsidiary, the exercise price shall be no less than 110% of the Fair Market Value per Share on the date of grant.

(B) granted to any other Employee, the per Share exercise price shall be no less than 100% of the Fair Market Value per Share on the date of grant.

(iii) In the case of a Nonstatutory Stock Option

(A) granted to a Participant who, at the time of grant of such Option, owns stock representing more than ten percent (10%) of the voting power of all classes of stock of the Company or any Parent or Subsidiary, the exercise price shall be no less than 110% of the Fair Market Value per Share on the date of grant.

(B) granted to any other Participant, the per Share exercise price shall be no less than 85% of the Fair Market Value per Share on the date of grant.

(iv) Notwithstanding the foregoing, Options may be granted with a per Share exercise price other than as required above pursuant to a merger or other corporate transaction.

(v) The consideration to be paid for the Shares to be issued upon exercise of an Option, including the method of payment, shall be determined by the Administrator (and, in the case of an Incentive Stock Option, shall be determined at the time of grant). Such consideration may consist of (1) cash, (2) check, (3) promissory note, (4) other Shares which (a) in the case of Shares acquired upon exercise of an Option, have been owned by the Optionee for more than six months on the date of surrender, and (b) have a Fair Market Value on the date of surrender equal to the aggregate exercise price of the Shares as to which such Option shall be exercised, (5) consideration received by the Company under a cashless exercise program implemented by the Company in connection with the Plan, or (6) any combination of the foregoing methods of payment. In making its determination as to the type of consideration to accept, the Administrator shall consider if acceptance of such consideration may be reasonably expected to benefit the Company.

(d) Exercise of Option.

(i) Procedure for Exercise; Rights as a Shareholder. Any Option granted hereunder shall be exercisable according to the terms hereof at such times and under such conditions as determined by the Administrator and set forth in the Award Agreement. Except in the case of Options granted to Officers, Directors and Consultants, Options shall become exercisable at a rate of no less than 20% per year over five (5) years from the date the Options are granted. Unless the Administrator provides otherwise, vesting of Options granted hereunder shall be tolled during any unpaid leave of absence. An Option may not be exercised for a fraction of a Share. An Option shall be deemed exercised when the Company receives: (a) written or electronic notice of exercise (in accordance with the Award Agreement) from the person entitled to exercise the Option, and (b) full payment for the Shares with respect to which the Option is exercised. Full payment may consist of any consideration and method of payment authorized by the Administrator and permitted by the Award Agreement and the Plan. Shares issued upon exercise of an Option shall be issued in the name of the Optionee or, if requested by the Optionee, in the name of the Optionee and his or her spouse. Until the Shares are issued (as evidenced by the appropriate entry on the books of the Company or of a duly authorized transfer agent of the Company), no right to vote or receive dividends or any other rights as a shareholder shall exist with respect to the Shares, notwithstanding the exercise of the Option. The Company shall issue (or cause to be issued) such Shares promptly after the Option is exercised. No adjustment will be made for a dividend or other right for which the record date is prior to the date the Shares are issued, except as provided in Section 12 of the Plan. Exercise of an Option in any manner shall result in a decrease in the number of Shares thereafter available, both for purposes of the Plan and for sale under the Option, by the number of Shares as to which the Option is exercised.

(ii) Termination of Employment. If an Optionee ceases to be employed by the Company, such Optionee may exercise his or her Option within such period of time as is specified in the Award Agreement (of at least thirty [30] days) to the extent that the Option is vested on the date of termination (but in no event later than the expiration of the term of the Option as set forth in the Award Agreement). In the absence of a specified time in the Option Agreement, the Option shall remain exercisable for three (3) months following the Optionee's termination. If, on the date of termination, the Optionee is not vested as to his or her entire Option, the Shares covered by the unvested portion of the Option shall revert to the Plan. If, after termination, the Optionee does not exercise his or her Option within the time specified by the Administrator, the Option shall terminate, and the Shares covered by such Option shall revert to the Plan.

(e) Disability of Optionee. If an Optionee ceases to be employed by the Company as result of the Optionee's Disability, the Optionee may exercise his or her Option within such period of time as is specified in the Award Agreement (of at least six [6] months) to the extent the Option is vested on the date of termination (but in no event later than the expiration of the term of such Option as set forth in the Award Agreement). In the absence of a specified time in the Award Agreement, the Option shall remain exercisable for twelve (12) months following the Optionee's termination. If, on the date of termination, the Optionee is not vested as to his or her entire Option, the Shares covered by the unvested portion of the Option shall revert to the Plan. If, after termination, the Optionee does not exercise his or her Option within the time specified herein, the Option shall terminate, and the Shares covered by such Option shall revert to the Plan.

(f) Death of Optionee. If an Optionee dies while employed by the Company, the Option may be exercised within such period of time as is specified in the Award Agreement (of at least six [6] months) to the extent that the Option is vested on the date of death (but in no event later than the expiration of the term of such Option as set forth in the Award Agreement) by the Optionee's estate or by a person who acquires the right to exercise the Option by bequest or inheritance. In the absence of a specified time in the Award Agreement, the Option shall remain exercisable for twelve (12) months following the Optionee's termination. If, at the time of death, the Optionee is not vested as to the entire Option, the Shares covered by the unvested portion of the Option shall immediately revert to the Plan. If the Option is not so exercised within the time specified herein, the Option shall terminate, and the Shares covered by such Option shall revert to the Plan.

(i) Buyout Provisions. The Administrator may at any time offer to buy out for a payment in cash or Shares, an Option previously granted, based on such terms and conditions as the Administrator shall establish and communicate to the Optionee at the time that such offer is made.

(g) Non-Transferability of Options. The Options may not be sold, pledged, assigned, hypothecated, transferred, or disposed of in any manner other than by will or by the laws of descent or distribution and may be exercised, during the lifetime of the Optionee, only by the Optionee.

8. Stock Appreciation Rights

(a) SARs may be granted at a price determined by the Administrator, and may be granted in tandem with an Option, such that the exercise of the SAR or related Option will result in a forfeiture of the right to exercise the related Option for an equivalent number of shares, or independently of any Option.

(b) An SAR may be exercised at such times as may be specified in an Award Agreement, in whole or in installments, which may be cumulative and shall expire at such time as the Administrator shall determine at the time of grant; provided that no SAR shall be exercisable later than ten (10) years after the date granted. The Administrator may amend any SAR to accelerate the dates after which the SAR may be executed in whole or in part.

(c) SARs shall be exercised by the delivery of a written notice of exercise to the Company setting forth the number of Shares with respect to which the SAR is to be exercised.

9. Restricted Stock

(a) Restricted Stock may be granted alone or in conjunction with other Awards under the Plan and may be conditioned upon continued employment for a specified period, the attainment of specific performance goals or such factors as the Administrator may determine. In making an Award of Restricted Stock, the Administrator will determine the restrictions that will apply, the period during which the Award is subject to such restrictions, and the price, if any, payable by a recipient. The Administrator may amend any Award of Restricted Stock to accelerate the dates after which such Award may be executed in whole or in part.

(b) Nontransferability. Shares of Restricted Stock shall not be transferable until after removal of the legend with respect to such shares.

10. Stock Purchase Rights.

(a) Rights to Purchase. Stock Purchase Rights may be issued either alone, in addition to, or in tandem with other awards granted under the Plan and/or cash awards made outside of the Plan. After the Administrator determines that it will offer Stock Purchase Rights under the Plan, it shall advise the offeree in writing or electronically of the terms, conditions and restrictions related to the offer, including the number of Shares that such person shall be entitled to purchase, the price to be paid, and the time within which such person must accept such offer. The terms of the offer shall comply in all respects with Section 260.140.42

of Title 10 of the California Code of Regulations. The offer shall be accepted by execution of a Restricted Stock purchase agreement in the form determined by the Administrator.

(b) Repurchase Option. Unless the Administrator determines otherwise, the Restricted Stock purchase agreement shall grant the Company a repurchase option exercisable upon the voluntary or involuntary termination of the purchaser's service with the Company for any reason (including death or disability). The purchase price for Shares repurchased pursuant to the Restricted Stock purchase agreement shall be the original price paid by the purchaser and may be paid by cancellation of any indebtedness of the purchaser to the Company. The repurchase option shall lapse at such rate as the Administrator may determine. Except with respect to Shares purchased by Officers, Directors and Consultants, the repurchase option shall in no case lapse at a rate of less than 20% per year over five (5) years from the date of purchase.

(c) Other Provisions. The Restricted Stock purchase agreement shall contain such other terms, provisions and conditions not inconsistent with the Plan as may be determined by the Administrator in its sole discretion.

(d) Rights as a Shareholder. Once the Stock Purchase Right is exercised, the purchaser shall have rights equivalent to those of a shareholder and shall be a shareholder when his or her purchase is entered upon the records of the duly authorized transfer agent of the Company. No adjustment shall be made for a dividend or other right for which the record date is prior to the date the Stock Purchase Right is exercised, except as provided in Section 12 of the Plan.

11. Other Stock-Based Awards

(a) The Administrator shall have complete discretion in determining the number of Shares subject to Other Stock-Based Awards, the consideration for such Awards and the terms, conditions and limitations pertaining to same including, without limitation, restrictions based upon the achievement of specific business objectives, tenure, and other measurements of individual or business performance, and/or restrictions under applicable federal or state securities laws, and conditions under which such Awards will lapse.

(b) Payment of Other Stock-Based Awards may be in the form of cash, shares, other Awards, or in such combinations thereof as the committee shall determine at the time of grant, and with such restrictions as it may impose. Payment may be made in a lump sum or in installments as prescribed by the Administrator. The Administrator may also require or permit Participants to elect to defer the issuance of Shares or the settlement of Awards in cash under such rules and procedures as it may establish under the Plan. The Administrator may also provide that deferred settlements include the payment or crediting of interest on the deferred amounts or the payment or crediting of dividend equivalent to deferred amounts denominated in Shares.

(c) The Administrator may, at its sole discretion, direct the Company to issue Shares subject to such restrictive legends and/or stop transfer instructions as the administrator deems appropriate.

12. Adjustments Upon Changes in Capitalization, Merger or Asset Sale.

(a) Changes in Capitalization. Subject to any required action by the shareholders of the Company, the number of shares of Common Stock covered by each outstanding Award, and the number of shares of Common Stock which have been authorized for issuance under the Plan but as to which no Award has yet been granted or which has been returned to the Plan upon cancellation or expiration of an Award, as well as the price per share of Common Stock covered by each such outstanding Award, shall be proportionately adjusted for any increase or decrease in the number of issued shares of Common Stock resulting from a stock split, reverse stock split, stock dividend, combination or reclassification of the Common Stock, or any other increase or decrease in the number of issued shares of Common Stock effected without receipt of consideration by the Company. The conversion of any convertible securities of the Company shall not be deemed to have been "effected without receipt of consideration." Such adjustment shall be made by the Board, whose determination in that respect shall be final, binding and conclusive. Except as expressly provided herein, no issuance by the Company of shares of stock of any class, or securities convertible into shares of stock of any class, shall affect, and no adjustment by reason thereof shall be made with respect to, the number or price of shares of Common Stock subject to an Award.

(b) Dissolution or Liquidation. In the event of the proposed dissolution or liquidation of the Company, the Administrator shall notify each Participant as soon as practicable prior to the effective date of such proposed transaction. The Administrator in its discretion may provide for a Participant to have the right to exercise his or her Award until fifteen (15) days prior to such transaction as to all of the Shares covered thereby, including Shares as to which the Award would not otherwise be exercisable. In addition, the Administrator may provide that any Company repurchase option applicable to any Shares purchased upon exercise of an Award shall lapse as to all such Shares, provided the proposed dissolution or liquidation takes place at the time and in the manner contemplated. To the extent it has not been previously exercised, an Award will terminate immediately prior to the consummation of such proposed action

(c) Merger or Asset Sale. In the event of a merger of the Company with or into another corporation, or the sale of substantially all of the assets of the Company, each outstanding Award shall be assumed or an equivalent option or right substituted by the successor corporation or a Parent or Subsidiary of the successor corporation. In the event that the successor corporation refuses to assume or substitute for the Award, the Participant shall fully vest in and have the right to exercise the Award as to all of the Shares, including Shares as to which it would not otherwise be vested or exercisable. If an Award becomes fully vested and exercisable in lieu of assumption or substitution in the event of a merger or sale of assets, the Administrator shall notify the Participant in writing or electronically that the Award shall be fully exercisable for a period of fifteen (15) days from the date of such notice, and the Award shall terminate upon the expiration of such period. For the purposes of this paragraph, the Award shall be considered assumed if, following the merger or sale of assets, the option or right confers the right to purchase or receive, for each Share subject to the Award immediately prior to the merger or sale of assets, the consideration (whether stock, cash, or other securities or property) received in the merger or sale of assets by holders of Common Stock for each Share held on the effective date of the transaction (and if holders were offered a choice of consideration, the type of consideration chosen by the holders of a majority of the outstanding Shares); provided, however, that if such consideration received in the merger or sale of assets is not solely common stock of the successor corporation or its Parent, the Administrator may, with the consent of the successor corporation, provide for the consideration to be received upon the exercise of the Award, for each Share subject to the Award, to be solely common stock of the successor corporation or its Parent equal in fair market value to the per share consideration received by holders of Common Stock in the merger or sale of assets.

13. Amendment and Termination of the Plan.

    (a) Amendment and Termination. The Board may at any time amend, alter, suspend or terminate the Plan.

    (b) Shareholder Approval. The Board shall obtain shareholder approval of any Plan amendment to the extent necessary and desirable to comply with Applicable Laws.

    (c) Effect of Amendment or Termination. No amendment, alteration, suspension or termination of the Plan shall impair the rights of any Participant, unless mutually agreed otherwise between the Participant and the Administrator, which agreement must be in writing and signed by the Participant and the Company. Termination of the Plan shall not affect the Administrator's ability to exercise the powers granted to it hereunder with respect to Awards granted under the Plan prior to the date of such termination.

14. Conditions Upon Issuance of Shares.

    (a) Legal Compliance. Shares shall not be issued pursuant to the exercise of an Option unless the exercise of such Option and the issuance and delivery of such Shares shall comply with Applicable Laws and shall be further subject to the approval of counsel for the Company with respect to such compliance.

(b) Investment Representations. As a condition to the exercise of an Option, the Administrator may require the person exercising such Option to represent and warrant at the time of any such exercise that the Shares are being purchased only for investment and without any present intention to sell or distribute such Shares if, in the opinion of counsel for the Company, such a representation is required.

15. Inability to Obtain Authority. The inability of the Company to obtain authority from any regulatory body having jurisdiction, which authority is deemed by the Company's counsel to be necessary to the lawful issuance and sale of any Shares hereunder, shall relieve the Company of any liability in respect of the failure to issue or sell such Shares as to which such requisite authority shall not have been obtained.

16. Reservation of Shares. The Company, during the term of this Plan, shall at all times reserve and keep available such number of Shares as shall be sufficient to satisfy the requirements of the Plan.

17. Shareholder Approval. The Plan shall be subject to approval by the shareholders of the Company within twelve (12) months after the date the Plan is adopted. Such shareholder approval shall be obtained in the degree and manner required under Applicable Laws.

18. Information to Participants. The Company shall provide to each Participant, not less frequently than annually during the period such Participant has one or more Awards outstanding, and, in the case of an individual who acquires Shares pursuant to the Plan, during the period such individual owns such Shares, copies of annual financial statements. The Company shall not be required to provide such statements to key employees whose duties in connection with the Company assure their access to equivalent information.

# PARSAP PLAN

Form of ____ Stock Incentive Plan

Company Name ______________________________

Year _______STOCK INCENTIVE PLAN

1. PURPOSE. __________________________. _______ Stock Incentive Plan (the "Plan") is intended to provide incentives which will attract, retain and motivate highly competent persons as officers and employees of, and consultants and advisors to, ______________________ (the "Company") and its subsidiaries and affiliates, by providing them opportunities to acquire shares of the Company's common stock, par value $_______ per share (the "Common Stock"), or to receive monetary payments based on the value of such shares pursuant to the Benefits (as defined below) described herein. Additionally, the Plan is intended to assist in further aligning the interests of the Company's officers, employees and consultants and advisors to those of its other stockholders.

2. ADMINISTRATION.

   (a) The Plan will be administered by a committee (the "Committee") appointed by the Board of Directors of the Company from among its members (which may be the Compensation Committee) and shall be comprised, unless otherwise determined by the Board of Directors, solely of not less than two members who shall be (i) "Non-Employee Directors" within the meaning of Rule 16b-3 (b) (3) (or any successor rule) promulgated under the Securities Exchange Act of 1934, as amended (the "Exchange Act") and (ii) "outside directors" within the meaning of Treasury Regulation Section 1.162-27(e)(3) under Section 162(m) of the Internal Revenue Code of 1986, as amended (the "Code"). The Committee is authorized, subject to the provisions of the Plan, to establish such rules and regulations as it deems necessary for the proper administration of the Plan and to make such determinations and interpretations and to take such action in connection with the Plan and any Benefits granted hereunder as it deems necessary or advisable. All determinations and interpretations made by the Committee shall be binding and conclusive on all participants and their legal representatives. No member of the Committee and no employee of the Company shall be liable for any act or failure to act hereunder, except in circumstances involving his or her bad faith, gross negligence or willful misconduct, or for any act or failure to act hereunder by any other member or employee or by any agent to whom duties in connection with the administration of this Plan have been delegated. The Company shall indemnify members of the Committee and any agent of the Committee who is an employee of the Company, a subsidiary or an affiliate against any and all liabilities or expenses to which they may be subjected by reason of any act or failure to act with respect to their duties on behalf of the Plan, except in circumstances involving such person's bad faith, gross negligence or willful misconduct.

(b) The Committee may delegate to one or more of its members, or to one or more agents, such administrative duties as it may deem advisable, and the Committee, or any person to whom it has delegated duties as aforesaid, may employ one or more persons to render advice with respect to any responsibility the Committee or such person may have under the Plan. The Committee may employ such legal or other counsel, consultants and agents as it may deem desirable for the administration of the Plan and may rely upon any opinion or computation received from any such counsel, consultant or agent. Expenses incurred by the Committee in the engagement of such counsel, consultant or agent shall be paid by the Company, or the subsidiary or affiliate whose employees have benefited from the Plan, as determined by the Committee.

3. PARTICIPANTS. Participants will consist of such officers and employees of, and such consultants and advisors to, the Company and its subsidiaries and affiliates as the Committee in its sole discretion determines to be important or responsible for the success and future growth

and profitability of the Company and whom the Committee may designate from time to time to receive Benefits under the Plan. Designation of a participant in any year shall not require the Committee to designate such person to receive a Benefit in any other year or, once designated, to receive the same type or amount of Benefit as granted to the participant in any other year. The Committee shall consider such factors as it deems pertinent in selecting participants and in determining the type and amount of their respective Benefits.

4. TYPE OF BENEFITS. Benefits under the Plan may be granted in any one or a combination of (a) Stock Options, (b) Stock Appreciation Rights, (c) Stock Awards, (d) Performance Awards and (e) Stock Units (each as described below, and collectively, the "Benefits"). Stock Awards, Performance Awards, and Stock Units may, as determined by the Committee in its discretion, constitute Performance-Based Awards, as described in Section 11 hereof. Benefits shall be evidenced by agreements (which need not be identical) in such forms as the Committee may from time to time approve; provided, however, that in the event of any conflict between the provisions of the Plan and any such agreements, the provisions of the Plan shall prevail.

5. COMMON STOCK AVAILABLE UNDER THE PLAN. The aggregate number of shares of Common Stock that may be subject to Benefits, including Stock Options, granted under this Plan shall be __________ shares of Common Stock, which may be authorized and unissued or treasury shares, subject to any adjustments made in accordance with Section 13 hereof. The maximum number of shares of Common Stock with respect to which Benefits may be granted or measured to any individual participant under the Plan during the term of the Plan shall not exceed ________ provided, however, that the maximum number of shares of Common Stock with respect to which Stock Options and Stock Appreciation Rights may be granted to an individual participant under the Plan during the term of the Plan shall not exceed __________ (in each case, subject to adjustments made in accordance with Section 13 hereof). Any shares of Common Stock subject to a Stock Option or Stock Appreciation Right which for any reason is cancelled or terminated without having been exercised, any shares subject to Stock Awards, Performance Awards or Stock Units which are forfeited, any shares subject to Performance Awards settled in cash or any shares delivered to the Company as part or full payment for the exercise of a Stock Option

or Stock Appreciation Right shall again be available for Benefits under the Plan. The preceding sentence shall apply only for purposes of determining the aggregate number of shares of Common Stock subject to Benefits but shall not apply for purposes of determining the maximum number of shares of Common Stock with respect to which Benefits (including the maximum number of shares of Common Stock subject to Stock Options and Stock Appreciation Rights) that may be granted to any individual participant under the Plan.

6. STOCK OPTIONS. Stock Options will consist of awards from the Company that will enable the holder to purchase a number of shares of Common Stock, at set terms. Stock Options may be "incentive stock options" ("Incentive Stock Options"), within the meaning of Section 422 of the Code, or Stock Options that do not constitute Incentive Stock Options ("Nonqualified Stock Options"). The Committee will have the authority to grant to any participant one or more Incentive Stock Options, Nonqualified Stock Options, or both types of Stock Options (in each case with or without Stock Appreciation Rights). Each Stock Option shall be subject to such terms and conditions consistent with the Plan as the Committee may impose from time to time, subject to the following limitations:

   (a) EXERCISE PRICE. Each Stock Option granted hereunder shall have such per-share exercise price as the Committee may determine at the date of grant; provided, however, subject to subsection (d) below, that the per-share exercise price shall not be less than 100% of the Fair Market Value (as defined below) of the Common Stock on the date the Stock Option is granted.

   (b) PAYMENT OF EXERCISE PRICE. The option exercise price may be paid in cash or, in the discretion of the Committee, by the delivery of shares of Common Stock of the Company then owned by the participant, or by delivery to the Company of (i) irrevocable instructions to deliver directly to a broker the stock certificates representing the shares for which the Option is being exercised, and (ii) irrevocable instructions to such broker to sell such shares for which the Option is being exercised, and promptly deliver to the Company the portion of the proceeds equal to the Option exercise price and any amount necessary to satisfy the Company's obligation for withholding taxes, or any combination thereof. For purposes of making payment in shares of Common Stock, such shares shall be valued at their Fair Market Value on the date of exercise of the Option and shall have been held by the Participant for at least six months. To facilitate the foregoing, the Company may enter into agreements for coordinated procedures with one or more brokerage firms. The Committee may prescribe any other method of paying the exercise price that it determines to be consistent with applicable law and the purpose of the Plan, including, without limitation, in lieu of the exercise of a Stock Option by delivery of shares of Common Stock of the Company then owned by a participant, providing the Company with a notarized statement attesting to the number of shares owned, where upon verification by the Company, the Company would issue to the participant only the number of incremental shares to which the participant is entitled upon exercise of the Stock Option or by the Company retaining from the shares of Common Stock to be delivered upon the exercise of the Stock Option that number of shares having a Fair Market Value on the date of exercise equal to the option price of the number of shares with respect to which the Participant exercises the Stock Option.

(c) EXERCISE PERIOD. Stock Options granted under the Plan shall be exercisable at such time or times and subject to such terms and conditions as shall be determined by the Committee; provided, however, that no Stock Option shall be exercisable later than ten years after the date it is granted except in the event of a participant's death, in which case, the exercise period of such participant's Stock Options may be extended beyond such period but no later than one year after the participant's death. All Stock Options shall terminate at such earlier times and upon such conditions or circumstances as the Committee shall in its discretion set forth in such option agreement at the date of grant; provided, however, the Committee may, in its sole discretion, later waive any such condition.

(d) LIMITATIONS ON INCENTIVE STOCK OPTIONS. Incentive Stock Options may be granted only to participants who are employees of the Company or one of its subsidiaries (within the meaning of Section 424[f] of the Code) at the date of grant. The aggregate Fair Market Value (determined as of the time the Stock

Option is granted) of the Common Stock with respect to which Incentive Stock Options are exercisable for the first time by a participant during any calendar year (under all option plans of the Company and of any parent corporation or subsidiary corporation [as defined in Sections 424(e) and (f) of the Code, respectively]) shall not exceed $100,000. For purposes of the preceding sentence, Incentive Stock Options will be taken into account in the order in which they are granted. The per-share exercise price of an Incentive Stock Option shall not be less than 100% of the Fair Market Value of the Common Stock on the date of grant, and no Incentive Stock Option may be exercised later than ten years after the date it is granted; provided, however, Incentive Stock Options may not be granted to any participant who, at the time of grant, owns stock possessing (after the application of the attribution rules of Section 424[d] of the Code) more than 10% of the total combined voting power of all classes of stock of the Company or any parent or subsidiary corporation of the Company, unless the exercise price is fixed at not less than 110% of the Fair Market Value of the Common Stock on the date of grant and the exercise of such option is prohibited by its terms after the expiration of five years from the date of grant of such option. In addition, no Incentive Stock Option may be issued to a participant in tandem with a Nonqualified Stock Option.

(e) POST-EMPLOYMENT EXERCISES. The exercise of any Stock Option after termination of employment of a participant with the Company, a subsidiary of the Company or with any company or person providing consulting or advisory services to the Company shall be subject to such conditions as imposed by the Committee at the time of the grant and satisfaction of the conditions precedent that the participant neither (i) competes with, or takes other employment with or renders services to a competitor of, the Company, its subsidiaries or affiliates without the written consent of the Company; provided that this clause (i) shall not apply to consultants or advisors of the Company, nor (ii) conducts himself or herself in a manner adversely affecting the Company; provided, however, that the Committee, in its sole discretion, may waive any conditions imposed in the grant letter or as set forth in (i) and (ii) above relating to the exercise of options after the date of termination of employment during the term of the option.

7. STOCK APPRECIATION RIGHTS.

(a) The Committee may, in its discretion, grant Stock Appreciation Rights to the holders of any Stock Options granted hereunder. In addition, Stock Appreciation Rights may be granted independently of, and without relation to, Stock Options. A Stock Appreciation Right means a right to receive a payment in cash, Common Stock or a combination thereof, in an amount equal to the excess of (i) the Fair Market Value, or other specified valuation, of a specified number of shares of Common Stock on the date the right is exercised over (ii) the Fair Market Value, or other specified valuation (which shall be no less than the Fair Market Value) of such shares of Common Stock on the date the right is granted, all as determined by the Committee; provided, however, that if a Stock Appreciation Right is granted in tandem with or in substitution for a Stock Option, the designated Fair Market Value in the award agreement may be the Fair Market Value on the date such Stock Option was granted. Each Stock Appreciation Right shall be subject to such terms and conditions as the Committee shall impose from time to time.

(b) Stock Appreciation Rights granted under the Plan shall be exercisable at such time or times and subject to such terms and conditions as shall be determined by the Committee; provided, however, that no Stock Appreciation Right shall be exercisable later than ten years after the date it is granted except in the event of a participant's death, in which case, the exercise period of such participant's Stock Appreciation Right may be extended beyond such period but no later than one year after the participant's death. All Stock Appreciation Rights shall terminate at such earlier times and upon such conditions or circumstances as the Committee shall in its discretion set forth in such right at the date of grant.

(c) The exercise of any Stock Appreciation Right after termination of employment of a participant with the Company, a subsidiary of the Company or with any company or person providing consulting or advisory services to the Company shall be subject to satisfaction of the conditions precedent that the participant neither (i) competes with, or takes other employment with or renders services to a competitor of, the Company, its subsidiaries or affiliates without the written consent of the Company; provided that this clause (i) shall not apply to consultants or advisors of the Company, nor (ii) conducts himself or herself in a manner adversely affecting the Company; provided, however, that the Committee, in its sole discretion, may waive any conditions imposed in the grant letter or as set forth in (i) and (ii) above relating to the exercise of options after the date of termination of employment during the term of the option.

8. STOCK AWARDS. The Committee may, in its discretion, grant Stock Awards (which may include mandatory payment of bonus incentive compensation in stock) consisting of Common Stock issued or transferred to participants with or without other payments therefore. Stock Awards may be subject to such terms and conditions as the Committee determines appropriate, including, without limitation, vesting, restrictions on the sale or other disposition of such shares, the right of the Company to reacquire such shares for no consideration upon termination of the participant's employment within specified periods, and may constitute Performance-Based Awards, as described in Section 11 hereof. The Committee may require the participant to deliver a duly signed stock power, endorsed in blank, relating to the Common Stock covered by such an Award. The Committee may also require that the stock certificates evidencing such shares be held in custody or bear restrictive legends until the restrictions thereon shall have lapsed. The Stock Award shall specify whether the participant shall have, with respect to the shares of Common Stock subject to a Stock Award, all of the rights of a holder of shares of Common Stock of the Company, including the right to receive dividends and to vote the shares.

9. PERFORMANCE AWARDS

(a) Performance Awards may be granted to participants at any time and from time to time, as shall be determined by the Committee. Performance Awards may constitute Performance-Based Awards, as described in Section 11 hereof. The Committee shall have complete discretion in determining the number, amount and timing of awards granted to each participant. Such Performance

Awards may be in the form of shares of Common Stock or Stock Units. Performance Awards may be awarded as short-term or long-term incentives. Performance targets may be based upon, without limitation, Company-wide, divisional and/or individual performance.

(b) With respect to those Performance Awards that are not intended to constitute Performance-Based Awards, the Committee shall have the authority at any time to make adjustments to performance targets for any outstanding Performance Awards which the Committee deems necessary or desirable unless at the time of establishment of such targets the Committee shall have precluded its authority to make such adjustments.

(c) Payment of earned Performance Awards shall be made in accordance with terms and conditions prescribed or authorized by the Committee. The participant may elect to defer, or the Committee may require or permit the deferral of, the receipt of Performance Awards upon such terms as the Committee deems appropriate.

10. STOCK UNITS

(a) The Committee may, in its discretion, grant Stock Units to participants hereunder. The Committee shall determine the criteria for the vesting of Stock Units. Stock Units may constitute Performance-Based Awards, as described in Section 11 hereof. A Stock Unit granted by the Committee shall provide payment in shares of Common Stock at such time as the award agreement shall specify. Shares of Common Stock issued pursuant to this Section 10 may be issued with or without other payments therefore as may be required by applicable law or such other consideration as may be determined by the Committee. The Committee shall determine whether a participant granted a Stock Unit shall be entitled to a Dividend Equivalent Right (as defined below).

(b) Upon vesting of a Stock Unit, unless the Committee has determined to defer payment with respect to such unit or a participant has elected to defer payment under subsection (c) below, shares of Common Stock representing the Stock Units shall be distributed to the participant unless the Committee provides for the payment of the Stock Units in cash or partly in cash and partly in shares of Common Stock equal to the value of the shares of Common Stock which would otherwise be distributed to the participant.

(c) Prior to the year with respect to which a Stock Unit may vest, the participant may elect not to receive a distribution upon the vesting of such Stock Unit and for the Company to continue to maintain the Stock Unit on its books of account. In such event, the value of a Stock Unit shall be payable in shares of Common Stock pursuant to the agreement of deferral.

(d) A "Stock Unit" means a notional account representing one share of Common Stock. A "Dividend Equivalent Right" means the right to receive the amount of any dividend paid on the share of Common Stock underlying a Stock Unit, which shall be payable in cash or in the form of additional Stock Units.

11. PERFORMANCE-BASED AWARDS. Certain Benefits granted under the Plan may be granted in a manner such that the Benefits qualify for the performance-based compensation exemption of Section 162(m) of the Code ("Performance-Based Awards"). As determined by the Committee in its sole discretion, either the granting or vesting of such Performance-Based Awards shall be based on achievement of various key performance indicators in one or more business criteria that apply to the individual participant, one or more business units or the Company as a whole. The business criteria shall be as follows, individually or in combination: (i) net sales; (ii) net earnings; (iii) earnings per share; (iv) net sales growth; (v) market share; (vi) net operating profit; (vii) expense targets; (viii) working capital targets relating to inventory and/or accounts receivable; (ix) operating margin; (x) return on equity; (xi) return on assets; (xii) planning accuracy (as measured by comparing planned results to actual results); (xiii) market price per share; and (xiv) total return to stockholders. In addition, Performance-Based Awards may include comparisons to the performance of other companies, such performance to be measured by one or more of the foregoing business criteria. With respect to Performance-Based Awards, (i) the Committee shall establish in writing (a) the performance goals applicable to a given period, and such performance goals shall state, in terms of an objective formula or standard, the method for computing the amount of compensation payable to the participant if such performance goals are obtained and (b) the individual employees or class of

employees to which such performance goals apply no later than 90 days after the commencement of such period (but in no event after 25% of such period has elapsed) and (ii) no Performance-Based Awards shall be payable to or vest with respect to, as the case may be, any participant for a given period until the Committee certifies in writing that the objective performance goals (and any other material terms) applicable to such period have been satisfied. With respect to any Benefits intended to qualify as Performance-Based Awards, after establishment of a performance goal, the Committee shall not revise such performance goal or increase the amount of compensation payable thereunder (as determined in accordance with Section 162[m] of the Code) upon the attainment of such performance goal. Notwithstanding the preceding sentence, the Committee may reduce or eliminate Benefits payable upon the attainment of such performance goal.

12. FOREIGN LAWS. The Committee may grant Benefits to individual participants who are subject to the tax laws of nations other than the United States, which Benefits may have terms and conditions as determined by the Committee as necessary to comply with applicable foreign laws. The Committee may take any action that it deems advisable to obtain approval of such Benefits by the appropriate foreign governmental entity; provided, however, that no such Benefits may be granted pursuant to this Section 12 and no action may be taken which would result in a violation of the Exchange Act, the Code or any other applicable law.

13. ADJUSTMENT PROVISIONS; CHANGE IN CONTROL.

    (a) If there shall be any change in the Common Stock of the Company or the capitalization of the Company through merger, consolidation, reorganization, recapitalization, stock dividend, stock split, reverse stock split, split up, spin-off, combination of shares, exchange of shares, dividend in kind or other like change in capital structure or distribution (other than normal cash dividends) to stockholders of the Company in order to prevent dilution or enlargement of participants' rights under the Plan, the Committee, in its sole discretion, shall adjust, in an equitable manner, as applicable, the number and kind of shares that may be issued under the Plan, the number and kind of shares subject to outstanding Benefits, the exercise price applicable to outstanding Benefits, and the Fair Market Value of the Common Stock and other value determinations applicable to outstanding Benefits; provided, however, that any such arithmetic adjustment to a Performance-Based Award shall not cause the amount of compensation payable thereunder to be increased from what otherwise would have been due upon attainment of the unadjusted award. Appropriate adjustments may also be made by the Committee in the terms of any Benefits under the Plan to reflect such changes or distributions and to modify any other terms of outstanding Benefits on an equitable basis, including modifications of performance targets and changes in the length of performance periods; provided, however, that any such arithmetic adjustment to a Performance-Based Award shall not cause the amount of compensation payable thereunder to be increased from what otherwise would have been due upon attainment of the unadjusted award. In addition, other than with respect to Stock Options, Stock Appreciation Rights, and other awards intended to constitute Performance-Based Awards, the Committee is authorized to make adjustments to the terms and conditions of, and the criteria included in, Benefits in recognition of unusual or nonrecurring events affecting the Company or the financial statements of the Company, or in response to changes in applicable laws, regulations, or accounting principles. Notwithstanding the foregoing, (i) each such adjustment with respect to an Incentive Stock Option shall comply with the rules of Section 424(a) of the Code, and (ii) in no event shall any adjustment be made which would render any Incentive Stock Option granted hereunder other than an incentive stock option for purposes of Section 422 of the Code. The determination of the Committee as to the foregoing adjustments, if any, shall be conclusive and binding on participants under the Plan.

(b) Notwithstanding any other provision of this Plan, if there is a Change in Control of the Company, all then outstanding Stock Options and Stock Appreciation Rights shall immediately vest and become exercisable. For purposes of this Section 14(b), a "Change in Control" of the Company shall be deemed to have occurred upon any of the following events:

(i) a change in control of the Company that would be required to be reported in response to Item 6(e) of Schedule 14A of Regulation 14A promulgated under the Exchange Act; or

(ii) during any period of two (2) consecutive years, the individuals who at the beginning of such period constitute the Company's Board of Directors or any individuals who would be "Continuing Directors" (as hereinafter defined) cease for any reason (other than due to death or voluntary resignation) to constitute at least a majority thereof; or

(iii) the Company's Common Stock shall cease to be publicly traded after initially being publicly traded; or

(iv) the Company's Board of Directors shall approve a sale of all or substantially all of the assets of the Company, and such transaction shall have been consummated; or

(v) the Company's Board of Directors shall approve any merger, consolidation, or like business combination or reorganization of the Company, the consummation of which would result in the occurrence of any event described in Section 13(b)(i) above, and such transaction shall have been consummated.

For purposes of this Section 13(b), "Continuing Directors" shall mean (a) the directors of the Company in office on the Effective Date (as defined below) and (b) any successor to any such director and any additional director who after the Effective Date was nominated or selected by a majority of the Continuing Directors of the Company (or the Nominating Committee of the Board of Directors) in office at the time of his or her nomination or selection.

The Committee, in its discretion, may determine that, upon the occurrence of a Change in Control of the Company, each Stock Option and Stock Appreciation Right outstanding hereunder shall terminate within a specified number of days after notice to the holder, and such holder shall receive, with respect to each share of Common Stock subject to such Stock Option or Stock Appreciation Right, an amount equal to the excess of the Fair Market Value of such shares of Common Stock immediately prior to the occurrence of such Change in Control or such other event over the exercise price per share of such Stock Option or Stock Appreciation Right; such amount to be payable in cash, in one or more kinds of property (including the property, if any, payable in the transaction) or in a combination thereof, as the Committee, in its discretion, shall determine. The provisions contained in the preceding sentence shall be inapplicable to a Stock Option or Stock Appreciation Right granted within six (6) months before the occurrence of a Change in Control if the holder of such Stock Option or Stock Appreciation Right is subject to the reporting requirements of Section 16(a) of the Exchange Act and no exception from liability under Section 16(b) of the Exchange Act is otherwise available to such holder.

14. NONTRANSFERABILITY. Each Benefit granted under the Plan to a participant shall not be transferable otherwise than by will or the laws of descent and distribution, and shall be exercisable, during the participant's lifetime, only by the participant. In the event of the death of a participant, each Stock Option or Stock Appreciation Right theretofore granted to him or her shall be exercisable during such period after his or her death as the Committee shall in its discretion set forth in such option or right at the date of grant and then only by the executor or administrator of the estate of the deceased participant or the person or persons to whom the deceased participant's rights under the Stock Option or Stock Appreciation Right shall pass by will or the laws of descent and distribution. Notwithstanding the foregoing, at the discretion of the Committee, an award of a Benefit other than an Incentive Stock Option may permit the transferability of a Benefit by a participant solely to the participant's spouse, siblings, parents, children and grandchildren or trusts for the benefit of such persons or partnerships, corporations, limited liability companies or other entities owned solely by such persons, including trusts for such persons, subject to any restriction included in the award of the Benefit.

15. OTHER PROVISIONS. The award of any Benefit under the Plan may also be subject to such other provisions (whether or not applicable to the Benefit awarded to any other participant) as the Committee deter-

mines appropriate, including, without limitation, for the installment purchase of Common Stock under Stock Options, for the installment exercise of Stock Appreciation Rights, to assist the participant in financing the acquisition of Common Stock, for the forfeiture of, or restrictions on resale or other disposition of, Common Stock acquired under any form of Benefit, for the acceleration of exercisability or vesting of Benefits in the event of a change in control of the Company, for the payment of the value of Benefits to participants in the event of a change in control of the Company, or to comply with federal and state securities laws, or understandings or conditions as to the participant's employment in addition to those specifically provided for under the Plan. The Committee shall have full discretion to interpret and administer the Plan.

16. FAIR MARKET VALUE. For purposes of this Plan and any Benefits awarded hereunder, Fair Market Value shall be the closing price of the Company's Common Stock on the date of calculation (or on the last preceding trading date if Common Stock was not traded on such date) if the Company's Common Stock is readily tradeable on a national securities exchange or other market system, and if the Company's Common Stock is not readily tradeable, Fair Market Value shall mean the amount determined in good faith by the Committee as the fair market value of the Common Stock of the Company.

17. WITHHOLDING. All payments or distributions of Benefits made pursuant to the Plan shall be net of any amounts required to be withheld pursuant to applicable federal, state and local tax withholding requirements. If the Company proposes or is required to distribute Common Stock pursuant to the Plan, it may require the recipient to remit to it or to the corporation that employs such recipient an amount sufficient to satisfy such tax withholding requirements prior to the delivery of any certificates for such Common Stock. In lieu thereof, the Company or the employing corporation shall have the right to withhold the amount of such taxes from any other sums due or to become due from such corporation to the recipient as the Committee shall prescribe. The Committee may, in its discretion and subject to such rules as it may adopt (including any as may be required to satisfy applicable tax and/or non-tax regulatory requirements), permit an optionee or award- or right-holder to pay all or a portion of the federal, state and local withholding taxes arising in connection with any Benefit consisting of

shares of Common Stock by electing to have the Company withhold shares of Common Stock having a Fair Market Value equal to the amount of tax to be withheld, such tax calculated at rates required by statute or regulation.

18. TENURE. A participant's right, if any, to continue to serve the Company or any of its subsidiaries or affiliates as an officer, employee, or otherwise, shall not be enlarged or otherwise affected by his or her designation as a participant under the Plan.

19. UNFUNDED PLAN. Participants shall have no right, title, or interest whatsoever in or to any investments which the Company may make to aid it in meeting its obligations under the Plan. Nothing contained in the Plan, and no action taken pursuant to its provisions, shall create or be construed to create a trust of any kind, or a fiduciary relationship between the Company and any participant, beneficiary, legal representative or any other person. To the extent that any person acquires a right to receive payments from the Company under the Plan, such right shall be no greater than the right of an unsecured general creditor of the Company. All payments to be made hereunder shall be paid from the general funds of the Company and no special or separate fund shall be established and no segregation of assets shall be made to assure payment of such amounts except as expressly set forth in the Plan. The Plan is not intended to be subject to the Employee Retirement Income Security Act of 1974, as amended.

20. NO FRACTIONAL SHARES. No fractional shares of Common Stock shall be issued or delivered pursuant to the Plan or any Benefit. The Committee shall determine whether cash, or Benefits, or other property shall be issued or paid in lieu of fractional shares or whether such fractional shares or any rights thereto shall be forfeited or otherwise eliminated.

21. DURATION, AMENDMENT AND TERMINATION. No Benefit shall be granted more than ten years after the Effective Date. The Committee may amend the Plan from time to time or suspend or terminate the Plan at any time. No amendment of the Plan may be made without approval of the stockholders of the Company if the amendment will: (i) disqualify any Incentive Stock Options granted under the Plan; (ii) increase the aggregate number of shares of Common Stock that may be delivered through Stock Options under the Plan; (iii) increase either of

the maximum amounts which can be paid to an individual participant under the Plan as set forth in Section 5 hereof; (iv) change the types of business criteria on which Performance-Based Awards are to be based under the Plan; or (v) modify the requirements as to eligibility for participation in the Plan.

22. GOVERNING LAW. This Plan, Benefits granted hereunder and actions taken in connection herewith shall be governed and construed in accordance with the laws of the State of ________ (regardless of the law that might otherwise govern under applicable ________ principles of conflict of laws).

23. EFFECTIVE DATE.

    (a) The Plan shall be effective as of ________________, the date on which the Plan was adopted by the Committee (the "Effective Date"), provided that the Plan is approved by the stockholders of the Company at an annual meeting, any special meeting or by written consent of stockholders of the Company within 12 months of the Effective Date, and such approval of stockholders shall be a condition to the right of each participant to receive any Benefits hereunder. Any Benefits granted under the Plan prior to such approval of stockholders shall be effective as of the date of grant (unless, with respect to any Benefit, the Committee specifies otherwise at the time of grant), but no such Benefit may be exercised or settled and no restrictions relating to any Benefit may lapse prior to such stockholder approval, and if stockholders fail to approve the Plan as specified hereunder, any such Benefit shall be cancelled.

    (b) This Plan shall terminate on __________________ (unless sooner terminated by the Committee).

Exhibit F

Form of Amended Non-Employee Director Stock Option Plan

---

## NON-EMPLOYEE DIRECTOR STOCK OPTION PLAN

1. PURPOSE. The purpose of this Plan is to help attract, retain and compensate highly qualified individuals who are not current employees of ____________________ (the "Company") as members of the Board of Directors and, by encouraging ownership of a stock interest in the Company, to gain for the Company the advantages inherent in directors having a greater personal financial investment in the Company.

2. DEFINITIONS. As used herein, the following terms shall have the meanings indicated:

   "Annual Meeting Date" means 5:OO p.m. on the date of the annual meeting of the Company's shareholders at which the Directors are elected.

   "Board" means the Company's Board of Directors,

   "Common Stock" means the Common Stock, par value $.01 per share, of the Company.

   "Company" refers to ____________________, a ________________ corporation, or any successor thereof.

   "Director" means a member of the Board.

   "Effective Date" is the date specified in Section 16.1.

   "Eligible Director" means any person who is a member of the Board and who, at the time of the grant, is not an "employee" of the Company and/or any of its subsidiaries, within the meaning of the Employee Retirement Security Act of 1974, as amended ("ERISA").

   "Fair Market Value" of the Common Stock on any date of reference means it shall be determined in good faith by the Board and may, among other methods, be the Closing Price of the Common Stock preceding the grant date or the average of the Closing Prices of the Common Stock on each of the 30 business days immediately preceding such date. For this purpose, the Closing Price of the Common Stock on any business day shall be (i) if such Common Stock is listed or admitted for trading on any United States national securities exchange, or if actual transactions are otherwise reported on a consolidated transaction reporting system, the last reported sale price of Common Stock on such exchange or reporting system, as reported in any newspaper of general circulation; (ii) if the Common Stock is quoted on the National Association of Securities Dealers Automated Quotations System ("NASDAQ"), or any similar system of automated dissemination of quotations of securities prices in common use, the closing bid quotation for such day of the Common Stock on such system; or (iii) if neither clause (i) or (ii) is applicable, the mean between the high bid and low ask quotations for the Common Stock as reported by the National Quotation Bureau, Incorporated, if at least two securities dealers have inserted both bid and ask quotations for the Common Stock on at least 5 of the 10 preceding days.

"Initial Grant Date" means the date on which a person is first elected as a member of the Board.

"Option" (when capitalized) means any stock option granted under this Plan.

"Option Agreement" means the agreement between the Company and the Optionee for the grant of an option.

"Option Period" means the ten-year period between the date an Option is granted and the expiration date of the Option.

"Optionee" means a person to whom a stock option is granted under this Plan or any person who succeeds to the rights of such person under this Plan by reason of the death of such person.

"Plan" shall mean this Non-Employee Director Stock Option Plan for the Company.

"Share(s)" shall mean a share or shares of the Common Stock.

3. SHARES AND OPTIONS. Subject to Section 11 of this Plan, the maximum number of shares of Common Stock, which may be issued pursuant to Options granted under the Plan, shall be ________ shares.

Shares of Common Stock shall be made available for issuance pursuant to the Plan either from shares of Common Stock reacquired by the Company (either directly or indirectly through an agent, trustee or other person or entity) or from authorized but unissued shares. Any shares of Common Stock with respect to which Options have expired or terminated for any reason other than exercise of such Options, shall again be available for issuance pursuant to the Plan, to the extent permitted under Rule 16b-3 promulgated under the Securities Exchange Act of 1934, as amended (the "Exchange Act").

4. GRANTS OF OPTIONS. Each Eligible Director elected after the Effective Date shall receive an initial grant of an Option to purchase ________ Shares on the Initial Grant Date. In addition, commencing in _____ and provided that a sufficient number of shares remain available under this Plan, each Eligible Director who is re-elected to serve as a director on the Annual Meeting Date, shall be granted an option to purchase ________ shares each year on the Annual Meeting Date. Upon the grant of each Option, the Company and the Eligible Director shall enter into an Option Agreement, which shall specify the grant date and the exercise price and shall include or incorporate by reference the substance of this Plan and such other provisions consistent with this Plan as the Board may determine. The options to be granted under this Plan shall be nonqualified stock options (stock options which do not constitute "incentive stock options" within the meaning of Section 422A of the Code).

5. EXERCISE PRICE. The exercise price per Share of any Option shall be the Fair Market Value of the Shares underlying such Option on the date such Option is granted.

6. EXERCISE OF OPTIONS. An Option shall be deemed exercised when (1) the Company has received written notice of such exercise in accordance with the terms of the Option; (ii) full payment of the aggregate exercise price of the Shares as to which the Option is exercised has been made; and (iii) arrangements that are satisfactory to the Board in its sole discretion have been made for the Optionee's payment to the Company of the amount that is necessary for the Company to withhold in accordance with applicable Federal or state tax withholding requirements. The exercise price of any Shares purchased, and any required tax payment, shall be paid, at the election of the Company, in cash, by the

tender of Shares, or both. If payment is made in cash, it may be made by certified or official bank check, personal check or money order. If payment is made by the tender of Shares, the Fair Market Value of each Share shall be determined as of the day the Shares are tendered for payment or, if no sale or bid has been made on such date, then on the last preceding day on which such sale or bid shall have been made. Any excess of the value of the tendered Shares over the purchase price will be returned to the Optionee as follows:

(i) any whole Shares remaining in excess of the purchase price will be returned to the Optionee in kind, and may be represented by one or more certificates as determined by the Company in its sole discretion;

(ii) any partial Shares remaining in excess of the purchase price will be returned to the Optionee in cash.

No Optionee shall be deemed to be a holder of any Shares subject to an Option unless and until a stock certificate or certificates for such Shares are issued to such person(s) under the terms of the Plan. No adjustment shall be made for dividends (ordinary or extraordinary, whether in cash, securities or other property) or distributions or other rights for which the record date is prior to the date such stock certificate is issued, except as expressly provided in Section 11 hereof.

7. ISSUANCE OF SHARES. No shares shall be issued and delivered upon exercise of any option unless and until in the opinion of the Company's legal counsel, any applicable registration requirements of the Securities Act of 1933, as amended, any applicable listing requirements of any national securities exchange on which stock of the same class is then listed, and any other requirements of law or of any regulatory bodies having jurisdiction over such issuance and delivery, shall have been fully complied with.

8. VESTING; EXERCISABILITY.

8.1 Each Option granted hereunder on an Annual Meeting Date shall vest and become nonforfeitable on the next Annual Meeting Date, if the Optionee has continued to serve as a Director until that meeting. An Option granted other than on an Annual Meeting Date shall vest and become nonforfeitable on the first anniversary of the day on which such Option was granted, if the Optionee has continued to serve as a Director until that day. An Option shall on that day and thereafter be exercisable, subject only to Section 8.2.

8.2 The expiration date of an Option shall be 10 years from the date of grant of the Option, subject to earlier termination pursuant to Section 10.

9. CHANGE OF CONTROL PROVISIONS. Notwithstanding any other provision of the Plan, the following acceleration provisions shall apply in the event of a "Change of Control" as defined in this Section 9:

9.1 Any Option previously granted under the Plan to an Eligible Director on the date of a "Change of Control" (as defined in Section 9.2) automatically shall become fully exercisable and vested, subject only to legal restrictions on the issuance of Shares set forth in Section 13 and the provisions of the next sentence. Unless an Optionee can transfer an Option or Shares issued upon exercise of an Option without incurring liability under Section 16(b) of the Exchange Act, at least six months shall elapse from the date of acquisition of the Option to the date of disposition of the Option (other than upon exercise) or the underlying Shares.

9.2 For purposes of Section 9.1, a "Change of Control" shall mean:

(a) Individuals who, as of the effective date of the Plan, constitute the Board (the "Incumbent Board") cease for any reason to constitute at least a majority of the Board; provided, however, that any individual becoming a director subsequent to the date hereof whose election, or nomination for election by the Company's shareholders, was approved by a vote of at least a majority of the directors then comprising the Incumbent Board shall be considered as though such individual were a member of the Incumbent Board, but excluding, for this purpose, any such individual whose initial assumption of office occurs as a result of either an actual or threatened solicitation to which Rule 14a-11 of Regulation 14A promulgated under the Exchange Act applies or other actual or threatened solicitation of proxies or consents; or

(b) Approval by the shareholders of the Company of a reorganization, merger or consolidation, in each case, with respect to which all or substantially all of the individuals and entities who were the beneficial owners, respectively, of the Outstanding Company Common Stock and Outstanding Company Voting Securities immediately prior to such reorganization, merger or consolidation do not, following such reorganization, merger or consolidation beneficially own, directly or indirectly, more than 51% of, respectively, the then outstanding shares of common stock and the combined voting power of the then outstanding voting securities entitled to vote generally in the election of directors, as the case may be, of the corporation resulting from such organization, merger or consolidation; or

(c) Approval by the shareholders of the Company of (i) a complete liquidation or dissolution of the Company; or (ii) the sale or other disposition of all or substantially all of the assets of the Company, other than to a corporation, with respect to which following such sale or other disposition, more than 51% of, respectively, the then outstanding shares of common stock of such corporation and the combined voting power of the then outstanding voting securities of such corporation entitled to vote generally in the election of directors is then beneficially owned, directly or indirectly, by all or substantially all of the individuals and entities who were the beneficial owners, respectively, of the Outstanding Company Common Stock and Outstanding Company Voting Securities immediately prior to such sale or other disposition. The term "the sale or other disposition of all or substantially all of the assets of the Company" shall mean a sale or other disposition transaction or series of related transactions involving assets of the Company or of any direct or indirect subsidiary of the Company (including the stock of any direct or indirect subsidiary of the Company) in which the value of the assets or stock being sold or otherwise disposed of (as measured by the purchase price being paid therefore or by such other method as the Board determines is appropriate in a case where there is no readily ascertainable purchase price) constitutes more than two-thirds of the fair market value of the Company (as hereinafter defined). The "fair market value of the Company" shall be the aggregate market value of the then Outstanding Company Common Stock (on a fully diluted basis) plus the aggregate market value of the Company's other outstanding equity securities. The aggregate market value of the shares of Outstanding Company Common Stock shall be determined by multiplying the number of shares of Outstanding Company Common Stock (on a fully diluted basis) outstanding on the date of the execution and delivery of a definitive agreement with respect to the transaction or series of related transactions (the "Transaction Date") by the average Fair Market Value per share for the ten trading days immediately preceding the Transaction Date. The aggregate market value of any other equity securities of the Company shall be determined in a manner similar to that prescribed in the preceding sentence for determining the aggregate market value of the shares of Outstanding Company Common Stock.

10. TERMINATION OF OPTION PERIOD. An Optionee whose directorship terminates for any reason other than death or disability (as defined in Section 105[d][4] of the Code) shall be entitled to exercise any Options which are then exercisable only within the six-month period after the date he ceases to serve as a director; after such six-month period, such Options shall be null and void. In the case of termination of the directorship by reason of the Director's death or disability within the meaning of Section 105(d)(4) of the Code, the Option or any portion thereof which was not exercisable on the date of termination shall be accelerated and become immediately exercisable, and the period to exercise such Option shall be twelve months, subject to the earlier expiration of the Option Period. The estate of an Optionee who dies, or a person who acquires the right to exercise an Option, including any portion of such Option which was not exercisable at the time of death, by bequest or inheritance or by reason of the death of the Optionee, may exercise the Option only within the twelve-month period after the death of the Optionee, subject to the earlier expiration of the Option Period.

11. ADJUSTMENT OF SHARES.

11.1 Option Agreements evidencing Options shall be subject to adjustment by the Board as to the number and price of Shares subject to such Options in the event of changes in the outstanding Shares by reason of stock dividends, stock splits, recapitalizations, reorganizations, mergers, consolidations, combinations, exchanges, or other relevant changes in capitalization occurring after the date of grant of any such Option. In the event of any such change in the outstanding Shares, the aggregate number of Shares available under the Plan shall be appropriately adjusted by the Board, whose determination shall be conclusive.

11.2 Except as otherwise expressly provided herein, the issuance by the Company of shares of its capital stock of any class, or securities convertible into shares of capital stock of any class, either in connection with a direct sale or upon the exercise of rights or warrants to subscribe therefore, or upon conversion of shares or obligations of the Company convertible into such shares or other securities, shall not affect, and no adjustment by reason thereof shall be made with respect to, the number or exercise price of the Shares then subject to outstanding Options granted under the Plan.

11.3 Without limiting the generality of the foregoing, the existence of outstanding Options granted under the Plan shall not affect in any manner the right or power of the Company to make, authorize or consummate (i) any or all adjustments, recapitalizations, reorganizations or other changes in the Company's capital structure or its business; (ii) any issue by the Company of debt securities, or preferred stock or (iii) any merger or consolidation of preferred stock that would rank above the Shares subject to outstanding Options; (iv) the dissolution or liquidation of the Company; (v) any sale, transfer or assignment of all or any part of the assets or business of the Company; or (vi) any other corporate act or proceedings, whether of a similar character or otherwise.

12. TRANSFERABILITY OF OPTIONS. Each Option shall provide that such Option shall not be transferable by the Optionee otherwise than by will or the descent and distribution, and each Option shall be exercis-

able during the Optionee's lifetime only by the Optionee.

13. ISSUANCE OF SHARES. As a condition of any sale or issuance of Shares upon exercise of any Option, the Board may require such agreements or undertakings, if any, as the Board may deem necessary or advisable to assure compliance with any applicable law or regulation including, but not limited to, the following:

    (a) a representation and warranty by the Optionee to the Company, at the time any Option is exercised, that Optionee is acquiring the Shares to be issued for investment and not with a view to, or for sale in connection with, the distribution of any such Shares; and

    (b) a representation, warranty and/or agreement to be bound by any legends that are, in the opinion of the Board, necessary or appropriate to comply with the provisions of any securities law deemed by the Board to be applicable to the issuance of the Shares and are endorsed upon the Share certificates.

14. ADMINISTRATION OF THE PLAN. The Plan shall be administered by the Board, which shall have the authority to adopt such rules and regulations and to make such determinations as are not inconsistent with the Plan and as are necessary or desirable for the implementation and administration of the Plan, provided that the Board does not have any discretion with respect to the grant of options under the Plan.

15. INTERPRETATION.

    15.1 If any provision of the Plan should be held invalid or illegal for any reason, such determination shall not affect the remaining provisions hereof, but instead the Plan shall be construed and enforced as if such provision had never been included in the Plan. Without limiting the generality of the foregoing, transactions under this Plan are intended to comply with all applicable conditions of Rule 16b-3 or its successors promulgated under the Exchange Act, and this Plan is intended to constitute a "Formula Plan" pursuant to Rule 16b-3(c)(Z)(ii) under the Exchange Act. To the extent any provision of the Plan or action by the Board hereunder is inconsistent with the foregoing requirements, it shall be deemed null and void, to the extent permitted by law and deemed advisable by the Board.

15.2 The determinations and the interpretation and construction of any provision of the Plan by the Board shall be final and conclusive. This Plan shall be governed by the laws of the State of __________. Headings contained in this Plan are for convenience only and shall in no manner be construed as part of this Plan. Any reference to the masculine, feminine, or neuter gender shall be a reference to such other gender as is appropriate.

16. TERM OF PLAN; AMENDMENT AND TERMINATION OF THE PLAN.

16.1 This Plan is effective as of ________________; provided, however, that within one year after such date, the Plan shall have been approved by the affirmative vote of the holders of a majority of the shares of Common Stock present or represented and entitled to vote at a meeting of the Company's shareholders, of any adjournment thereof. This Plan shall continue in effect until all Options granted hereunder have expired or been exercised, unless sooner terminated under the provisions relating thereto. No Option shall be granted after 10 years from the Effective Date. Any Option granted under this Plan prior to the date that shareholder approval is obtained pursuant to this Section 16.1 shall be deemed to have been granted as of the date such shareholder approval is obtained.

16.2 The Board may from time to time amend, terminate or suspend the Plan or any Option; provided, however, that except to the extent provided in Section 10, no such amendment may (i) without approval by the Company's shareholders, increase the number of Shares reserved for Options or change the class of persons eligible to receive Options or involve any other change or modification requiring shareholder approval under Rule 16b-3 of the Exchange Act; (ii) permit the granting of Options that expire beyond the maximum 10-year period described in Section 8.2; (iii) extend the termination date of the Plan as set forth in Section 16.1; or (iv) give the directors discretion with respect to the grant of options; and, provided further, that except to the extent otherwise specifically provided in Section 10, no amendment, termination or suspension of the Plan or any Option issued hereunder shall substantially impair any Option previously granted to any Optionee without the consent of such

Optionee. Any termination or suspension of the Plan shall not affect Options already granted and such Options shall remain in full force and effect as if this Plan had not been terminated or suspended. No Option may be granted while the Plan is suspended or after it is terminated.

16.3 Notwithstanding anything else contained herein, the provisions of this Plan which govern the number of Options to be awarded to Directors, the exercise price per share under each such Option, when and under what circumstances an Option will be granted, and the period within which each Option may be exercised, shall not be amended more than once every six months (even with shareholder approval), other than to conform to changes in the Code, or the rules promulgated thereunder, and under ERISA, or the rules promulgated thereunder, or with rules promulgated by the Securities and Exchange Commission.

17. NO RIGHT TO SERVICE. Except as provided in this Plan, no Eligible Director shall have any claim or right to be granted a stock option under the Plan. Neither the Plan nor any action pursuant thereto shall be construed as giving any Eligible Director a right to be retained in the service of the Company. The adoption of this Plan shall not affect any other compensation, retirement or other benefit plan or program in effect for the Company.

18. RESERVATION OF SHARES. The Company, during the term of the Plan, will at all times reserve and keep available a number of Shares as shall be sufficient to satisfy the requirements of the Plan.

As adopted by the Board of Directors on ____________________, and amended on ________________________________________.

# Restricted Stock Plan

______________________________RESTRICTED STOCK PLAN

FOR NON-EMPLOYEE DIRECTORS

ARTICLE I. DEFINITIONS

1.1. Definitions

As used herein, the following terms shall have the meanings hereinafter set forth unless the context clearly indicates to the contrary:

(a) "Age for Board Retirement" shall mean the age for mandatory retirement of members of the Board as specified in the Bylaws of the Company, as applied to Eligible Directors on the date of such Eligible Directors' retirement from the Board.

(b) "Assumed Award" shall mean a restricted stock grant, restricted stock unit or other equity-based arrangement that was granted by __________ to one of its non-employee directors for his or her service as such and which is assumed by the Company in connection with the Distribution, as such award has been adjusted or amended pursuant to the terms thereof.

(c) "Award" shall mean an award of Restricted Stock and/or Restricted Units pursuant to the provisions of Article V or Article VI hereof.

(d) "Awardee" shall mean an Eligible Director to whom Restricted Stock has been awarded hereunder.

(e) "Board" shall mean the Board of Directors of the Company.

(f) "Change of Control" of the Company shall be deemed to have occurred if (i) a third person, including a "group" as defined in Section 13(d) (3) of the Securities exchange Act of 1934, acquires shares of the Company having twenty-five percent or more of the total number of votes that may be cast for the election of directors of the Company; or (ii) as the result of any cash tender or exchange offer, merger or other business combination, or any combination of the foregoing transactions (a "Transaction"), the persons who were directors of the Company before the Transaction shall cease to constitute a majority of the Board of the Company or any successor to the Company.

(g) "Committee" shall mean the administrative body provided for in Section 4.1.

(h) "Company" shall mean ______________________ and, with respect to periods of time prior to the date of the Distribution, ______________________________.

(i) "Distribution" shall have the meaning set forth in Section 2.2.

(j) "Eligible Director" shall mean a director of the Company who is not and never has been an employee of the Company or any of its Subsidiaries.

(k) "__________ Stock Price" shall mean, as of any date, the closing sale price for shares of Stock quoted for such date on The New York Stock Exchange.

(l) "Plan" shall mean the Restricted Stock Plan fox Non-Employee Directors, the current terms of which are set forth herein.

(m) "Plan Effective Date" shall mean the date upon which the Plan becomes effective in accordance with the provisions of Section 2.3.

(n) "Restricted Stock Agreement" and " Restricted Unit Agreement " shall mean the agreement between the Company and the Awardee with respect to Restricted Stock and Restricted Units, respectively, awarded hereunder.

(o) "Restricted Stock Award" shall mean Stock that is awarded to an Eligible Director by the Committee pursuant to Article V hereof, which is nontransferable and subject to a substantial risk of forfeiture until specific conditions are met.

(p) "Restricted Unit Award" shall mean amounts awarded pursuant to Article VI hereof.

(q) "Stock" shall mean the Common Stock of the Company or, in the event that the outstanding shares of Stock are hereafter changed into or exchanged for shares of a different stock or securities of the Company or some other corporation, such other stock or securities.

(r) "Subsidiary" shall mean any corporation, the majority of the outstanding capital stock of which is owned, directly or indirectly, by the Company or any partnership or joint venture in which either the Company or such a corporation is at least a twenty percent (20%) equity participant.

ARTICLE II. GENERAL

2.1 Name

This Plan shall be known as the "________________________ Restricted Stock Plan for Non-Employee Directors." The purpose of the Plan is to advance the interests of the Company and its stockholders by affording to Eligible Directors of the Company an opportunity to acquire or increase their proprietary interest in the Company by the grant to such directors of Awards under the terms set forth herein. By encouraging non-employee directors to become owners of Company shares, the Company seeks to increase their incentive for enhancing stockholder value and to motivate, retain and attract those highly competent individuals upon whose judgment, initiative, leadership and continued efforts the success of the Company in large measure depends.

2.2 Effective Date

The Plan shall become effective upon its approval by ____________, as sole stockholder of the Company.

2.3 Limitations

Subject to adjustment pursuant to the provisions of Section 8.1 hereof, the aggregate number of shares of Stock, which may be issued as Awards, shall not exceed __________. Any such shares may be either authorized as unissued shares or shares issued and thereafter acquired by the Company.

2.4 Awards Granted under Plan

For purposes of Section 2.4, the aggregate number of shares of Stock issued under this Plan at any time shall equal only the number of shares actually issued pursuant to all Awards and shall not count any shares returned to the Company upon cancellation, expiration or forfeiture of an Award or delivered (either actually or by attestation) in payment or satisfaction of the tax obligation of an Award.

ARTICLE III. PARTICIPANTS

3.1 Eligibility

Any Eligible Director shall be eligible to participate in the Plan

ARTICLE IV. ADMINISTRATION

4.1 Composition of Committee

The Plan shall be administered by the Organization and Compensation Committee of the Board of Directors, and/or by the Board of Directors or another committee of the Board of Directors of the Company, as appointed from time to time by the Board of Directors (any such administrative body, the "Committee"). The Board of Directors shall fill vacancies on, and from time to time may remove or add members to, the Committee. The Committee shall act pursuant to a majority vote or unanimous written consent.

4.2 Duties and Powers of the Committee

Subject to the express provisions of this Plan, the Committee shall be authorized and empowered to do all things necessary or desirable in connection with the administration of this Plan with respect to the Awards over which such Committee has authority, including, without limitation, the following:

(a) to prescribe, amend and rescind rules and regulations relating to this Plan and to define terms not otherwise defined herein;

(b) to determine the number of Shares subject to Awards;

(c) to prescribe and amend the terms of the agreements or other documents evidencing Awards made under this Plan;

(d) to determine whether, and the extent to which, adjustments are required pursuant to Section 8.1 hereof;

(e) to interpret and construe this Plan, any rules and regulations under the Plan and the terms and conditions of any Award granted hereunder, and to make exceptions to any such provisions in good faith and for the benefit of the Company; and

(f) to make all other determinations deemed necessary or advisable for the administration of the Plan.

4.3 Determinations of the Committee

All decisions, determinations and interpretations by the Committee or the Board regarding the Plan shall be final and binding on all current or former directors of the Company and their beneficiaries, heirs, successors and assigns. The Committee or the Board, as applicable, shall consider such factors as it deems relevant, in its sole and absolute discretion, to making such decisions, determinations and interpretations including, without limitation, the recommendations or advice of any officer of the Company or Eligible Director and such attorneys, consultants and accountants as it may select.

4.4 Company Assistance

The Committee may designate the Secretary of the Company or other Company employees to assist the Committee in the administration of the Plan, and may grant authority to such persons to execute agreements evidencing Awards made under this Plan or other documents entered into under this Plan on behalf of the Committee or the Company. The Company shall supply full and timely information to the Committee on all matters relating to Eligible Directors, their death, retirement, disability or removal or resignation from the Board and such other pertinent facts as the Committee may require. The Company shall furnish the Committee with such clerical and other assistance as is necessary in the performance of its duties.

ARTICLE V. RESTRICTED STOCK AWARDS

5.1 Awards under the Plan

The Committee may provide for a one-time Restricted Stock Award to any Eligible Director that shall be granted on a date determined by the Committee, in its sole discretion, in connection with such Eligible Director first being appointed or elected to the Board. The Committee shall grant to each Eligible Director that is a member of the Board during all or any portion of each calendar year during the term of the Plan a Restricted Stock Award, which shall be granted on a date determined by the Committee, in its sole discretion. The number of shares of Stock subject to a one-time Restricted Stock Award shall be set by the Committee but shall not exceed ________ and the number of shares of Stock subject to an annual Restricted Stock Award shall be set by the Committee but shall not exceed ___________.

An Assumed Award is a restricted stock grant, restricted stock unit or other equity-based arrangement that was granted by ___________ to its non-employee directors for their service as such and assumed by the Company in connection with the Distribution, as adjusted or amended pursuant to the terms thereof. Assumed Awards may be settled with Stock authorized and issued under this Plan. Notwithstanding any provision to the contrary in this Plan and except as provided in this sentence, the terms of Assumed Awards shall be subject to the terms and conditions set forth in the grant agreement and/or other document(s) evidencing such Award and, to the extent provided therein, to terms equivalent to the terms of the plan under which such Award was originally granted; provided, however, that all Assumed Awards shall be administered by the Committee, which shall have the power and authority provided for in Section 4 of this Plan.

Each Award granted hereunder must be granted within ten years from the effective date of the Plan. The Awardee shall be entitled to receive the Stock subject to such Award only if the Company and the Awardee, within the time period specified by the Committee, enter into a written Restricted Stock Agreement dated as of the date of the Award, which Agreement shall set forth such terms and conditions as may be determined by the Committee consistent with the Plan.

5.3 Restrictions on Sale or Other Transfer

Each share of Stock granted under a Restricted Stock Award shall be subject to acquisition by the Company, and may not be sold or otherwise transferred except to the following provisions:

(a) The shares of Stock represented by the Restricted Stock Agreement shall be held in book entry form with the Company's transfer agent until the restrictions lapse in accordance with the conditions established by the Committee pursuant to Section 5.4 hereof, or until the shares of Stock are forfeited pursuant to paragraph (c) of this Section 5.3. Notwithstanding the foregoing, the Awardee may request that, prior to the lapse of the restrictions or forfeiture of the shares, certificates evidencing such shares be issued in his name and delivered to him, and each such certificate shall bear the following legend:

"The shares of ________________ common stock evidenced by this certificate are subject to acquisition by __________________, and such shares may not be sold or otherwise transferred except pursuant to the provisions of the Restricted Stock Agreement by and between __________________ and the registered owner of such shares."

(b) No such shares may be sold, transferred or otherwise alienated or hypothecated so long as such shares are subject to the restriction provided for in this Section 5.3.

(c) All of the Awardee's Restricted Stock remaining subject to any restriction hereunder shall be forfeited to, and be acquired at no cost by, the Company in the event that the Committee determines that any of the following circumstances has occurred:

(i) the Awardee has engaged in knowing and willful misconduct in connection with his or her service as a member of the Board;

(ii) the Awardee, without the consent of the Committee, at any time during his or her period of service as a member of the Board, becomes a principal of, serves as a director of, or owns a material interest in, any business that directly or through a controlled subsidiary competes with the Company or any Subsidiary; or

(iii) the Awardee does not stand for reelection to, or voluntarily quits or resigns from, the Board for any reason, except under circumstances that would cause such restrictions to lapse under Section 5.4.

5.4 Lapse of Restrictions

(a) Unless provided otherwise by the Committee, the restrictions imposed under Section 5.3 above upon a one-time Restricted Stock Award shall lapse to the extent of 20% of the number of shares subject to such Award on such date as shall be designated by the Committee and thereafter, the restrictions on the remaining shares subject to such Award will lapse in four equal increments on the succeeding anniversary dates following the date of lapsing of restrictions on the first 20 percent of the shares.

(b) Unless provided otherwise by the Committee, the restrictions imposed under Section 5.3 above upon an annual Restricted Stock Award shall lapse once such Restricted Stock is held by the Awardee for at least six months, the Awardee completes six years of service on the Board of the Company and any of the following occurs:

(i) the Awardee attains the Age for Board Retirement or obtains Board approval of early retirement in accordance with Section 5.5;

(ii) the Awardee dies or becomes permanently and totally disabled; or

(iii) any Change of Control occurs.

(c) Notwithstanding the foregoing, the Committee may provide that the restrictions imposed under Section 5.3 will lapse over or upon satisfaction of a fewer number of years of service on the Board of the Company, except that the Committee may not provide for full lapsing of all such restrictions for less than three (3) years' service on the Board of the Company, other than upon the Awardee's retirement, death or disability, or upon a Change of Control.

5.5 Early Retirement

An Awardee who leaves the Board prior to the Age for Board Retirement may, upon application to and in the sole discretion of the Committee, be granted early retirement status.

5.6 Rights as Stockholder

Subject to the provisions of Section 5.3 hereof, upon the issuance to the Awardee of Restricted Stock hereunder, the Awardee shall have all the rights of a stockholder with respect to such Stock, including the right to vote the shares and receive all dividends and other distributions paid or made with respect thereto.

5.7 Stock Certificates

The Company shall not be required to issue or deliver any certificate for shares of Stock received as Restricted Stock pursuant to a Restricted Stock Agreement executed hereunder, prior to fulfillment of all of the following conditions:

(a) the admission of such shares to listing on all stock exchanges on which the Stock is then listed;

(b) the completion of any registration or other qualification of such shares under any federal or state law or under the rulings or regulations of the Securities and Exchange Commission or any other governmental regulatory body, which the Committee shall in its sole discretion deem necessary or advisable;

(c) the obtaining of any approval or other clearance from any federal or state governmental agency, which the Committee shall in its sole discretion determine to be necessary or advisable; and

(d) the lapse of such reasonable period of time following the execution of the Restricted Stock Agreement as the Committee from time to time may establish for reasons of administrative convenience.

ARTICLE VI. RESTRICTED UNIT AWARDS

The Committee may in its discretion provide that Restricted Units be awarded in conjunction with Restricted Stock Awards. Each Restricted Unit Award granted hereunder shall be evidenced by minutes of a meeting or the written consent of the Committee and by a written Restricted Unit Agreement dated as of the date of grant and executed by the Company and the Awardee, which Agreement shall set forth such terms and conditions as may be determined by the Committee consistent with the Plan.

6.1 Award Terms and Conditions

Each Restricted Unit Award shall have a value equal to the value of a corresponding number of shares of Stock on the date that such Award, or portion thereof, becomes earned and payable. Each Restricted Unit Award shall become earned and payable on the dates upon which a portion of the restrictions lapse on any associated Restricted Stock Award, or upon such other terms and conditions as may be determined by the Committee. The proceeds of each Restricted Unit Award shall be applied in payment of applicable federal and state withholding taxes arising from the lapse of restrictions on the related Restricted Stock and from such award (or portion thereof) becoming earned and payable, with the balance, if any, to be remitted to the Awardee.

6.2 Effect of Forfeiture of Restricted Stock Award

Unless provided otherwise by the Committee, upon all or any part of a

Restricted Stock Award being forfeited pursuant to Section 5.3(c), any associated Restricted Unit Award shall be forfeited and cancelled, without any payment to the Awardee, to the same extent as such Restricted Stock Award.

ARTICLE VII. TERMINATION AMENDMENT AND MODIFICATION OF PLAN

The Committee may at any time terminate, and may at any time and from time to time and in any respect amend or modify, the Plan provided that, if under applicable laws or the rules of any securities exchange upon which the Company's common stock is listed, the consent of the Company's stockholders is required for such amendment or modification, such amendment or modification shall not be effective until the Company obtains such consent, and provided, further, that no termination, amendment or modification of the Plan shall in any manner affect any Award theretofore granted pursuant to the Plan without the consent of the Awardee.

ARTICLE VIII. MISCELLANEOUS

(a) Subject to Section 8.1 (b) below, if the outstanding shares of Stock of the Company are increased, decreased, or exchanged for a different number or kind of shares or other securities, or if additional shares or new or different shares or other securities are distributed with respect to such shares of Stock or other securities, through merger, consolidation, sale of all or substantially all of the assets of the Company, reorganization, recapitalization, reclassification, stock dividend, stock split, reverse stock split or other distribution with respect to such shares of Stock or other securities, an appropriate and proportionate adjustment may be made in (i) the maximum number and kind of shares provided in Sections 2.4 and 5.1, and (ii) the number and kind of shares or other securities subject to the outstanding Awards,

(b) Adjustments under Section

8.1 (a) will be made by the Committee, whose determination as to what adjustments will be made and the extent thereof will be final, binding, and conclusive. No fractional interests will be issued under the Plan resulting from any such adjustments.

8.2 Continuation of Board Service

Nothing in the Plan or in any instrument executed pursuant to the Plan will confer upon any Eligible Director any right to continue to serve on the Board.

8.3 Compliance with Government Regulations

No shares of Stock will be issued hereunder unless and until all applicable requirements imposed by federal and state securities and other laws, rules, and regulations and by any regulatory agencies having jurisdiction and by any stock exchanges upon which the Stock may be listed have been fully met. As a condition precedent to the issuance of shares of Stock pursuant hereto, the Company may require the Eligible Director to take any reasonable action to comply with such requirements.

8.4 Privileges of Stock Ownership

No director and no beneficiary or other person claiming under or through such person will have any right, title, or interest in or to any shares of Stock allocated or reserved under the Plan or subject to any Award except as to such shares of Stock, if any, that have been issued to such director.

8.5 Withholding

The Company may make such provisions as it deems appropriate to withhold any taxes the Company determines it is required to withhold in connection with any Award. The Company may require the Eligible Director to satisfy any relevant tax requirements before authorizing any issuance of Stock to the director. Such settlement may be made in cash or Stock, at the discretion of the Committee.

8.6 Non-Transferability

For so long as it is subject to any restrictions pursuant to this Plan, an Award may be owned during the life of the director solely by the director or the director's duly appointed guardian or personal representative. No Award and no other right under the Plan, contingent or otherwise, will be assignable or subject to any encumbrance, pledge, or charge of any nature.

8.7 Other Compensation Plans

The adoption of the Plan shall not affect any other stock option or incentive or other compensation plans in effect for the Company or any Subsidiary, nor shall the Plan preclude the Company from establishing any other forms of incentive or other compensation for employees or directors of the Company or any Subsidiary.

8.8 Plan Binding on Successors

The Plan shall be binding upon the successors and assigns of the Company.

8.9 Singular, Plural; Gender

Whenever used herein, nouns in the singular shall include the plural, and the masculine pronoun shall include the feminine gender.

8.10 Headings, etc., Not Part of Plan

Headings of Articles and Sections hereof are inserted for convenience and reference; they constitute no part of the Plan.

8.11 Governing Law

This Plan and any Awards hereunder shall be governed by and interpreted and construed in accordance with the laws of the State of _________ and applicable federal law. Any reference in this Plan or in the agreement evidencing any Award to a provision of law or to a rule or regulation shall be deemed to include any successor law, rule or regulation of similar effect or applicability.

# Restricted Stock Unit Plan

______________________________ STOCK INCENTIVE PLAN

Table of Contents

ARTICLE I

GENERAL



ARTICLE II

AWARDS UNDER THE PLAN

ARTICLE III

MISCELLANEOUS

## ______________________________ STOCK INCENTIVE PLAN

## ARTICLE I

## GENERAL

1.1 Purpose

The purpose of _________________________Stock Incentive Plan is to attract, retain and motivate officers, directors, employees (including prospective employees), consultants and others who may perform services for the Firm, to compensate them for their contributions to the long-term growth and profits of the Firm, and to encourage them to acquire a proprietary interest in the success of the Firm.

1.2 Definitions of Certain Terms

1.2.1 "Award" means an award made pursuant to the Plan.

1.2.2 "Award Agreement" means the written document by which each Award is evidenced.

1.2.3 "Board" means the Board of Directors of ___________________

1.2.4 "Certificate" means a stock certificate (or other appropriate document or evidence of ownership) representing shares of Common Stock of _____________.

1.2.5 "Code" means the Internal Revenue Code of 1986, as amended from time to time, and the applicable rulings and regulations thereunder

1.2.6 "Committee" means the committee appointed by the Board to administer the Plan pursuant to Section 1.3.

1.2.7 "Common Stock" means common stock of __________, par value $________ per share.

1.2.8 "Employment" means a grantee's performance of services for the Firm, as determined by the Committee. The terms "employ" and "employed" shall have their correlative meanings.

1.2.9 "Exchange Act" means the Securities Exchange Act of 1934, as amended from time to time, and the applicable rules and regulations thereunder.

1.2.10 "Fair Market Value" means, with respect to a share of Common

Stock on any day, the fair market value as determined in accordance with a valuation methodology approved by the Committee.

1.2.11 "Firm" means ____________ and its subsidiaries and affiliates.

1.2.12 "__________" means __________________, and any successor thereto.

1.2.13 "Incentive Stock Option" means an Option that is intended to qualify for special federal income tax treatment pursuant to Sections 421 and 422 of the Code, as now constituted or subsequently amended, or pursuant to a successor provision of the Code, and which is so designated in the applicable Award Agreement.

1.2.14 "Nonqualified Stock Option" means an Option that is not an Incentive Stock Option.

1.2.15 "Option" means an Incentive Stock Option or a Nonqualified Stock Option or both, as the context requires.

1.2.16 "Plan" means The Goldman Sachs 1999 Stock Incentive Plan, as described herein and as hereafter amended from time to time.

1.3 Administration

1.3.1 Subject to Section 1.3.4, the Plan shall be administered by a committee appointed by the Board whose members shall serve at the pleasure of the Board. To the extent required for transactions under the Plan to qualify for the exemptions available under Rule 16b-3 promulgated under the Exchange Act, all actions relating to Awards to persons subject to Section 16 of the Exchange Act may be taken by the Board or a committee or subcommittee of the Board composed of two or more members, each of whom is a "non-employee director" within the meaning of Exchange Act Rule 16b-3. To the extent required for compensation realized from Awards under the Plan to be deductible by ____________ pursuant to Section 162(m) of the Code, such Awards may be granted by a committee or subcommittee of the Board composed of two or more members, each of whom is an "outside director" within the meaning of Code Section 162 (m).

1.3.2 The Committee shall have complete control over the administration of the Plan and shall have the authority in its discretion to (a) exercise all of the powers granted to it under the Plan, (b) construe, interpret and implement the Plan and any Award Agreements, (c) prescribe, amend and rescind rules and regulations relating to the Plan, including rules governing its own operations, (d) make all determinations necessary or advisable in administering the Plan, (e) correct any defect, supply any omission and reconcile any inconsistency in the Plan, (f) amend the Plan to reflect changes in applicable law (whether or not the rights of the grantee of any Award are adversely affected, unless otherwise provided in such grantee's Award Agreement), (g) unless otherwise provided in an Award Agreement, amend any outstanding Award Agreement in any respect, whether or not the rights of the grantee of such Award are adversely affected, including, without limitation, to accelerate the time or times at which the Award becomes vested, unrestricted or may be exercised, waive or amend any goals, restrictions or conditions set forth in such Award Agreement, or impose new goals, restrictions and conditions, or reflect a change in the grantee's circumstances (e.g., a change to part-time employment status), or to permit ________________ to utilize the pooling-of-interests accounting method and (h) determine whether, to what extent and under what Circumstances and method or methods (1) Awards may be (A) settled in cash, shares of Common Stock, other securities, other Awards or other property, (B) exercised or (C) canceled, forfeited or suspended; (2) shares of Common Stock, other securities, other Awards or other property, and other amounts payable with respect to an Award may be deferred either automatically or at the election of the grantee thereof or of the Committee; (3) loans (whether or not secured by Common Stock) may be extended by the Firm with respect to any Awards; and (4) Awards may be settled by ______________, any of its subsidiaries or affiliates or any of its or their designees.

1.3.3 Actions of the Committee may be taken by the vote of a majority of its members. Any action may be taken by a written instrument signed by a majority of the Committee members, and action so taken shall be fully as effective as if it had been taken by a vote at a meeting. The determination of the Committee on all matters relating to the Plan or any Award Agreement shall be final, binding and conclusive. The Committee may allocate among its members and delegate to any person who is not a member of the Committee any of its administrative responsibilities.

1.3.4 Notwithstanding anything to the contrary contained herein: (a) until the Board shall appoint the members of the Committee, the PI shall be administered by the Board and (b) the Board may, in its sole discretion, at any time and from time to time, grant Awards or administer the Plan. In either of the foregoing events, the Board shall have all of the authority and responsibility granted to the Committee herein.

1.3.5 No member of the Board or the Committee or any employee of the Firm shall be liable for any action or determination made in good faith with respect to the Plan or any Award thereunder. Each such person shall be indemnified and held harmless by ____________ against and from any loss, cost, liability, or expense that may be imposed upon or incurred by such person in connection with or resulting from any action, suit or proceeding to which such person may be a party or in which such person may be involved by reason of any action taken or failure to act under the Plan or any Award Agreement and against and from any and all amounts paid by such person, with __________'s approval, in settlement thereof, or paid by such person in satisfaction of any judgment in any such action, suit or proceeding against such person, provided that _________ shall have the right, at its own expense, to assume and defend the same. The foregoing right of indemnification shall not be available to a person to the extent that a final judgment or other final adjudication binding upon such person establishes that the acts or omissions of such person giving rise to the indemnification claim resulted from such person's bad faith, fraud or willful criminal act or omission. The foregoing right of indemnification shall not be exclusive of any other rights of indemnification to which such persons may be entitled under ___________'s Certificate of Incorporation or Bylaws, as a matter of law, or otherwise, or any other power that __________ may have to indemnify such persons or hold them harmless.

1.4 Persons Eligible for Awards

Awards under the Plan may be made to such officers, directors, employees (including prospective employees), consultants and other individuals who may perform services for the Firm, as the Committee may select.

1.5 Types of Awards Under Plan

Awards may be made under the Plan in the form of (a) Options, (b) stock appreciation rights, (c) dividend equivalent rights, (d) restricted stock, (e) restricted stock units and (f) other equity-based or equity-related Awards which the Committee determines to be consistent with the purpose of the Plan and the interests of the Firm. No Incentive Stock Option (other than an Incentive Stock Option that may be assumed or issued by ____________ in connection with a transaction to which Section 424[a] of the Code applies) may be granted to a person who is not eligible to receive an Incentive Stock Option under the Code.

1.6 Shares Available for Awards

1.6.1 Total shares available. Subject to adjustment pursuant to Section 1.6.2, the total number of shares of Common Stock which may be delivered pursuant to Awards granted under the Plan through ___________'s fiscal year ending in ________ shall not exceed _______________ shares and pursuant to Awards granted in each fiscal year thereafter shall not exceed _______ percent (_____%) of the issued and outstanding shares of Common Stock, determined as of the last day of the immediately preceding fiscal year, increased by the number of shares available for Awards in previous fiscal years but not covered by Awards granted in such years. If, after the effective date of the Plan, any Award is forfeited or otherwise terminates or is canceled without the delivery of shares of Common Stock, shares of Common Stock are surrendered or withheld from any Award to satisfy a grantee's income tax or other withholding obligations, or shares of Common Stock owned by a grantee are tendered to pay the exercise price of any Award granted under the Plan, then the shares covered by such forfeited, terminated or canceled Award or which are equal to the number of shares surrendered, withheld or tendered shall again become available for transfer pursuant to Awards granted or to be granted under this Plan. Notwithstanding the foregoing, but subject to adjustment as provided in Section 1.6.2., no more than _______________ shares of Common Stock shall be delivered pursuant to the exercise of Incentive Stock Options. The maximum number of shares of Common Stock with respect to which Options or stock appreciation rights may be granted to an individual grantee (i) in __________'s fiscal year ending in ________ shall equal $_________ shares of Common Stock and (ii) in each subsequent fiscal year shall equal _________% of the maximum number for the preceding fiscal year. Any shares of Common Stock (a) delivered by ____________, (b) with respect to which Awards are made by ___________ and (c) with respect to which ________ becomes obligated to make Awards, in each case through the assumption of, or in substitution for, outstanding awards previously granted by an acquired entity, shall not be counted against the shares of Common Stock available for Awards under this Plan. Shares of Common Stock, which may be delivered pursuant to Awards, may be authorized but unissued Common Stock or authorized and issued Common Stock held in _________'s treasury or otherwise acquired for the purposes of the Plan.

1.6.2 Adjustments. The Committee shall have the authority (but shall not be required) to adjust the number of shares of Common Stock authorized pursuant to Section 1.6.1 and to adjust equitably (including, without limitation, by payment of cash) the terms of any outstanding Awards (including, without limitation, the number of shares of Common Stock covered by each outstanding Award, the type of property to which the Award is subject and the exercise or strike price of any Award), in such manner as it deems appropriate to preserve the benefits or potential benefits intended to be made available to grantees of Awards, for any increase or decrease in the number of issued shares of Common Stock resulting from a stock split, reverse stock split, stock dividend, spinoff, splitup, combination or reclassification of the Common Stock, or any other event the Committee determines in its sole discretion affects the capitalization of __________, including any extraordinary dividend or distribution. After any adjustment made pursuant to this Section 1.6.2, the number of shares of Common Stock subject to each outstanding Award shall be rounded to the nearest whole number.

1.6.3 Except as provided in this Section 1.6 or under the terms of any applicable Award Agreement, there shall be no limit on the number or the value of shares of Common Stock that may be subject to Awards to any individual under the Plan.

1.6.4 There shall be no limit on the amount of cash, securities (other than shares of Common Stock as provided in this Section 1.6) or other property that may be delivered pursuant to any Award.

## ARTICLE II

## AWARDS UNDER THE PLAN

2.1 Agreements Evidencing Awards

Each Award granted under the Plan shall be evidenced by a written document, which shall contain such provisions and conditions, as the Committee deems appropriate. The Committee may grant Awards in tandem with or in substitution for any other Award or Awards granted under this Plan or any award granted under any other plan of the Firm. By accepting an Award pursuant to the Plan, a grantee thereby agrees that the Award shall be subject to all of the terms and provisions of the Plan and the applicable Award Agreement.

2.2 No Rights as a Shareholder

No grantee of an Award shall have any of the rights of a shareholder of ___________ with respect to shares subject to such Award until the delivery of such shares. Except as otherwise provided in Section 1.6.2, no adjustments shall be made for dividends, distributions or other rights (whether ordinary or extraordinary, and whether in cash, Common Stock, other securities or other property) for which the record date is prior to the date such shares are delivered.

2.3 Grant of Options and Stock Appreciation Rights

The Committee may grant (a) Options to purchase shares of Common Stock from _______ and (b) stock appreciation rights, in such amounts and subject to such terms and conditions as the Committee may determine.

2.4 Exercise of Options and Stock Appreciation Rights

2.4.1 Any acceptance by the Committee of an optionee's written notice of exercise of an Option shall be conditioned upon payment for the shares being purchased. Such payment may be made in cash or by such other method as the Committee may from time to time prescribe.

2.4.2 After receiving payment from the optionee of the full Option exercise price, or after receiving notice from the grantee of the exercise of a stock appreciation right for which payment will be made by ________ partly or entirely in shares of Common Stock, ________ shall, subject to the provisions of the Plan or any Award Agreement, deliver the shares of Common Stock.

2.5 Grant of Restricted Stock

The Committee may grant or offer for sale restricted shares of Common Stock in such amounts and subject to such terms and conditions, as the Committee shall determine. Upon the delivery of such shares, the grantee shall have the rights of a shareholder with respect to the restricted stock, subject to any restrictions and conditions as the Committee may include in the applicable Award Agreement. In the event that a Certificate is issued in respect of restricted shares of Common Stock, such Certificate may be registered in the name of the grantee but shall be held by ____________________ or its designated agent until the time the restrictions lapse.

2.6 Grant of Restricted Stock Units

The Committee may grant Awards of restricted stock units in such amounts and subject to such terms and conditions as the Committee shall determine. A grantee of a restricted stock unit will have only the rights of a general unsecured creditor of ____________________ until delivery of shares of Common Stock, cash or other securities or property is made as specified in the applicable Award Agreement. On the delivery date, the grantee of each restricted stock unit not previously forfeited shall receive one share of Common Stock, or cash, securities or other property equal in value to a share of Common Stock or a combination thereof, as specified by the Committee.

2.7 Other Stock-Based Awards

The Committee may grant other types of equity-based or equity-related

Awards (including the grant or offer for sale of unrestricted shares of Common Stock) in such amounts and subject to such terms and conditions, as the Committee shall determine. Such Awards may entail the transfer of actual shares of Common Stock to Plan participants, or payment in cash or otherwise of amounts based on the value of shares of Common Stock, and may include, without limitation, Awards designed to comply with or take advantage of the applicable local laws of jurisdictions other than the United States.

2.8 Grant of Dividend Equivalent Rights

The Committee may include in the Award Agreement with respect to any Award a dividend equivalent right entitling the grantee to receive amounts equal to all or any portion of the dividends that would be paid on the shares of Common Stock covered by such Award if such shares had been delivered pursuant to such Award. The grantee of a dividend equivalent right will have only the rights of a general unsecured creditor of ____________________ until payment of such amounts is made as specified in the applicable Award Agreement. In the event such a provision is included in an Award Agreement, the Committee shall determine whether such payments shall be made in cash, in shares of Common Stock or in another form, whether they shall be conditioned upon the exercise of the Award to which they relate, the time or times at which they shall be made, and such other terms and conditions as the Committee shall deem appropriate.

## ARTICLE III

## MISCELLANEOUS

3.1 Amendment of the Plan

3.1.1 Unless otherwise provided in an Award Agreement, the Board may from time to time suspend, discontinue, revise or amend the Plan in any respect whatsoever, including in any manner that adversely affects the rights, duties or obligations of any grantee of an Award.

3.1.2 Unless otherwise determined by the Board, shareholder approval of any suspension, discontinuance, revision or amendment shall be obtained only to the extent necessary to comply with any applicable law, rule or regulation.

3.2 Tax Withholding

3.2.1 As a condition to the delivery of any shares of Common Stock pursuant to any Award or the lifting or lapse of restrictions on any Award, or in connection with any other event that gives rise to a federal or other governmental tax withholding obligation on the part of ____________________ or any of its subsidiaries or affiliates relating to an Award (including, without limitation, FICA tax), (a) ____________________ may deduct or withhold (or cause to be deducted or withheld) from any payment or distribution to a grantee whether or not pursuant to the Plan or (b) the Committee shall be entitled to require that the grantee remit cash to ____________________ or any of its subsidiaries or affiliates (through payroll deduction or otherwise), in each case in an amount sufficient in the opinion of ____________________ to satisfy such withholding obligation.

3.2.2 If the event giving rise to the withholding obligation involves a transfer of shares of Common Stock, then, unless the applicable Award Agreement provides otherwise, at the discretion of the Committee, the grantee may satisfy the withholding obligation described under Section 3.2.1 by electing to have ____________________ withhold shares of Common Stock (which withholding, unless otherwise provided in the applicable Award Agreement, will be at a rate not in excess of the statutory minimum rate) or by tendering previously owned shares of Common Stock, in each case having a Fair Market Value equal to the amount of tax to be withheld (or by any other mechanism as may be required or appropriate to conform with local tax and other rules). For this purpose, Fair Market Value shall be determined as of the date on which the amount of tax to be withheld is determined (and ____________________ may cause any fractional share amount to be settled in cash).

3.3 Required Consents and Legends

3.3.1 If the Committee shall at any time determine that any consent (as hereinafter defined) is necessary or desirable as a condition of, or in connection with, the granting of any Award, the delivery of shares of Common Stock or the delivery of any cash, securities or other property under the Plan, or the taking of any other action thereunder (each such action being hereinafter referred to as a "plan action"), then such plan action shall not be taken, in whole or in part, unless and until such consent shall have been effected or obtained to the full satisfaction of the Committee. The Committee may direct that any Certificate evidencing shares delivered pursuant to the Plan shall bear a legend setting forth such restrictions on transferability as the Committee may determine to be necessary or desirable, and may advise the transfer agent to place a stop order against any legended shares.

3.3.2 The term "consent" as used herein with respect to any plan action includes (a) any and all listings, registrations or qualifications in respect thereof upon any securities exchange or under any federal, state, or local law, or law, rule or regulation of a jurisdiction outside the United States, (b) any and all written agreements and representations by the grantee with respect to the disposition of shares, or with respect to any other matter, which the Committee may deem necessary or desirable to comply with the terms of any such listing, registration or qualification or to obtain an exemption from the requirement that any such listing, qualification or registration be made, (c) any and all other consents, clearances and approvals in respect of a plan action by any governmental or other regulatory body or any stock exchange or self-regulatory agency and (d) any and all consents or authorizations required to comply with, or required to be obtained under, applicable local law or otherwise required by the Committee. Nothing herein shall require ____________________ to list, register or qualify the shares of Common Stock on any securities exchange.

3.4 Nonassignability

Except to the extent otherwise expressly provided in the applicable Award Agreement, no Award (or any rights and obligations thereunder) granted to any person under the Plan may be sold, exchanged, transferred, assigned, pledged, hypothecated or otherwise disposed of (including through the use of any cash-settled instrument) (each such action being hereinafter referred to as an "assignment"), whether voluntarily or involuntarily, other than by will or by the laws of descent and distribution, and all such Awards (and any rights thereunder) shall be exercisable during the life of the grantee only by the grantee or the grantee's legal representative. Notwithstanding the immediately preceding sentence, the Committee may permit, under such terms and conditions that it deems appropriate in its sole discretion, a grantee to transfer any Award to any person or entity that the Committee so determines. Any assignment in violation of the provisions of this Section 3.4 shall be void. All of the terms and conditions of this Plan and the Award Agreements shall be binding upon any such permitted successors and assigns.

3.5 Requirement of Consent and Notification of Election Under Section 83(b) of the Code or Similar Provision

No election under Section 83(b) of the Code (to include in gross income in the year of transfer the amounts specified in Code Section 83(b)) or under a similar provision of the law of a jurisdiction outside the United States may be made unless expressly permitted by the terms of the Award Agreement or by action of the Committee in writing prior to the making of such election. If a grantee of an Award, in connection with the acquisition of shares of Common Stock under the Plan or otherwise, is expressly permitted under the terms of the Award Agreement or by such Committee action to make any such election and the grantee makes the election, the grantee shall notify the Committee of such election within ten (10) days of filing notice of the election with the Internal Revenue Service or other governmental authority, in addition to any filing and notification required pursuant to regulations issued under Code Section 83(b) or other applicable provision.

3.6 Requirement of Notification Upon Disqualifying Disposition Under Section 421(b) of the Code If any grantee shall make any disposition of shares of Common Stock delivered pursuant to the exercise of an Incentive Stock Option under the circumstances described in Section 421(b) of the Code (relating to certain disqualifying dispositions), such grantee shall notify ____________________ of such disposition within 10 days thereof

3.7 Change in Control

3.7.1 The Committee may provide in any Award Agreement for provisions relating to a "change in control" of ____________________ or any of its subsidiaries or affiliates (as such term is defined by the Committee in any such Award Agreement), including, without limitation, the acceleration of the exercisability of, or the lapse of restrictions or deemed satisfaction of goals with respect to, any outstanding Awards.

3.7.2 Unless otherwise provided in the applicable Award Agreement, in the event of a merger, consolidation, mandatory share exchange or other similar business combination of ____________________ with or into any other entity ("successor entity") or any transaction in which another person or entity acquires all of the issued and outstanding Common Stock of ____________________, or all or substantially all of the assets of ____________________, outstanding Awards may be assumed or an equivalent Award may be substituted by such successor entity or a parent or subsidiary of such successor entity.

3.8 Right of Discharge Reserved

Nothing in the Plan or in any Award Agreement shall confer upon any grantee the right to continued Employment by the Firm or affect any right, which the Firm may have to terminate such Employment.

3.9 Nature of Payments

3.9.1 Any and all grants of Awards and deliveries of Common Stock, cash, securities or other property under the Plan shall be in consideration of services performed or to be performed for the Firm by the grantee. Awards under the Plan may, in the discretion of the Committee, be made in substitution in whole or in part for cash or other compensation otherwise payable to an Employee.

3.9.2 All such grants and deliveries shall constitute a special discretionary incentive payment to the grantee and shall not be required to be taken into account in computing the amount of salary or compensation of the grantee for the purpose of determining any contributions to or any benefits under any pension, retirement, profit-sharing, bonus, life insurance, severance or other benefit plan of the Firm or under any agreement with the grantee, unless the Firm specifically provides otherwise.

3.10 Non-Uniform Determinations

The Committee's determinations under the Plan and Award Agreements need not be uniform and may be made by it selectively among persons who receive, or are eligible to receive, Awards under the Plan (whether or not such persons are similarly situated). Without limiting the generality of the foregoing, the Committee shall be entitled, among other things, to make non-uniform and selective determinations under Award Agreements, and to enter into nonuniform and selective Award Agreements, as to (a) the persons to receive Awards, (b) the terms and provisions of Awards and (c) whether a grantee's Employment has been terminated for purposes of the Plan.

3.11 Other Payments or Awards

Nothing contained in the Plan shall be deemed in any way to limit or restrict ____________________ from making any award or payment to any person under any other plan, arrangement or understanding, whether now existing or hereafter in effect.

3.12 Plan Headings

The headings in this Plan are for the purpose of convenience only and are not intended to define or limit the construction of the provisions hereof.

3.13 Date of Adoption and Term of Plan

The Plan was adopted by the Board on__________________. Unless sooner terminated by the Board, the provisions of the Plan respecting the grant of Incentive Stock Options shall terminate on the day before the _______ anniversary of the adoption of the Plan by the Board, and no Incentive Stock Options shall thereafter be granted under the Plan. The Board reserves the right to terminate the Plan at any time; provided, however, that all Awards made under the Plan prior to its termination shall remain in effect until such Awards have been satisfied or terminated in accordance with the terms and provisions of the Plan and the applicable Award Agreements.

3.14 Governing Law

ALL RIGHTS AND OBLIGATIONS UNDER THE PLAN AND EACH AWARD AGREEMENT SHALL BE GOVERNED BY AND CONSTRUED IN ACCORDANCE WITH THE LAWS OF THE STATE OF ________________, WITHOUT REGARD TO PRINCIPLES OF CONFLICT OF LAWS.

3.15 Severability; Entire Agreement

If any of the provisions of this Plan or any Award Agreement is finally held to be invalid, illegal or unenforceable (whether in whole or in part), such provision shall be deemed modified to the extent, but only to the extent, of such invalidity, illegality or unenforceability and the remaining provisions shall not be affected thereby; provided, that if any of such provisions is finally held to be invalid, illegal, or unenforceable because it exceeds the maximum scope determined to be acceptable to permit such provision to be enforceable, such provision shall be deemed to be modified to the minimum extent necessary to modify such scope in order to make such provision enforceable hereunder. The Plan and any Award Agreements contain the entire agreement of the parties with respect to the subject matter thereof and supersede all prior agreements, promises, covenants, arrangements, communications, representations and warranties between them, whether written or oral with respect to the subject matter thereof.

3.16 Waiver of Claims

Each grantee of an Award recognizes and agrees that prior to being selected by the Committee to receive an Award he or she has no right to any benefits hereunder. Accordingly, in consideration of the grantee's receipt of any Award hereunder, he or she expressly waives any right to contest the amount of any Award, the terms of any Award Agreement, any determination, action or omission hereunder or under any Award Agreement by the Committee, ____________________ or the Board, or any amendment to the Plan or any Award Agreement (other than an amendment to this Plan or an Award Agreement to which his or her consent is expressly required by the express terms of an Award Agreement).

3.17 No Third Party Beneficiaries

Except as expressly provided therein, neither the Plan nor any Award Agreement shall confer on any person other than the Firm and the grantee of any Award any rights or remedies thereunder.

3.18 Successors and Assigns of ____________________

The terms of this Plan shall be binding upon and inure to the benefit of ____________________ and its successors and assigns.

IN WITNESS WHEREOF, and as evidence of the adoption of this Plan effective as of __________, _______ by __________________, it has caused the same to be signed by its duly authorized officer this _____________ day of _____________, ____________.

____________________________________

By:__________________________________

Name:

Title:

# Glossary

**10-K**

A required annual SEC filing for a public company that provides certain financial and related business information.

**162(m)**

A provision of the IRC dealing with the deductibility of compensation expenses on a publicly owned company's tax return of compensation to a named individual in excess of $1 million. Certain exceptions which permit compensation over the threshold to be deducted are allowed for incentive type compensations determined by IRS regulations.

**415**

Section of the Internal Revenue Code (IRC) that contains the benefits limits and contributions limits applicable to individual plan participants in tax-qualified pension and profit-sharing plans. Commonly referred to as the "415 limits."

## A

**Accounting Principles Board (APB)**

Source of authority regarding rules and conventions for accounting from 1959 to 1973, when it was replaced by the Financial Accounting Standards Board (FASB).

**accrual accounting**

The accounting concept whereby revenues and expenses are recorded in the period to which they apply irrespective of the cash flows. As an example, a manufacturing company records a sale when a product is shipped to the customer even if the sale was on credit. It also records at that time all expenses associated with that sale, whether the actual cash has been transferred or not.

**affiliated director**

A member of the Board of Directors of a company who, although not a current employee of the organization, is either a retired employee and/or does business with the company (such as a financial or legal consultant or advisor).

**alternative minimum tax**

Introduced in the tax act of 1969, the alternative minimum tax (AMT) requires that any person with "preference" income as defined in the Internal Revenue Code must complete the AMT calculation and pay the larger of that or the regular income tax. Under the AMT calculation, unrealized gain on exercise of an Incentive Stock Option is considered preference income and must be included in income for AMT calculations. In addition several regular deductions such as state income and real estate taxes cannot be deducted in AMT calculations.

**American Stock Exchange (AMEX)**

An organization that oversees the buying and selling of publicly owned shares of stock listed on the exchange.

**annual incentive**

Usually a lump-sum payment (cash or stock) made in addition to an employee's normal pay for a fiscal or calendar year, based on performance (individual, business unit and/or company). May also be called an annual bonus.

**APB 25**

An accounting provision promulgated by the Accounting Principles Board providing rules for measuring expense to be recorded by a company with respect to stock issued to employees. The expense is determined on the measurement date based on the difference in the value of the stock and what the employee will pay. (See measurement date.)

## B

**beta**

(1) A measure of volatility of a stock, normally ranging from 0.55 to 2.0, used in determining the cost of capital for a company. (2) In multiple regression, the weights of coefficients that apply to the model after all the variables (xs and ys) have been transformed to a common metric of z-scores. Beta weights indicate the strength of the relationship between an independent variable and the dependent variable. They also are known as standardized partial regression weights

**binomial option pricing model**

A mathematical formula that determines a theoretical value for an option on stock subject to trade on an option exchange. May be used by a company that chooses to apply the FAS123 rule to stock granted to employees.

**Black-Scholes Model**
A mathematical model originally developed by Fisher Black and Myron Scholes to value stock options traded on public markets. It estimates the theoretical price an individual would pay for a traded option and considers the stock price on grant date, option exercise price, number of years or terms of the option, dividend yield, risk free rate of return and stock price volatility.

**bonus guarantee**
A payment in addition to base salary that is made regardless of performance (e.g., an incentive award that is guaranteed, usually to a new hire or to a newly promoted person). It is usually nonrecoverable by the company.

**bonus progressivity**
See progressivity of incentives.

**bonus-eligible**
A term referring to groups or classes of employees who are eligible to participate in a bonus program.

**book unit award plan**
A type of long-term incentive plan in which an employee is awarded stock units valued at the book value per share. In a book value appreciation plan, an increase in the book value of the stock accrues to the benefit of the employee. In a full value book value plan, the full value of the book value units accrues to the benefit of the employee, usually after fulfilling a vesting period.

**book value (BV)**
Total shareholders' equity divided by the number of common shares outstanding. Book value sometimes is used in incentive plans in privately owned companies in which a fair market value of shares is not readily known.

**book value purchase plans**
An incentive program in which employees purchase shares of their organization at book value per share. They subsequently can sell the shares back to the organization at the then book value.

## C

**capital gains taxation**
The taxes applicable to gains realized on the sale of capital assets such as real estate or company shares. Tax laws specify time periods for holding assets to qualify for long-term capital gains tax rates, which usually have been lower

than ordinary tax rates or rates for short term capital gains. Congress periodically changes rates applicable to various types of income.

**cash option exercise**
When an individual pays cash for the option exercise price of a number of shares exercised to purchase the shares.

**cashless option exercise**
When an individual exercises an option through an outside broker or dealer with the broker in effect making simultaneous purchases and sales of the underlying option shares and delivering cash or stock to the individual for the option profit.

**change in control provision**
A provision related to a stated percentage change in ownership whereby provisions of an employment contract may cause an increase or an acceleration of specified payments or benefits

**charge to earnings**
When an organization recognizes an expense in the income statement, GAPP accounting requires an organization to expense executive compensation programs over the time periods when services are actually performed, not necessarily when the compensation is paid.

**cliff vesting**
A vesting provision where 100% of the vesting requirements occur at one time.

**common shares**
In corporate finance, the form in which an owner's interest is represented - distributed in units known as shares with voting rights and possibly dividends. Appreciation and dividends are not fixed or guaranteed.

**common stock**
See common shares.

**compensation committee**
A committee at the board of director level that approves pay and incentive award programs involving senior management of the company.

**compensation committee report**
A narrative description of the policies, philosophies, considerations and events that influence the committee's pay decisions with respect to the chief executive officer and other senior managers in a company. The SEC requires this report to be included in the company's proxy statement.

**constructive receipt**

The controlling tax principle for determining the timing of tax liability in case of a deferred payment. The law provides that when an individual can "reach out and take" compensation is the time when it is taxed even if the employees choose not to take it at that time. There are ways of legally deferring income without coming under the concept of constructive receipt.

**corporate-owned life insurance (COLI)**

Life insurance policies that insure the lives of selected executive-level employees where the company is either owner and beneficiary or ownership and beneficial interest is split with the executive. The organization pays the premiums, retains ownership of the insurance and receives tax-free proceeds when the participants die. The amount of the insurance purchased is calculated to recover the cost of executive benefits to be provided under a nonqualified plan. However, the death-benefit proceeds may be used by the organization for any purpose.

## D

**deferred compensation**

Any of a number of compensation payments that are payable to an employee at some point in the future. These include voluntary deferral of earned incentives, mandatory deferrals of earned incentives, as well as earnings and retirement plan vehicles.

**deferred option grants**

An individual defers compensation and the amount deferred is used to reduce or "buy down" the option price of option shares by a specified amount, leaving the remainder to be paid when the option is exercised.

**derivative security**

A security that may become a share of common stock. Included are stock options, warrants, and convertible securities among others.

**diluted earnings per share**

A calculation that assumes conversion of all common stock equivalents to common shares and calculates earnings per share, using the treasury stock method. A publicly owned company must report diluted earnings per share if it has common stock equivalents. (See also basic earnings per share.)

**dilution (percent)**

The decrease in ownership percentage of current owners when additional shares of stock are issued. Dilution of ownership decreases earnings per share, because of the additional shares having been issued. Dilution occurs when a company issues additional shares either in a share offering or to settle stock option or stock plan requirements.

**director and officer (D&O) liability insurance**
Insurance to protect members of boards of directors and key officers against law suits for various types of malpractice or oversight.

**discounted restricted stock purchase**
Purchase of restricted stock by the employee, at a price below the current market price of the stock on date of purchase.

**discounted stock option**
A stock option granted at an exercise price less than 100% of fair market value on date of grant disqualifying disposition (of an ISO) Sale of IS0 shares before the completion of the required holding period: one year after exercise and two years after grant. A disqualifying disposition changes the tax treatment of the IS0 so that it is taxed the same way as a nonqualified option.

**dividend equivalents**
In some incentive plans, participants are paid an amount of money equal to the dividends that are paid per share of common stock.

**dividends**
Payments to shareholders by a corporation that are paid from the company's retained earnings. Not all companies pay dividends. Dividends may be in cash or in shares of stock.

**Dow Jones Industrial Average (DJIA)**
The most widely quoted stock market index. It is comprised of 30 widely held New York Stock Exchange listed large industrial company common stocks. It is often consider a barometer of overall market activity.

## E

**economic benefit**
A concept in the tax law whereby if there is a promise by the employer to pay some amount in the future which has been funded and thus there is no substantial risk of forfeiture, there will be a current tax liability. If there is a substantial risk of forfeiture, such as the organization's creditors may attach the funds in case of bankruptcy, there is no economic benefit and no tax liability until the money is paid to the employee.

**Emerging Issues Task Force**
A task force created by FASB that deals with issues not precisely covered by GAAP. Many questions about handling stock issued to employees have been decided by the EITF.

**Employee Retirement Income Security Act of 1974 (ERISA)**
An act regulating private employer pension and welfare programs. The act has provisions that cover eligibility for participation, reporting and disclosure requirements, establishing fiduciary standards for the financial management of retirement funds, setting up tax incentives for funding pension plans rather than having them on a pay-as-you-go basis, and establishing the Pension Benefits Guarantee Corp. (PBGC) as an agency to insure pension plans against financial failure.

**Employee stock option**
See stock option

**employment contract**
A contract that provides an incoming employee with a written guarantee of receiving certain rewards, regardless of the results produced on the job. The employee also may agree not to (1) compete with the present employer for the duration of employment and some reasonable time period thereafter, (2) disclose or discuss secret formulas, etc., that are of value to the employer, and (3) hold another job.

**equity investment**
A financial investment that results in an ownership position and no fixed return or guarantee of the principal amount.

**evergreen authorization**
Shares made available for future grants under an option plan that represents a specified percentage of outstanding shares for each year of the plan. Unused shares from any year usually are carried forward for possible use in later years.

**evergreen plan**
No termination date is specified after which grants can no longer be made. Normally such a plan would remain in effect until canceled by the board of directors.

**exercise (of a share option or other executive-plan feature)**
The occasion when the holder takes possession of the shares, rights or proceeds determined by a plan's provisions (e.g., the actual purchase of stock under the terms of the stock option plan).

**exercise period**

The date or dates specific when stock options are available for purchase by the option holder.

**expiration date**

The last day of an option term at which point the option is cancelled if not exercised.

## F

**fair market value (FMV)**

Stock price, usually measured as the simple average of the high and low market prices of a share of a company's stock on a recognized stock exchange on a particular day.

**FAS 123**

A statement issued by the Financial Accounting Standards Board in 1995. The statement permits a company to choose between using APB 25 or to use an option pricing model such as the Black-Scholes or the Binomial model to determine the accounting expense to be recorded with respect to stock issued to employees. If a company chooses APB 25 for its income statement, it must show the costs per the pricing model in the footnotes to the financial statements. All stock-related plans for employees must be evaluated on the same approach.

**Financial Accounting Standards Board (FASB)**

The organization that promulgates the "generally accepted accounting principles" (GAAP) that govern accounting for publicly held U.S. companies. It is of particular importance in determining the rules connected with the accounting for stock and stock-related incentive programs, as well as accounting for pensions and other post-retirement programs.

**fixed share authorization**

Shares made available for grants as part of an option plan that represents a specified number of shares or a specified percentage of outstanding shares on a specified date over the life of the plan.

**form of payment (of an award or incentive)**

The method used to pay out an incentive that may be cash, stock, a combination of both, or some other valuable consideration.

**front-end bonus**

A specific bonus given at the beginning of a service period, usually for accepting an employment offer. It could also be used at the beginning of a new reward program. Also called a signing bonus, it typically is used to offset forfeited benefits left behind.

**full value (plans)**
Executive compensation plans under which a participant receives full value of the employer's capital share or equivalent; e.g., restricted stock, phantom share without any investment or purchase required. Value may be based on market price, book value or determined by a formula.

## G

**gain multiple**
See targeted gain.

**generally accepted accounting principals (GAAP)**
The principals and rules of accounting applicable to U.S. companies, as prescribed by the Financial Accounting Standards Board (FASB) and its predecessors, and as deemed required to apply to all public companies by rules established and enforced by the Securities and Exchange Commission (SEC).

**golden handcuffs**
Employee benefits and/or payments or incentives linked to an individual's continued employment with an organization. Leaving the organization results in forfeiting the value.

**golden parachute**
A provision in an employment contract that provides for an increase or acceleration of certain benefits, payments, vesting or other rights in the event the employee (usually an executive) loses his or her position due to a merger or takeover. Golden parachutes are sometimes a part of an anti-takeover strategy.

**graded vesting**
A vesting provision where 100% of the vesting requirements occur over a gradual period of time (i.e., 25% each year for four years).

**grant date**
See option grant date

**grant multiple**
In stock option plans, the number used at a given salary level to determine the grant size. This is done by multiplying the number times the salary and dividing the product by the current stock price.

**grant price**
The price an executive will pay to exercise a market-based incentive device (typically stock options). The grant price for an incentive stock option is at least 100 percent, or the fair market value at the time of grant of the option

**gross up**
The practice of increasing the amount of a cash payment to offset the tax impact on the individual resulting from the cash payment.

## H

**highly compensated employee**
Any employee who meets one or more of the following definitions: (1) owns 5 percent or more of the company in the current or prior year, (2) earns more than $80,000 or more in the preceding plan year, (3) at the employer's election is in the top 20 percent of the organization's employees in terms of pay. The Internal Revenue Code determines tax status of benefit programs on the basis of how the plan treats highly compensated employees, compared to other employees, and comparative eligibility and participation rates.

## I

**incentive compensation**
Variable rewards for performance or achievement of short-term or long-term goals. Designed to stimulate employee performance.

**incentive eligible**
A term referring to groups or classes of employees who are eligible to participate in an incentive plan.

**incentive progressivity**
A concept whereby the percentage target potential of an incentive award is higher at higher income levels. May be applicable to either or both short term and long-term incentives.

**incentive stock option (SO)**
A stock option that qualifies for favorable tax treatment (no tax at exercise and long-term capital gains treatment, if shares are held for one year after exercise and two years after grant before sale) and which meets other rules as specified by legislation. The applicable section of the Internal Revenue Code is Section 422.

**indexed options**
Options granted which are tied to a specified index or formula and not known on the grant date.

**insider**
A shareholder who owns 10 percent or more of a company's stock, a member of the board of directors or an elected officer in a senior policy-making role of a corporation, or anyone else who possesses information that is not publicly known about the company, but which is important in valuing its stock. Securities and Exchange Commission regulations place restrictions on stock purchases and sales by insiders. Violations can result in fines or prison sentences. The SEC also imposes filing requirements on insiders with respect to their ownership and changes in ownership of company shares.

**Internal Revenue Code (IRC)**
The tax laws passed by Congress and administered by the IRS.

**Internal Revenue Service (IRS)**
The agency of the federal government responsible for interpretation of tax laws, collection of income tax, and enforcement of the Internal Revenue Code. Compliance with IRS rules is an extremely important consideration in the design of compensation and benefit programs.

## J

**jumbo stock grant/option**
When a company awards an executive a large number of restricted shares or option shares. The key issue is that size of the award compared with other normal awards is several times larger. When restricted stock is involved there may be a longer than usual vesting period. Often times the jumbo award is in lieu of awards that would otherwise be made in future years.

## K

**Keogh Plan**
A plan that enables a self-employed individual to establish a qualified tax-deductible pension or profit-sharing plan, subject to meeting IRS requirements. Also known as an H.R. 10 plan.

## L

**leverage stock option**

The company matches a multiple of stock options to the executive's purchase of fixed number of shares; e.g., company provides four options for every one share purchased.

**liquidity**

An indicator of a company's ability to procure ready assets to meet short-term financial obligations. Cash is the most liquid asset.

**long-term incentive plan**

Any incentive plan (usually limited to executives) that requires sustained performance of the firm for a period longer than one fiscal year for maximum benefit to the employee. Some plans are based on capital shares of the organization and may require investment by the employee, while others are based on financial performance.

**lump-sum incentive award**

An incentive award that is paid in a single cash payment.

## M

**market capitalization**

Also called "market cap." It is the result of multiplying the stock price times the number of shares outstanding. Thus if the stock price is $50 per share and the number of shares is 10 million, the market capitalization would be $500 million. Companies are often referred to as large cap, mid cap, small cap or micro cap, depending on the size of their market capitalization.

**measurement date**

Used to determine compensation expense in stock option and award plans. It is the first date on which both the number of shares and the purchase price are known. This is defined in APB 25 issued by the Accounting Principles Board (APB).

**measurement principle**

Related to compensation for services that a corporation receives as consideration for stock issued through employee stock option, stock purchase and stock award plans. Compensation is measured by the quoted market price of the stock at the measurement date less the amount, if any, to be paid by the employee. APB 25.

**mix of pay**
The profile of various components of direct pay expressed as a percentage of the total (e.g., 50 percent base salary, 35 percent short-term incentives, 15 percent long-term incentives).

# N

**named individuals**
Those persons who are named in a company's proxy statement and whose compensation are shown based on SEC disclosure requirements.

**National Association of Securities Dealers Automated Quotation System (NASDAQ)**
An organization that facilitates the trading of shares of stock in publicly traded companies.

**New York Stock Exchange (NYSE)**
The largest and most established stock trading organization. The NYSE is located on Wall Street in New York City. It is also referred to as the "Big Board."

**noncompete agreements**
A provision, or separate employment contract, that prohibits an employee from competing with the employer after termination of employment (or the contract) for a specified period of time. The agreement typically sets limitations regarding customers, products, services, or an industry (or a combination), after employment terminates.

# O

**Omnibus plans**
A stock plan that allows administrators (usually the board compensation committee in a public company) to make various types of grants and to specify grant provisions without plan-related limitations except as specifically required for regulatory or shareholder approval purposes.

**option exercise price (or option price)**
The stated price to be paid by an optionee to purchase shares covered by a stock option.

**option exercise proceeds**
Cash, stock or other value received by a company as a result of stock option exercises including cash or stock paid by individuals to exercise and company

cash savings on taxes because of deductibility of non-statutory option profits at exercise.

**option grant date**
The date the stock option becomes effective and the option term begins.

**option performance vesting**
When an option becomes exercisable during its term based on achieving pre-determined performance objectives.

**option profit**
The excess of price at exercise of shares over the exercise price.

**option repricing**
This occurs when the exercise price on outstanding options is changed other than by recapitalization type of adjustment. When done it is usually to reduce the price of underwater options.

**outside directors**
Members of the board of directors of an organization who are not current employees of the organization. (See affiliated directors.)

**over the counter**
Securities in companies which are publicly traded, but not on one of the established stock exchanges such as the NYSE, AMEX, NASDAQ or one of the regional exchanges.

**overhang**
A measure of potential dilution from stock compensation plans equal to: the number of shares in outstanding grants plus those remaining available for grants divided by common shares outstanding. Expressed as a percentage, overhang is often a measure considered by shareholders in assessing company requests for additional shares for stock plans.

## P

**peer comparison**
A concept used in some incentive plans where a company's results in specified financial measures are compared with those of a group of other companies determined to be peer companies. The comparative results can be used in incentive formulas.

**performance period**
A predetermined span of time during which individual (or group) performance is measured.

**performance share plan**
A stock (or stock unit) grant/award plan in which the payout is contingent upon achievement of certain predetermined external or internal performance goals during a specified period (e.g., three to five years) before the recipient has rights to the stock. The employee receiving the shares pays ordinary income tax on the value of the award at the time of earning it. These grants are subject to the variable accounting provisions of APB 25 as the measurement date is the date on which the shares or cash is paid to the participant.

**performance unit plan (PUP)**
Similar to a performance share plan, except that unit value is not related to stock price. The actual award payment may be in cash, stock or a combination.

**Performance-Accelerated Restricted-Stock Award Plan (PARSAP) or Performance Accelerated Stock Option Plan (PASOP)**
A restricted-stock award or grant that vests eventually in any event based on continued employment, but vesting can occur on an accelerated basis, if preset and stated objectives or performance levels are reached. Favorable grant date accounting treatment applies due to the vesting occurring with continued employment whether the performance objectives are met or not. Occasionally referred to as time-accelerated restricted stock award plan (TARSAP).

**performance-based restricted stock**
Restricted shares of stock awarded to an executive in which the shares are contingent on the achievement of either internal or external performance measures or an increase in the company's stock price. This is similar to a performance share plan and subject to the "variable" accounting provisions of APB 25 and FAS 28.

**perquisite**
A benefit or "perk" tied to a specific key or management level job (e.g., a company car for personal use, free meals, financial counseling or use of company facilities). A perk's status value often exceeds its financial value.

**phantom options**
Options on units equivalent to shares but not real shares, or rights to the appreciation on shares without related option rights.

**phantom stock (full value)**
A long-term incentive plan in which the participant receives a payment in

cash based on a formula. Under a full value plan the full value of the formula is paid. The formula may or may not involve the actual stock price.

**phantom stock (incremental value)**
Similar in concept to the full value phantom stock grant, except that the amount paid is the increase or appreciation in the value as calculated in the formula. The formula may or may not involve the actual stock price.

**premium stock option**
An option whereby the exercise price is set above the FMV at the date of grant.

**present value**
The value of an amount of money at the present time or at the beginning of a specific period of time. The concept recognizes that receipt of a dollar in five years is less desirable than receipt of a dollar today. Present value formulas take into account assumptions about interest rates to produce an estimate of the current worth of the guaranteed delivery of a dollar at some specified point in the future. Present value formulas and variants are used in determining funding requirements for several compensation and benefits programs.

**price at exercise**
The stock price at the time an individual exercises an option. This determines the option price after the option exercise price is subtracted.

**price-earnings ratio (P-E ratio)**
The ratio of a stock's market price to its net earnings per share, sometimes used as an index of the financial performance of an organization.

**profit-sharing**
A plan providing for employee participation in the profits of an organization. The plan normally includes a predetermined and defined formula for allocating profit shares among participants, and for distributing funds accumulated under the plan. However, some plans are discretionary. Funds may be distributed in cash, deferred as a qualified retirement program or distributed in a cash/deferred combination.

**progressivity of incentives**
See incentive progressivity.

**prospectus (1)**
A required SEC filing to register shares authorized for grants under a stock option plan, which must be filed before the options become exercisable. Prospectuses are also required for other reasons by SEC.

**proxy statement**

A document required by the Securities and Exchange Commission (SEC) for a publicly owned company that notifies shareholders of the company's annual (or any special) meeting, and which transmits information relevant to matters that will be voted upon by shareholders including election officers. Also included in the statement is information about compensation of the company's highest paid executive officers.

## Q

**qualified plan (pension or profit-sharing)**

A pension or profit-sharing plan that meets (qualifies under) certain IRS statutory requirements, and consequently has certain tax advantages for employer and/or employee. (Namely, deferral of employee tax to a future date while still allowing for a current tax deduction for the employer.) To qualify, a plan must not discriminate in favor of highly compensated employees. It may be either a defined-benefit or a defined-contribution plan.

**qualified stock option**

A type of stock option specifically authorized by tax legislation. This type of option no longer exists under this name. Currently the form of option that may have favorable tax treatment is the "Incentive Stock Option." It can be stated that it is a "qualified" form of option because it does qualify for long-term capital gains tax treatment if all legal requirements are followed.

## R

**rabbi trust**

A nonqualified trust established by an employer to provide some "psychic" security to employees where the employer promises to pay deferred compensation in the form of cash and/or other assets in the future. The trust is irrevocable and inaccessible to present or future management, and it may or may not be currently funded. It protects against a "change of heart" or a "change of control" in risking nonpayment of promised amounts. However, the funds belong to the corporation and, in the event of bankruptcy, they are specifically within the reach of the organization's creditors. The first such trust approved by the IRS was for a rabbi.

**reload options**

When a company provides an employee additional stock options equal to the number of shares that the executive delivers to a company upon a stock-for-stock exercise of an option, with the term of exercisability of the reload option limited to the remaining term of the original option grant and the option price equal to the FMV at the time of exercise, which triggered the reload option.

**restricted stock**
Stock is given (or sold at a discount) to an employee, who is restricted from selling or transferring it for a specified time period (usually three to five years). The executive receives dividends, but must forfeit the stock if he/she terminates employment before the restriction period ends. If the employee remains in the employ of the company through the restricted period the shares vest, irrespective of employee or company performance.

**risk-free rate of return**
The yield on U.S. Treasury securities, which represents assured payment of interest and repayment of capital. Often used in determining the cost of capital.

## S

**scope**
A set of quantifiable job characteristics that ascribe value to a job. Typical measures include sales volume, asset size of the organization, number of subordinates and size of budget managed.

**Section 16**
A section of the SEC regulations which identifies "insiders," which precludes insiders from unfairly profiting from the purchase and sale of company stock, and which provides certain exceptions related to transactions involving stock for insiders.

**secular trust**
An irrevocable trust established for the exclusive purpose of holding assets to pay employees' nonqualified retirement and/or deferred compensation benefits. It has a design similar to that of a rabbi trust, but the assets contained within the trust are not subject to the claims of the company's general creditors in bankruptcy. It provides benefit payment security to an extent somewhat similar to that provided under a tax-qualified retirement plan trust. The executive is taxed and the company gets a deduction when money is put in the trust.

**Securities and Exchange Commission**
A federal agency that enforces the Securities and Exchange Act of 1934 and other securities acts and which issues rules and regulations on related matters, such as insider trading and required disclosures on executive compensation.

The agency establishes rules for companies reporting to shareholders about the financial and business results of the enterprise for publicly owned companies.

**sequential exercise**
The exercise of stock options in the order in which they were granted. It was a legal requirement for Incentive Stock Options that no longer applies.

**shareholder protection formula**
A formula related to a company's bonus plan that sets aside a specified portion of profit for shareholders before any portion of the excess is made available for bonus awards.

**shareholder value**
See total shareholder return.

**shareholders' equity**
Money provided to the company by the owners through the issuance of equity securities and/or through retained earnings. This also represents the book value of the company.

**short-term incentives**
Rewards that are based on the attainment of short-term results of 12 months or less (e.g., net income). Also, see annual incentive.

**split-dollar insurance**
An agreement between two parties in which each may share in annual insurance expenses and also may share (according to the terms of the agreement) in the equity and death benefits of the policy. It may be used to secure executive benefits for nonqualified arrangements; this form of split-dollar insurance is known as corporate-owned life insurance (COLI).

**Standard & Poors (S&P) 500**
An index of 500 widely held stocks used as a barometer of stock market activity, similar to the DJIA, except that not all of the stocks are listed on the New York Stock Exchange.

**statutory stock options**
See Incentive stock options.

**stock appreciation rights (SAR)**
An infrequently used incentive plan in which the corporation grants an executive the right to receive a dollar amount equal to the future appreciation of its stock. SARs are not used much except by U.S. companies operating in some foreign countries where tax and other laws preclude the use of stock options.

**stock for stock exercise**
An arrangement in which a holder of a stock option uses the FMV of stock already owned to finance the exercise of a stock option. A widely used technique. It is sometimes referred to as a stock-swap exercise. Stockholders cannot sell the stock for a defined period of time.

**stock for tax withholding**
When shares delivered to an individual upon settlement of an option exercise are reduced for the individual's withholding taxes.

**stock grant plans**
Plans that provide stock to employees without any cost to them. Stock grants take two basic forms: (1) stock-appreciation grants and (2) full-value grants. Stock-appreciation grants entitle the employee to the appreciated value of a share of stock (or number of shares or units) over a designated period of time. These grants may be qualified or nonqualified under IRS regulations. A full-value grant entitles the employee to a total value of the worth of the share of stock (or number of shares or units) over a predetermined period of time.

**stock option**
Rights to purchase company shares at a specified price during a specified period of time.

**stock purchase plan (nonqualified)**
A plan that is, in effect, a management stock purchase plan. It allows senior management or other key personnel to purchase stock in the business. There are, however, certain restrictions: (1) the stockholder must be employed for a certain period of time, (2) the business has the right to buy back the stock, (3) stockholders cannot sell the stock for a defined period of time.

**stock swap**
See stock for stock exercise.

**Supplementary Executive Retirement Plan (SERP)**
A form of nonqualified pension plan that need not be funded and can be lost if the corporation goes bankrupt. It offers the organization the ability to grant more liberal benefits and to ensure that retirement amounts beyond those authorized under the Employee Retirement Income Security Act of 1974 (ERISA) can be provided to the highly paid employee. SERPS that restore benefits lost under ERISA are called 415 plans, as that is the section in the IRS describing limits as qualified plans. Other SERPS are structured to provide

benefits (typically for short service) beyond that provided by the basic pension plan. In executive compensation programs, the supplemental benefits or perquisites provided to senior executives in excess of those provided to lower paid executives or employees.

## T

**targeted gain**
A future value method which can be used to determine the appropriate size of a stock option grant based on assumptions of increases in the stock price over a prescribed period. The projected increase in the value of a share is then divided into the total targeted gain to determine the number of shares to be awarded.

**targeted gain treasury shares or treasury stock**
Shares of a company's stock which have been purchased by the company for later re-issuance. Sometimes used in employee stock plans.

**Time-Accelerated Restricted Stock Award Plan (TARSAP)**
See performance-accelerated restricted-stock award plan (PARSAP).

**timing of payment**
Payment may either be current or deferred to some future date or a combination of current and deferred.

**top hat**
In executive compensation programs, the supplemental benefits or perquisites provided to senior executives in excess of those provided to lower paid executives or employees.

**total direct compensation**
In executive compensation, total annual cash compensation plus the annualized value of long-term incentives.

**Total Shareholder Return (TSR)**
The sum of the increase(s) or decrease(s) in stock price and dividend(s) paid over time.

**treasury stock method**
The method used in calculating diluted earnings per share whereby common stock equivalents such as unexercised stock options exist. Generally accepted accounting principles require that this method be used in calculating and reporting to shareholders whenever common stock equivalents exist.

## U

**underwater options**
An outstanding option where the option price is above the stock's current market price.

**unexercised options/SARs**
The rights that have not yet been exercised. They may consist of both exercisable (vested) and nonexercisable (nonvested) rights.

**unreasonable (or excessive) compensation**
A potential tax issue in privately held or closely held companies is executive compensation. The IRS may challenge executive compensation in such organizations as excessive or unreasonable, and as a distribution of corporate profits rather than salary (IRS Sec. 162). If the IRS is sustained, the payment is a dividend and subject to double taxation as corporate income and as individual income.

## V

**vesting**
(1) Typically used in conjunction with a pension plan or a stock plan. Under a pension plan it assures that a participant will, after meeting certain requirements, retain a right to the benefits he or she has accrued (or some portion of them), even if employment under the plan terminates before retirement. Employee contributions are always fully vested. (2) For a stock option, it is the time when an executive's stock option or stock appreciation right becomes exercisable, or when other executive compensation becomes nonforfeitable.

## W

**window period**
The 10-day period, from the third to 12th day after public release of a company's quarterly financial statements, when insiders may exercise their stock-appreciation rights for cash without violating Securities and Exchange Commission rules for short-term trading.

# Y

## yield

The rate of return on an investment.  A yield on a bond (yield to maturity) will be determined by considering the market value of the bond, the stated rate of interest and the par value of the bond. The yield of a stock (dividend yield) is equal to the dividends paid divided by the market value of the stock.

# Glossary of Executive Compensation Abbreviations

| | |
|---|---|
| APB | Accounting Principals Board |
| ARB | Accounting Research Bulletin/Accounting Research Board |
| BV | Book value |
| CEO | Chief Executive Officer |
| CFO | Chief Financial Officer |
| COO | Chief Operating Officer |
| DEFRA | Deficit Reduction Act — 1984 |
| DER | Dividend equivalent right |
| DSO | Discounted Stock Option |
| EPS | Earnings per share |
| ERTA | Economic Recovery Tax Act — 1981 |
| FASB | Financial Accounting Standards Board |
| FMV | Fair market value |
| IASB | Internal Accounting Standards Board |
| IRC | Internal Revenue Code IRS Internal Revenue Service |
| ISO | Incentive stock option |
| LTI | Long-term incentive |
| LTIP | Long-term incentive plan/program |
| NQSO | Nonqualified stock option |
| PARSAP | Performance accelerated restricted stock plan |
| P/E | Price/earnings ratio |
| Perk | Perquisite |
| ROCE | Return on capital employed (same as ROTC) |

| | |
|---|---|
| ROE | Return on equity (same as ROSE) |
| ROI | Return on investment |
| ROS | Return on sales |
| ROSE | Return on shareholders' equity (same as ROE) |
| ROTC | Return on total capital (same as ROCE) |
| RSA | Restricted stock award |
| SAR | Stock appreciation right |
| SEC | Securities and Exchange Commission |
| SERP | Supplementary executive retirement plan |
| STI | Short-term incentive |
| TC | Total compensation |
| TCC | Total cash compensation |
| TDC | Total direct compensation |
| TEFRA | Tax Equity and Fiscal Responsibility Act of 1982 |
| TSR/TRS | Total shareholder return (stock price appreciation plus dividends) or Total return to shareholder |
| W-2 | The form an employer gives an individual at year's end which reports the individual's total earnings reported to the government, and which shows the total of all items withheld for federal, state, local and FICA taxes. |

# Selected References

## *Resources*

*Stock Option Alternatives: A Strategic and Technical Guide to Long-Term Incentives* (WorldatWork, 2003).

*Equity at Work: Constructing a Broad-based Stock Option Plan* (WorldatWork, 2001).

*Total Rewards Guidebook* (WorldatWork, 2000).

*Executive Compensation Answer Book*, Fifth Edition (Aspen Panel, 2002) Bruce Overton and Susan E. Stoffer.

*workspan* Magazine

*WorldatWork Journal*

WorldatWork courses:

T1: Total Rewards Management

T11: Fundamentals of Equity-based Rewards

C6: Elements of Executive Compensation

C6A: Advanced Concepts in Executive Compensation

C12: Variable Pay — Incentives, Recognition and Rewards

Barron, John M., and Waddell, Glen R. "Work Hard, Not Smart: Stock Options as Compensation." June 2003.

Brindisi, Louis, J. Jr. "Comeback for Restricted Stock Plans." *Harvard Business Review*, September 1977.

Carey, James F. "Successors to the Qualified Stock Option." *Harvard Business Review*, January 1978.

Ellig, Bruce R. "CEO Pay – A 20th Century Review." *WorldatWork Journal*, 3rd Quarter 2000.

Longnecker, Brent et. al. "America's Top Guns of Compensation." *WorldatWork Journal,* 3rd Quarter 2000.

Plunkett Research Ltd. "Plunkett's On-Line Trading, Finance & Investment Web Sites Almanac." January 2000.

Reifel, Kimberly. "Responding to Underwater Options." *workspan* Magazine, April 2001, Vol. 44. No. 4.

*Web sites*

About.com — www.about.com

AFL-CIO — www.aflcio.org/corporateamerica/paywatch/

Benefits Link — www.benefitslink.com

Bureau of Labor Statistics — www.bls.gov

Center for Advanced Human Resources Studies — www.ilr.cornell.edu/cahrs/Research.html

Center for Medicare and Medicaid Services (formerly Health Care Financing Administration — www.cms.hhs.gov)

Department of Labor — www.dol.gov

Employee Benefit Research Institute — www.ebri.org/

Families and Work Institute — www.familiesandworkinstitute.org

Foundation for Enterprise Development — http://www.fed.org/

HIPPA Online — www.cms.hhs.gov/hippa

HR Guide — www.hr-guide.com

Hrnext (note the Compensation and Benefits next tabs) — www2.hrnext.com/

HR Village — www.hrvillage.com

HRWorld — www.hrworld.com

InsidetheBoardroom.com — www.insidetheboardroom.com

International Telework Association and Council — www.telecommute.org

MyStockOptions.com — www.mystockoptions.com

The National Center for Employee Ownership — www.nceo.org/

The Official U.S. Government Site for Medicare Information — www.medicare.gov

Social Security Administration — www.ssa.gov

Society for Human Resources Management — www.shrm.org/

Stock Options.com — www.stock-options.com

The Todd Organization — www.toddorg.com

Work and Family Connection — www.workfamily.com

Workforce Magazine — www.workforce.com

WorldatWork — www.worldatwork.org

*Publications*

Bloomberg — www.about.com

Business Week — www.businessweek.com

CNN — www.cnn.com

Economist — www.economist.com

Fortune — www.fortune.com

Morningstar — www.morningstar.com

Reuters — www.reuters.com

Wall Street Journal — http://online.wsj.com/public/us

*Legislation and Regulations*

Foundation for Enterprise Development — http://www.fed.org/

Hrnext (note the Compensation and Benefits next tabs) — www2.hrnext.com/

Society for Human Resources Management — www.shrm.org/

WorldatWork — www.worldatwork.org

*Other*

Financial Accounting Standards Board — www.fasb.org

Institute of Management & Administration (IOMA) — www.ioma.com

Internal Revenue Service — www.irs.gov

Securities and Exchange Commission — www.sec.gov